Cheers for JOHN FEINSTEIN's

LAST DANCE
Behind the Scenes at the Final Four

"Though the Super Bowl has become America's most popular and significant sporting event, the Final Four has pushed — or perhaps surpassed — the once-almighty World Series for second place. Now John Feinstein, one of the best basketball writers around, has given us a fresh look at this annual springtime extravaganza. . . . Feinstein captures the excitement, tension, and color that make the first weekend in April a highlight of every sports year. *Last Dance* deserves to be read by anyone who is a college basketball fan and March Madness pool player."
— Dick Heller, *Washington Times*

"John Feinstein is college basketball's Boswell. . . . *Last Dance* is rewarding in its contents and rich in its details. . . . Feinstein captures the tremendous excitement of the tournament in compelling fashion by portraying the event through a wide gamut of characters — coaches, star players, benchwarmers, and organizers — and bringing the human element to center stage."
— CurledUp.com

"Feinstein is a type of bestseller factory, a man who over the past quarter century has become the victim of nearly as much professional envy as that visited upon Duke University coach Mike Krzyzewski. . . . Feinstein's not merely prolific; he's also quite good. . . . He manages just the right mix of sentimentality and irreverence. . . . The stars of this saga are the players, coaches, and even referees who have reached the pinnacle of the Final Four, the tournament's culminating weekend."
— John Ettore, *Christian Science Monitor*

W9-BVD-134

"Feinstein brings it all to life and, with a rare power of description, can convince even someone who didn't think basketball was all that important that the Big Dance is truly a big story. . . . A fascinating read."

— Albert Mohler, *Crosswalk*

"John Feinstein provides an inside look at college basketball's Final Four tournament as he tracks the teams that participated in 2005's games."

— Ron Berthel, Associated Press

"Feinstein obviously enjoys the company of basketball people, and he gets them to open up. Everyone from Bill Bradley to Mike Krzyzewski to a UNC benchwarmer gets a chance to talk about the Final Four in *Last Dance*. . . . If I had the chance to trail anyone around the Final Four, Feinstein would be near the top of my list. Since that won't happen, this book is an excellent substitute."

— Budd Bailey, *BookPage*

"Feinstein is not only a prolific author, he is one of the best around."

— Phil Tatman, *Orlando Sentinel*

"Feinstein takes a close look at the NCAA tournament by tracking last year's final four teams, and talking to the winners, the losers, their coaches, and the refs, too. As the two teams reach 'the last dance,' Feinstein makes explicit how March Madness is surpassed only by the frenzied attention surrounding the Super Bowl."

— Heather Fletcher, *New York Daily News*

"John Feinstein, author of 18 books on American sports, and fast becoming *the* authoritative voice on the subject, takes us inside the locker room with the likes of Georgetown's John Thompson and Duke's Mike Krzyzewski, onto the court to witness Christian Laettner's buzzer beater that iced his team's trip to the 1990 Final Four, and into media circles as well."

— Steve Goddard, HistoryWired.com

"*Last Dance* pulls back the televised veneer of the National Collegiate Athletic Association men's basketball tournament."

— Sam Schechner, *Wall Street Journal*

"John Feinstein captures all the tumult of the tournament to crown the NCAA basketball champions in his typically illuminating fashion. . . . Fans of college hoops, whether rabid or peripheral, will find *Last Dance* educational, entertaining, and a good way to keep in touch while waiting for the games to begin."

— Ron Kaplan, TeenReads.com

"Feinstein is one of the most readable writers around, and *Last Dance* breezes by, dropping a few interesting tidbits. Feinstein's rants about the selection committee's secrecy and frequent failures have real bite, and his mini-histories of how the tournament evolved are concise and useful."

— Noel Murray, *Onion A.V. Club*

"Feinstein, arguably the best book-length sports journalist working today, employs the 2005 weekend as the catalyst to discuss the history of the event, the key people, and, most significantly, the effect that involvement in the Final Four has had on participants' lives. . . . The anecdotes are entertaining, and the insights into the tournament's logistics fascinating, but what will linger are the remembrances of players, especially those who ended up on the losing side. The best books take us to places we've never been and let us feel what life there is like. Welcome to the Final Four, courtesy of John Feinstein."

— Wes Lukowsky, *Booklist*

ALSO BY JOHN FEINSTEIN

Tales from Q School

Next Man Up

Let Me Tell You a Story *(with Red Auerbach)*

Caddy for Life

Open

The Punch

The Last Amateurs

The Majors

A March to Madness

A Civil War

A Good Walk Spoiled

Play Ball

Hard Courts

Forever's Team

A Season Inside

A Season on the Brink

Last Shot
(A Final Four Mystery)

Running Mates
(A Mystery)

Winter Games
(A Mystery)

LAST DANCE

Behind the Scenes at the Final Four

JOHN FEINSTEIN

BACK BAY BOOKS
Little, Brown and Company
New York   Boston   London

This is for Esther Newberg, who is a wonderful agent, a better friend, and the world's absolute worst sport. Which is part of her charm.

Back Bay Books / Little, Brown and Company
Hachette Book Group USA
1271 Avenue of the Americas, New York, NY 10020
Visit our Web site at www.HachetteBookGroupUSA.com

Originally published in hardcover by
Little, Brown and Company, February 2006
First Back Bay paperback edition, February 2007

Library of Congress Cataloging-in-Publication Data

Feinstein, John.
  Last dance : behind the scenes at the Final Four / John Feinstein —
1st ed.
     p. cm.
  Includes index.
  ISBN-13: 978-0-316-16030-8 (hc) / 978-0-316-01425-0 (pb)
  ISBN-10: 0-316-16030-X (hc) / 0-316-01425-7 (pb)
  1. NCAA Basketball Tournament — History.   2. NCAA Basketball
Tournament — Anecdotes.   3. Basketball — Tournaments — United
States — History.   I. Title.

GV885.49.N37F45   2006
796.323'63'0973 — dc22   2005028478

                    10 9 8 7 6 5 4 3 2 1

                              Q-MART

                Printed in the United States of America

Contents

LAST DANCE

Introduction

Mike Krzyzewski

THERE WAS A TIME, a few years back, when it was very difficult for me to go to the Final Four when my team didn't make it there. Part of it, no doubt, was the disappointment I felt because we weren't still playing. I'm probably spoiled because we've made the Final Four on ten occasions since 1986, although I can honestly tell you that I have *never* taken getting there for granted. Each trip is special.

This past year, after we lost in the round of sixteen to Michigan State, I decided to make the trip to St. Louis. There were some meetings I felt I should attend and some people I wanted to see. As it turned out, making the trip was one of the best things I've done in a long time.

On Sunday morning I attended a new event that the National Association of Basketball Coaches started recently called the Past Presidents Brunch. It is, as you might have guessed, a brunch for all past presidents of the NABC. I was president in 1992, so I was invited.

When I sat down, I found myself next to Bill Foster. I have been given a lot of credit through the years for the success of Duke basketball. What a lot of people don't realize is that the foundation our program is built on was put in place by Bill Foster. In 1974 he became Duke's coach after the worst season in school history. The program was in shambles and Bill had to rebuild in what was, without question, the toughest basketball conference in America. North Carolina State had just won the national championship, North Carolina was coached by Dean Smith, Maryland was strong under Lefty Driesell, and Terry Holland was just arriving to build Virginia into a power. Within four years, Bill turned the program completely around. He recruited players such as Jim Spanarkel, Mike Gminski, Gene Banks, and Kenny Dennard. In 1978 Duke won the ACC Tournament and, with no seniors in the starting lineup (back then, that actually meant something), went all the way to the national championship game before losing to Kentucky.

My first truly great recruiting class included Johnny Dawkins, Mark Alarie, Jay Bilas, and David Henderson. All of them have told me they have memories of that '78 team, that they admired guys like Spanarkel and Gminski and Banks and Dennard, and that those players and that team first put Duke on their radar. If I don't recruit those four players, I'm probably not the coach at Duke today. If Bill Foster hadn't built the team and the program he did, I probably would not have gotten those four players. At that brunch I had a chance to sit and really talk to Bill about what he had to overcome and to tell him how much I appreciated what he had built. I got to look him in the eye and tell him that I honestly believed he deserved at least some of the credit for all that Duke has accomplished in the past twenty years. I think — I hope — that meant something to him.

As I was leaving the brunch, I ran into Marv Harshman. Like Bill Foster, Harshman is retired now, but years ago he was a great coach at the University of Washington. In fact, the first

NCAA Tournament game I coached was against a Marv Harshman–coached Washington team in 1984. We lost. Marv and I joked about the fact that he had started me on the road to having the most NCAA Tournament wins of any coach — with a loss.

I walked out of the brunch with a big smile on my face. Being in that room with so many of my colleagues from so many years and so many games was great. But to run into Foster and Harshman, two men who played a role in my life and were great coaches long before anyone thought to ask me to do a commercial for anything, was a great reminder to me of what the Final Four is all about. It is much bigger than the four teams and coaches who have the honor of playing in it in a given year. It has far more scope than three basketball games. It is about much more than wins and losses — although the wins and losses that occur will be remembered forever by the participants.

The Final Four is about understanding how lucky we all are to be part of college basketball. It is about people like me remembering how important Bill Foster and Marv Harshman are, not to mention John Wooden and Big House Gaines and Bill Russell and Bill Bradley and Dean Smith and John Thompson. And so many others. There's a tendency during the course of a basketball season for a coach to crawl into the cocoon of his team and the day-to-day, game-to-game pressures. Sometimes in April I feel a little bit like someone who has been locked in a cave all winter and I find myself blinking at the glare of Life Beyond Basketball. When I'm not still coaching at the Final Four — and, believe me, I prefer the years when I *am* still coaching — being there is a bridge back to reality. I'm reminded there's more to basketball than our practices, our games, and our rivalries. In spite of what some people might believe, Duke-Carolina is not the game's only great rivalry, although it is a pretty damn good one.

My first memories of the Final Four go back to listening to games on the radio as a kid growing up in Chicago. I always watched the Big Ten game of the week on television when I was young and I often went to games in the old Chicago Stadium. For some reason, a game I saw there between Duke and Notre Dame sticks out in my memory. Maybe there was some fate involved in that.

The first team I really remember well, though, is the Loyola of Chicago team that won the national championship in 1963. Those games, particularly the championship game against Cincinnati, stand out. I remember having the sense that what Loyola had done was a big deal even though I couldn't actually watch the games.

When I played at Army for Bob Knight in the late '60s, the National Invitation Tournament was as big a deal in our minds as the NCAAs were. My three years as a college player coincided with Lew Alcindor's three years at UCLA. (Alcindor, of course, later became Kareem Abdul-Jabbar.) I remember it sort of being accepted that no one was going to beat UCLA. We had very good teams at Army and we badly wanted to win a championship. In 1968 we were 20–4 and invited to the NCAAs. We knew we weren't going to beat UCLA and Alcindor, but we honestly thought we could win the NIT. So, Coach Knight decided to take the NIT bid. Unfortunately, we lost to Notre Dame (on St. Patrick's Day, as I am constantly reminded even now). The next year we went back to the NIT and shocked South Carolina, which had been ranked number two in the national polls for a lot of the season, in the quarterfinals before losing in the semis to Boston College.

My first Final Four was in 1973. I was still in the army but back home on leave in March. I had already talked to Coach Knight about joining his staff when I got out of the army the following year and I flew to St. Louis to watch Indiana play UCLA in the semifinals. I remember thinking *then* how big the event was and how amazing it was to stand in the lobby of the coaches' hotel and watch the parade of famous coaches as they came and went during the weekend. I didn't get to see Bill Walton shoot 21 of 22 for UCLA because I had to report back to my unit soon after the semifinals. I'm not sure if I'm right about this, but I don't think I would have been able to stay even if Indiana had won on Saturday.

A little more than a year later, I went to work for Coach Knight as a graduate assistant. That was the first year [1975] that he coached a team that went undefeated in the regular season. Unfortunately, Scott May broke his arm in February, and even though he was able to come back and play in the tournament, he wasn't the same player and we weren't the same team. We lost in the regional final to Kentucky, 92–90. To this day, I think Coach Knight would tell you that was his most disappointing loss because, with Scott healthy, that was probably his best team. Of course, Indiana, led by Scott, did go undefeated the next season and won the 1976 national championship.

I wasn't around — except as a spectator — when Indiana won that year in Philadelphia. By then I was back at Army as the head coach. I loved coaching at my alma mater, but deep down I knew I wanted to do what Coach Knight had done: take a team to the Final Four and win a national championship. The days when that was even remotely possible at Army were gone. The Vietnam War and big money coming into the NBA had changed recruiting at Army — even more so for football than basketball — and we had to set more realistic goals, such as getting to the postseason and getting into a conference where we could compete. The players I coached during my five years at Army are still among my closest friends today. But I knew there was going to come a time when, if I was successful, I was going to have to consider moving on.

That time came in 1980 when Tom Butters surprised me (and shocked the basketball world) by offering me the job at Duke. Had I known what the first three years were going to be like, I might have thought twice. I had to learn on the job how to coach — and recruit — in the ACC. Dean Smith was at his absolute zenith as a coach. My first game at Duke was against North Carolina in the old Big Four Tournament in Greensboro. Carolina had James Worthy and Sam Perkins and Al Wood on the court, and Dean had already gotten a commitment from a high school senior we knew was pretty good named Michael Jordan. They lost to Indiana in the national championship game that season. A year later, with Jordan, they were national champions. We were 10–17, the worst record in Duke history.

At the same time that I went to Duke, another young coach whom I knew pretty well took the North Carolina State job: Jim Valvano. Jimmy and I had coached against each other while I was at Army and he was at Iona. He had taken Iona to back-to-back NCAA Tournaments, and in 1980, his last year at Iona, my final year at Army, his team was the last one to beat Louisville, which won the national championship. They beat them by 17 in Madison Square Garden and Jimmy had his players cut down the nets. He said he was practicing for the day when he coached a team that cut down the nets at the Final Four. Typical Jimmy.

Of course, in his third year at State — my third year at Duke — Jimmy and his team did cut down the nets at the Final

Four in Albuquerque. While Jimmy and State were becoming national champions, we had improved from 10–17 to 11–17. We lost our last game that season to Virginia, 109–66. A lot of Duke people thought I was going to make a great coach — back at Army, where they thought I belonged.

I still remember that Final Four pretty vividly. Specifically, like a lot of people, I remember the semifinal game between Houston and Louisville. There was a stretch in the second half when it seemed as if every single play took place above the rim. Every player on the court appeared capable of jumping out of the building. They all looked like future NBA All-Stars. It was Roger Valdiserri, the longtime Notre Dame SID [sports information director], who famously commented after the game, "Welcome to basketball in the twenty-first century." I wasn't that much different from most people in New Mexico's Pit that day, in that I was awed by what I saw. The difference was, I was the coach at a school that had recent Final Four history — 1978 — and my goal as a coach was someday to be down on that floor coaching on Final Four Saturday. That's what was scary to me. I knew my team was a long way from being able to compete with what I was watching. It was one of the few times when I wondered if my dream of coaching in a Final Four might not come true.

A year later my four freshmen starters had become sophomores and we went 24–10. We beat North Carolina — with Jordan, Perkins, and Brad Daugherty — in the ACC Tournament semifinals and ended up losing to Washington and Marv Harshman in the NCAA Tournament. In 1986 we made it to the Final Four and beat a great Kansas team to get to Monday night. We lost that championship game to Louisville, 72–69, and if there is a game in my career I look back on with regret, it's that one. I just don't believe I gave my players as much help as I could have if I'd had more Final Four experience at that point. They were tired after the Kansas game, very tired, and I didn't find ways to use the bench early in the game to keep them fresh enough for the finish. Those four kids — Dawkins, Alarie, Bilas, and Henderson — deserved to win the national championship. I know they all feel as if they somehow came up short by not winning that night, but I've always felt that if anyone came up short, it was me. I do think they know that the three national championships we've won since would not have happened if not for them. That's why I honestly believe they have been national champions — because 1991, 1992, and 2001 could not have happened if not for 1986.

That 1986 team began a run that, as I look back on it now, was remarkable. We went to seven Final Fours in nine years. We upset number one seeds in the regional final in 1988 [Temple], 1989 [Georgetown], and 1990 [Connecticut]. In 1992 Christian Laettner hit the shot everyone remembers in Philadelphia to beat Kentucky. In 1994 we beat another number one seed [Purdue] in another regional final. I still remember Pete Gaudet, who was my associate coach throughout that run, joking after we beat UConn that he was going to have to withdraw from the annual coaches' golf tournament at the Final Four *again*. I told him I hoped he never got to play in it again.

When I was in St. Louis last year, I kept hearing people talk about all the pressure that was on Roy Williams because he hadn't won a national championship yet. I remember thinking how unfair that was. Roy was in his fifth Final Four last year — four with Kansas, one with North Carolina. No coach should feel pressure when his team is in the Final Four. He should feel great that his team is still playing on the last weekend of the season and be able to enjoy what they've accomplished. That doesn't mean you don't put everything you have into trying to win it all, because there is no feeling quite like cutting down the nets on Monday night. But getting to the Final Four should always be something you get to celebrate, not something that creates pressure. When I walk around at a Final Four, I'm constantly reminded how lucky you have to be to get to *one*. I see people like Lefty Driesell and Gene Keady and Norm Stewart and John Chaney, each of them a great basketball coach. They all made multiple regional finals; they all built programs that were excellent year in and year out for many years. None of them ever coached in a Final Four.

To get to one, you have to have a number of ingredients. You have to have been able to recruit very good players, you have to have a very patient family, you need excellent assistants, and you need luck. You need to keep key players healthy and, most of the time, you need to win at least one game that you probably deserve to lose. In 1986, when we were the number one seed in the eastern regional, we trailed number sixteen seed Mississippi Valley State with ten minutes left to play. We easily could have lost that game, but Johnny Dawkins made just enough plays to pull us through. Everyone remembers Christian Laettner's first buzzer-beater against Connecticut in 1990 that put us in that year's Final Four. A lot of people (not UConn fans, I know that) have forgotten that Tate George came within an inch or two of intercepting Bobby Hurley's pass downcourt just before the inbounds play that set up Christian's shot. We certainly could have lost to Kentucky in the regional final in 1992, and Quin Snyder's Missouri team easily could have taken us out in the second round in 2001. We managed to win and ended up winning the national title.

My point is this: I'm not sure you have to be a great coach to get to the Final Four. Probably you have to be a good one who catches a few key breaks — during the tournament, during the season, during a career. Sometimes I wonder where I would have ended up if I hadn't listened to Tom Rogers, my officer rep at Army, when I asked him if he thought I should take the Iowa State job when it was offered in 1980. "I think you need to follow this Duke thing through to the end," Colonel Rogers said. I guess it's fair to say he gave me good advice.

I was fortunate to have teachers in my life like Coach Knight, Henry Iba, and Pete Newell. All won national championships and all enjoyed counseling younger coaches. I hope now that I'm an older coach who has won national championships that I can do for some young coaches what my mentors did for me. When I think back now to 1983, I realize how fortunate I've been to have had players good enough to put us in a position to compete for championships.

Every time we've made the Final Four has been a thrill. There's no question I got a little bit spoiled when we had our run and made it seven times in nine years. It wasn't that I took getting there for granted, it was that I thought we would keep on going. When we didn't go for four straight seasons, it made getting back in 1999 that much sweeter. Not going really bothered me at first, especially in 1998, when we had a big lead in the regional final and lost to Kentucky. But what I have come to realize — finally, I'm a little slow sometimes figuring things out — is that you don't have to sulk when your team doesn't make the Final Four. There is too much about the weekend to enjoy, even when you aren't coaching.

Organizing a dinner for my former players and coaches is one of the better things I've done during my coaching career. To begin with, it's a lot of fun and it gives me a chance to spend time with guys who have been an important part of my life whom I don't get to see often. I think it's something everyone involved looks forward to. What's best about it is something I realized this year while we were all sitting around the restaurant, telling old stories and laughing at one another. By setting up this dinner, I have guaranteed myself one thing at every Final Four: regardless of what happens to my basketball team during that season, I will always have my team with me at the Final Four.

Some years I will coach my team. Other years I will drink wine with my team. But one way or the other, I'll always have my team with me. That's a pretty good deal for an old coach.

I'm already looking forward to Indianapolis. I'll be there with my team or with my team.

1

One Shining Moment

ROY WILLIAMS HAD THOUGHT ABOUT IT, planned it, even talked about it. He had told his children that when the moment came he knew just what he was going to do: throw his arms up in the air and walk around the court, arms raised in victory. But now, with the moment finally at hand, he knew that wasn't going to happen. He was looking at the clock and then at the court, the court and then the clock. He saw one final shot go up, knowing that even if it went in, it wouldn't change the outcome. It missed and Sean May had the ball in his hands, standing under the basket. Williams's eyes went back to the clock. Two . . . one . . .

And then there was bedlam. Williams had the sense that celebrations were breaking out all over the court, that his players were diving on top of one another, giving full vent to the emotions that had been pent up inside them for an entire basketball season. At that moment, one that he had waited for so long, the thought of raising his arms in triumph never crossed Williams's mind. There was an unshakable feeling of complete satisfaction, but also a coach's calm resolve to finish a job.

He took off his glasses, just as he did at every time-out, because he needed the glasses only for distance and when he looked his players in the eyes while speaking to them, he didn't want the glasses to blur his vision of their faces. Now he wanted to look into the eyes of the players and coaches from Illinois. He knew — from personal experience — that there was nothing he could say to make them feel any better at that moment, but he had always prided himself on handling victory and defeat with equal grace.

But May found him before he could find Coach Bruce Weber. He had a huge grin on his face, the kind of pure joy rarely seen in elite athletes. He had told Williams and his teammates that when North Carolina won the national championship, he was going to be the first one to hug Williams. Now he was fulfilling his promise. Williams was tingling as he hugged May, but he couldn't linger. He got untangled and began shaking hands with the kids in the orange and white uniforms. These were faces he had seen before, the blank stares that come when someone has put a lifetime into achieving something and been right on the doorstep of that achievement only to see it slide away. "New Orleans," he said. "I saw the faces of my Kansas players in New Orleans right after we lost to Syracuse. I wanted to say, 'I know how you feel' — because I did — but I knew it would be meaningless."

He settled for congratulating them on their season and on a great game. He knew they didn't hear a word he was saying. He found himself looking for Bruce Weber, because he wanted to say to him what Mike Krzyzewski had said to him in 1991 in Indianapolis, what Jim Boeheim had said to him in 2003 in New Orleans: your time will come. In '91, in just his third year as a head coach, he had no trouble believing it. Twelve years later it had been a lot more difficult. Weber was where Williams had been in '91. He had just completed his second season at Illinois.

And yet for him, the loss had to be tougher than the first time for Williams. Illinois had been ranked number one in the country since December. It had come within one victory of going undefeated in the regular season. It had matched the all-time NCAA record for wins — thirty-seven — coming into the final, and playing in St. Louis, a three-hour car ride from campus, this had clearly been Illinois' Final Four.

But someone had written the wrong ending to the Illini's script. The culprit had been Williams and his North Carolina team. Even though the circumstances had been different back in 1991, Williams knew what Weber was thinking and feeling. His Kansas team had been very good that season. It had entered the NCAA Tournament as a third seed in the southeast regional and had peaked at the right time, upsetting Indiana, Arkansas, and North Carolina en route to the championship game. Losing that night to Duke had hurt because he had believed his team was good enough to win and, well, because it was Duke — and if you are a graduate of North Carolina, losing to Duke always hurts. But deep down he had understood that it was Krzyzewski's time. Like Dean Smith, his own mentor, Krzyzewski had endured questions about why he seemed able to get to the Final Four but couldn't win that last game. Indianapolis had been Krzyzewski's fifth Final Four and his third title game. It had taken Smith seven Final Fours and four appearances on the last night of the season before he had, at last, cut the final net.

Williams had been on the bench that night in 1982 when Smith finally won his first national championship. He was thirty-one, in his third year as an assistant coach at his alma mater, making less than $10,000 a year and living his dream. He adored Dean Smith, thought him the best coach and the best man he had ever known. When Smith finally won that title, answering all those who said he couldn't win or wondered why he hadn't won, Williams cried. Smith was dry-eyed. Remarkably, Williams's career arc had, in many ways, mimicked those of his mentor and of his mentor's greatest rival, Krzyzewski. He had taken Kansas to the Final Four on four occasions and had twice reached the final. But, like Smith and Krzyzewski, he didn't win right away.

Like Smith and Krzyzewski, he had become defensive about being so successful without having achieved the ultimate success. Smith had actually had studies done to prove that it was statistically more difficult to reach multiple Final Fours than it was to win one. Krzyzewski became snappish when people asked about the monkey on his back. "There's no monkey on my back," he said repeatedly when the subject came up.

He was right. It was a gorilla.

Williams had inherited the gorilla. He was, without question, the BCNTHWTNC — Best Coach Never to Have Won the National Championship. In his fourteen seasons at Kansas, he had won more games than any coach in the history of the game had won in his first fourteen seasons. After the trip to the final in 1991, Kansas was a perennial power. In 1992 the Jayhawks spent the entire season ranked in the top five and went into the NCAA Tournament as the number one seed in the midwest regional, almost certain, most people believed, to return to the Final Four, very possibly to a rematch with Duke.

Except that, as often happens in the NCAA Tournament, Kansas was upset — in the second round by the University of Texas at El Paso. UTEP was coached by Don Haskins, who had coached the Miners to the most famous Final Four victory ever in 1966 when his team (then known as Texas Western) had upset all-powerful Kentucky in the title game. Kentucky, under Adolph Rupp, started five white players. Haskins started five black players. Books, documentaries, and movies still commemorate that game to this day. Haskins never again reached the Final Four after 1966, but on a Sunday afternoon in 1992, closing in on the end of his long career, Haskins's team upset Kansas and brought about a spate of stories reminding people about 1966 all over again.

Later that week, walking through an airport, Williams was stopped by a stranger. He girded himself for the words of comfort and sympathy he knew would come. "Don't worry, Coach, you'll get 'em next year." Or the dreaded "You had a great season anyway." This time, though, that wasn't what he got: "Do you realize what you've done to me?" the man shouted. "I had you guys winning the whole thing. You've completely ruined my bracket!"

Few people on earth are more polite than Roy Williams. Every once in a while, though, he cracks. This was one of those moments. "Ruined your bracket!" he shouted. "You think I care about your bracket? This is about my *life*."

That's what the NCAA Tournament does to college basketball coaches. Fairly or unfairly, they are judged almost solely on how their teams perform in March. A coach can win every game he plays during the regular season and it won't matter a bit unless his team wins in March — and, nowadays, in the first week in April, since the event dubbed "March Madness" now stretches further into the year. In fact, if a coach is highly successful in the regular season or even in the early rounds of the NCAA Tournament but can't win the whole thing, he is likely to be more scrutinized than a coach whose team is consistently decent but almost never very good or great.

Among elite coaches, there are numerous examples of this.

When Gary Williams arrived at Maryland in 1989, the basketball program at his alma mater was in complete shambles. It had been rocked by the 1986 cocaine-induced death of superstar Len Bias and then set back further by the school's decision to hire a high school coach who broke NCAA rules and then lied to investigators about breaking those rules. Less than a year after Williams took over, the school was hammered by the NCAA, given two years' probation because of Coach Bob Wade's transgressions, and quickly plummeted to the bottom of the Atlantic Coast Conference.

Williams dug in, started from square one, and by 1994 had the Terrapins not only back in the NCAA Tournament but, after a second-round upset of number two seed Massachusetts, back in the Sweet Sixteen for the first time since Bias's death. Celebrations broke out on campus. Williams was lionized. "It was as if we'd made the Final Four," he said. "It was one of the great feelings I've ever had in coaching." Maryland lost to Michigan the following week, but no one really cared. There was nothing but happiness in what people had taken to calling Garyland.

A year later the Terrapins made the Sweet Sixteen again — and lost to Connecticut. In 1998 they were there again, losing to Arizona. A year later same round, a loss to St. John's. There was no more joy in Garyland. People began referring to Williams as a "round of sixteen coach." There was no sweetness in that phrase. Williams wondered if they might be right. But he relentlessly pushed forward, and in 2001 his team won in the round of sixteen. Then they upset top-seeded Stanford in the regional final and — presto — Williams and Maryland were in the Final Four. Even a loss to archrival Duke a week later couldn't dull the sense of accomplishment. A year later Maryland made it back to the Final Four — and won the championship.

"The second time was entirely different than the first," Gary Williams remembered. "The first time there was this feeling that you were already a success because you were there. The second time, we would have felt like failures if we hadn't won the whole thing."

Roy Williams knew all about that feeling. Like Gary Williams, he remembered that first trip as a joyride, even after losing the championship game. Two years later a loss in the semifinals was mitigated by the fact that it was to Dean Smith, his old boss and mentor. It took nine years to get back. There were all sorts of near misses — most notably in 1997, when Kansas spent most of the season ranked number one in the country only to lose in the Not-So-Sweet-Sixteen to Arizona, which went on to win the title.

It was after that loss that Williams started telling people that winning the national championship wasn't so important to him. Yes, he wanted to win it. Yes, he would compete with every fiber in his being to try to win it. But if he didn't, he would be happy to walk away someday and just go coach his grandchildren. No doubt he believed it, because if he hadn't willed himself to believe it, he might never have slept at night. But no one else believed it, for the simple reason that no one gets to be as good at anything as Roy Williams was at coaching without burning to be the champion at the end of a season. At least once.

Anyone who had been there in 1982 on the night when Dean Smith finally won his first title on his seventh trip to the Final Four knew exactly how much Smith had wanted to win the minute he opened his mouth at his postgame press conference. "I guess we proved a very bright writer from Charlotte wrong tonight" were his very first words. Many — if not most — in the room looked at one another as if to say, "What the hell is he talking about?"

Those who knew Smith understood exactly what he was talking about. In 1980 Frank Barrows, a gifted feature writer for the *Charlotte Observer*, had written a lengthy story examining why Smith's program won with such remarkable consistency but couldn't win the national championship. Barrows's conclusion was that the very system that made the Tar Heels so good year in and year out prevented them from rising to the highest level when the pressure was greatest, in March. The Tar Heels, impeccably prepared by Smith for every game they played, were always good in November, good in December, good in January, good in February, good in March. But in March you had to be great. He noted that the two most spectacular college point guards of the 1970s were Michigan State's Earvin (Magic) Johnson and North Carolina's Phil Ford. "It would be impossible," Barrows wrote, "for a player at North Carolina to be nicknamed Magic. It simply wouldn't be allowed."

Barrows was right about that. In fact, in December of 1978, Michigan State and Johnson had played and lost at North Carolina. Johnson, as Smith often pointed out, turned the ball over eight times that night. But in March, North Carolina was eliminated in the second round of the NCAA Tournament by Pennsylvania. Michigan State — which beat Pennsylvania by 32 points in the semifinals — won the national title. Carolina had been the better team in December. Michigan State had been the great team in March.

Now, having finally won the title, Smith's first thought as he stood before the nation's media was of Barrows. "It was an immature comment," he said. "I always liked Frank. But I thought he was wrong about our system."

Whether Barrows was right or wrong wasn't the issue. The issue was whether Dean Smith, Hall of Fame coach, could win the national championship. The answer was yes, he could. And you can be damn sure that no matter how dry-eyed he was right then, there were few moments in his career more satisfying to Smith than that one.

Twenty-three years later, sitting in the stands in the Edward Jones Dome in St. Louis, Smith may have felt better for Williams than he had for himself on that night in New Orleans. As those final seconds ticked down, he didn't cry the way Williams had cried for him in New Orleans, but he did feel a surge of relief both for his onetime pupil and for his school. Three years earlier North Carolina had suffered through an unthinkable 8–20 season, a nadir that had led to Williams's return in the spring of 2003. By then, Williams had been to two more Final Fours (2002 and 2003) and had lost twice more, first to Gary Williams's Maryland team in the semifinals and then in a memorable final to Syracuse with rumors swirling everywhere that Williams was about to leave Kansas for his alma mater.

He had been offered the job in 2000 when Bill Guthridge, who had attempted to do the impossible in following Smith, retired. Guthridge had gone to two Final Fours in three years and, in return, had been pilloried by most of the school's fans. They all wanted Ol' Roy to come back, ride in on a white horse, and restore the Tar Heels to glory. Or at the very least, beat Duke. Guthridge had been 2–6 against the Blue Devils. That was unacceptable. But to the amazement of everyone in the college game, Williams had said no — no to North Carolina, no to Dean Smith, no to the shocked Carolina faithful who were ready to build a statue of him the minute he returned. He was adored in Kansas, abhorred in North Carolina. Some took to simply referring to him as "that man who coaches Kansas."

He became the Lord Voldemort of North Carolina: He Who Must Not Be Named.

Matt Doherty, who had played for Smith and coached under Williams, became the coach. He had one good year, winning 26 games, and then the program collapsed. It wasn't because Doherty couldn't recruit — he had recruited all five players who started in the '05 championship game — but those players turned on him and Dean Smith's famous Carolina "family" became dysfunctional.

Enter Williams. Or more accurately, reenter Williams. This time when Smith asked him to come home, he couldn't say no. The pain of being an outcast in his home state at his own school and among his close friends had worn on him. Three years after saying he would never leave Kansas, Williams left Kansas. He was greeted as a returning hero in North Carolina. All was forgiven. Not so in Kansas: he became the Voldemort of the Plains.

He walked into a team filled with talented but in some cases underachieving players. People began predicting an immediate return to greatness for Carolina in 2004. Seeing the predictions, Williams shook his head and said, "Ol' Roy isn't that good." Maybe not, but he was pretty damn good. Carolina returned to the NCAA Tournament that year and lost in the second round to Texas. Some found the season disappointing. Others saw it as a start. Williams recruited one of the top high school players in the country, Marvin Williams, and added him to what was now one of the more experienced teams in the nation, led by juniors Sean May, Raymond Felton, and the mercurial Rashad McCants.

There had been ups and downs throughout the season, but the Tar Heels had come together when it mattered. They had survived a one-point game in the round of sixteen against Villanova and had come from five points down at halftime in the semifinals against Michigan State to set up the championship game that made the most sense: Illinois, ranked number one almost the entire season, against Carolina, ranked number two at the end of the regular season and considered by those who watched basketball the most talented team in the country.

"I just wish people would stop saying we have the most talent," Dean Smith said on the eve of the final.

Very few coaches are comfortable in the role of favorite, but Smith had made an art form out of creating reasons why his team was the underdog. His approach had been best described years earlier by his old friend and rival Lefty Driesell, who once said of him, "Dean Smith's the only man in history who's won eight hundred games [879 to be exact] and been the underdog in every one of them."

In 1981, having reached his sixth Final Four, Smith found himself facing a Virginia team led by Ralph Sampson that had beaten Carolina twice during the regular season. "I think it's obvious," he said, "that they have a psychological advantage because they beat us twice. They've got to be very confident that they can beat us again since they've already done it."

Carolina won and faced Indiana in the final — a team it had beaten during the regular season. That didn't sway Smith. "I don't think there's any doubt Indiana has the psychological advantage," he said at the Sunday press conference. "Since we beat them, they'll want revenge."

Indiana won. Twenty-four years later, Smith was still upset about two quick fouls called in the first half on James Worthy, his star player. "Booker Turner," he said, remembering the referee who called both fouls. "On the second one, the ball wasn't even across midcourt and he called James for trying to get position under the basket. I'm not saying that cost us the game, but . . ."

"I am," Roy Williams said. "It certainly made it almost impossible for us to have a chance. Booker Turner. Wow. Maybe Coach Smith has forgiven him [he hasn't], but I certainly haven't."

On the eve of Williams's third championship game, his old coach didn't want people to see a loss as his failure. "Illinois is awfully good," he said. "They haven't won thirty-seven games because they were lucky."

No, they hadn't. The final was everything that makes college basketball special and the Final Four unique: two teams with one chance to make history. Most players who reach the championship game get only one opportunity to play on the most important Monday night there is on the sports calendar. Since the retirement in 1975 of the legendary John Wooden ended UCLA's dynasty, in which the Bruins won ten championships in twelve years, only a handful of players have been in more than one final. North Carolina played in the title game in 1981 and 1982, Houston went to back-to-back finals in 1983 and 1984, and Georgetown played in 1982, 1984, and 1985. Between 1990 and 1994, Duke played in four championship games in five seasons. Kentucky played in three straight title games between 1996 and 1998, and Duke was in the final again in both 1999 and 2001. That's a handful of players, perhaps 50 — out of about 750 who have suited up on Monday night since 1976 — who have gotten more than one chance. Among those players, only those who played for North Carolina in 1981, Duke in 1990, and Kentucky in 1997 came back after a loss in the final to win the championship a year later. All of which means that, as a player, one must assume there won't be a second chance.

That's what makes the championship game so intense. It is always a matchup of two teams that believe it is their destiny to win. More often than not they have had dominant seasons and had to win five games in the crucible of single-elimination play to get to the final game. On Saturday, in the semifinals, they have beaten teams that undoubtedly arrived in the Final Four city believing *they* were teams of destiny. That was certainly true of Illinois and North Carolina. The Illini were 37–1. They had overcome a 15-point deficit against Arizona in the last four minutes of their regional final, then had pulled away from a Louisville team that had also come from way behind to win its regional final. North Carolina was 32–4. It had trailed Michigan State by 5 points at halftime in the semifinals and then had turned the game into a blowout in the second half.

Two superb teams. But only one could win the national championship. The other would leave with an empty feeling — one that would never completely go away, regardless of how many games it had won en route to the final.

Jay Bilas, now a star analyst for both CBS and ESPN, was the starting center for Duke when it faced Louisville in the championship game in 1986. That Duke team was very much like this Illinois team. It had a dream season, winning thirty-seven games. Four of Duke's starters in that game were seniors, so there was no doubt that this was their one and only chance at a national title. It was a tired team, too, having played a draining semifinal on Saturday against Kansas. The game was decided, in the end, when Louisville's Pervis Ellison grabbed an airball by teammate Jeff Hall and scored what turned out to be the winning basket.

"What I can't forget is the feeling right after the game was over," Bilas said. "To sit there and realize you'd been so close and you hadn't closed the deal. There were all sorts of reasons why we didn't win that game, but none of them really matter. We lost. There aren't many days that go by when I don't think about that night. We did a lot of great things that year. In fact, if you go back and look, people were talking about us being one of the great teams of all time. Then we lost in the final and all of that went away. We were just another good team that came up short in the end. I'd be lying if I said that doesn't still hurt.

"Every year, when the championship game ends, I find myself looking at the players on the losing team. Not the coaches — they'll have other chances — but the players. I know how they feel, especially when it's a close game decided by a play or two at the finish. I know they're going to live with the feeling they've got in their stomachs right then for the rest of their lives. It'll always be there. You can talk all you want about how great your season was, the last memory is the one you carry inside you wherever you go, whatever you do, the rest of your life."

Carolina was in control of the game most of the night. Sean May simply wouldn't allow the Illini any sort of inside game and they took to flinging up three-point shots — by game's end they would attempt forty — and one shot after another chipped paint off the rim. But in the game's final minutes, Illinois showed its resiliency once more, rallying to tie the game at 70 after trailing by as many as 15 points. In the last two minutes, just when people were beginning to wonder if Williams was going to be denied yet again, it was Marvin Williams, the freshman — the one key player in the Carolina lineup Williams had recruited — who made the game's biggest play. After Rashad McCants had twisted to the basket and thrown up one of the worst shots ever seen in a championship game, an underhand flip that didn't come close to the rim, Williams came flying in from the outside to slam home the rebound.

That basket, with 1:13 left, was the game-winner. Illinois had chances but never scored again. Raymond Felton sealed the game with free throws. "After Raymond made the last one, I knew we had done it," Williams said. "I just kept going back and forth from the court to the clock. I saw the last shot miss; I saw Sean with the ball. I may have thought for a split second about throwing my arms up, but then I realized I didn't want to do that. I knew how Bruce [Weber] felt at that moment. I wanted to make sure I saw all the Illinois people before I celebrated."

And so, after May finally let him go, Williams looked around and realized that he hadn't seen Weber yet. In all the commotion, he had started to leave the floor, thinking Williams was going to join his team in the on-court party that had broken out. It wasn't hard to pick out Weber — he was wearing a bright orange jacket — so when Williams saw him leaving the court, he broke into a sprint. He caught him in the runway just before he got under the stands.

"You had a great year," he told Weber over the din. "You will be back here. Your time will come, you're a great basketball coach."

Weber smiled and thanked him as they shook hands. Williams knew his words, though heartfelt, were hollow at that moment. Because there's absolutely no guarantee that you will get back or that your moment will actually come.

"When you make the Final Four the first time, there's no doubt that you're going back," Digger Phelps, the former Notre Dame coach, often says. "At that moment, you're at the pinnacle of your career. You're a Final Four coach. You've built to that point. The question isn't if you're coming back, it's *when* you're coming back."

Phelps took Notre Dame to the Final Four in 1978 at the age of thirty-six. The Irish lost in the semifinals to Duke, rallying from 14 points down to have a shot to tie in the final seconds before losing. "We never figured out how to guard [Mike] Gminski," he said twenty-seven years later. "During the game, Bill Laimbeer says to me, 'We should be beating these guys, Coach.' I said, 'If you got an occasional stop on Gminski, we might beat them.'"

They never figured Gminski out. Disappointing as it was, Phelps knew he'd be back. He was wrong. He coached thirteen more seasons at Notre Dame and never made it back. The Duke team that beat Notre Dame that day lost the final to Kentucky. All five starters were underclassmen. As they left the court that night, the players heard their fans chanting, "We'll be back." They weren't. Nor was Bill Foster, who had coached them from last place in the ACC in 1977 to the championship game in 1978.

And so, while there was plenty of reason for Weber to believe he would be back at the pinnacle of his sport again in the future, there was no guarantee. The only guarantee for anyone who plays or coaches in the Final Four is that the memories will stay with you forever — one way or the other.

2

The Lobby

THE THREE BASKETBALL GAMES that decide the national championship are only a small part of what goes on during a Final Four. The event has evolved into a weeklong gathering of the entire basketball world. For years, the National Association of Basketball Coaches has held its annual convention during the Final Four, meaning that coaches gather from all over the country. The famous ones come and so do the not-so-famous. Retired coaches come and so do fired coaches. Coaches looking for work come and so do those who haven't worked for a while but still, deep down, wish they were.

The coaches — almost two thousand of them when you include all the college and high school coaches who gather at the Final Four site — are only one of the groups that show up. Because the Final Four has become one of *the* events in the cult of American sports — ranking behind only the Super Bowl as a gathering place for the sports world — thousands of people pour into the city where the Final Four is being held. More than 1,400 accredited media cover the event — and that doesn't include the 375 people sent by CBS or those who are turned down by the NCAA when they request credentials. Almost anyone with something to sell, from movie stars to shoe-company hucksters to ticket scalpers, shows up. Fans of the four teams show up and so do corporate high rollers willing to pay almost anything to get a ticket so they can say they were in the building when the national championship was decided.

For five days the city is transformed. The streets are jammed with people, many of them in the colors of the four teams that are playing. An entire brigade of men in sweatsuits can be seen on street corners and in hotel lobbies. Many are coaches, some are scalpers, others are hangers-on who want to corner a coach to tell him about the great player they can help him "acquire." Celebrity-spotting goes on constantly. Autograph seekers pour into the hotel designated for the coaches convention, hoping to spot Mike Krzyzewski or Jim Calhoun but happy to talk to Billy Tubbs or Rick Majerus.

"That's one of the problems nowadays," said Jim Boeheim, the Syracuse coach who has won one national championship and been to three Final Fours. "When I first started coming to the Final Four back in the seventies, we would stand around in the lobby for hours and hours and just talk basketball. You can't do that anymore. There are too many people who want something from you. If it isn't an autograph seeker, it's a ticket scalper. If it isn't a ticket scalper, it's someone from a radio show who just wants 'five minutes' of your time. If it isn't a radio producer, it's a coach who needs work or wants a recommendation. It never seems to stop."

There is no doubting the exponential growth of the Final Four, in every way. It began in 1939 as the National Collegiate Basketball Championship. In those days, it wasn't even the most important basketball tournament — the National Invitation Tournament was. Teams often played in both events — in 1950

City College of New York won them both — and winning the NIT carried as much prestige as winning the National Collegiate Championship until well into the 1950s. As late as 1970, it was not completely unheard-of for a team to turn down a chance to play in the NCAA Tournament to play in the NIT. In 1968 Bob Knight, then the coach at Army, chose the NIT over the NCAAs because he believed his team had a chance to win it — in part because the NIT was played in New York, forty-five minutes from West Point, in part because Lew Alcindor and UCLA were playing in the NCAAs. Army lost in the first round of the NIT to Notre Dame on St. Patrick's Day. Two years later Marquette coach Al McGuire was unhappy about the regional his team was being sent to by the NCAA basketball committee and turned them down, choosing to go to the NIT. The Warriors won the tournament.

The NCAA Tournament became a monolith in stages. The UCLA dynasty, which began in 1964, was a starting point. Texas Western's historic victory over Kentucky in 1966 — the only year between 1964 and 1973 when UCLA did not win the championship — was another touchstone. In 1968 NBC televised the semifinals and the championship game, marking the first time the tournament was on network TV. (The NIT final had already been on CBS for years by then.) In 1971 the finals were held in a dome for the first time — the Houston Astrodome. Then, in 1973 NBC took the championship game to prime time, moving it to Monday night for the first time. The gamble paid off when Bill Walton shot 21 of 22 from the field and scored 44 points, leading UCLA to an easy victory over Memphis State and its seventh straight title. Six years after that, Michigan State — led by Magic Johnson — and Indiana State — starring Larry Bird — met in what was the highest-rated final of all time. Earlier that same season a new cable TV network had been launched, one that was devoted to sports twenty-four hours a day. Desperate for programming, ESPN began televising any and all college basketball games it could gain the rights to. That included persuading the NCAA to allow it to televise first-round NCAA Tournament games and round-of-sixteen games — all the games that were played on weekdays, when NBC had no interest in televising them. Searching for a color commentator who would sound a little different, the fledgling network hired a recently fired coach named Dick Vitale to work many of its games.

Three years later CBS paid an astonishing $16 million a year to wrest the TV rights away from NBC, which had been paying $4 million a year. One of the first things CBS did was hire Billy Packer, who had been working for NBC as its lead color commentator since 1975. In fact, the team of Packer, play-by-play man Dick Enberg, and Al McGuire had become the face of college basketball. The notion that the trio would no longer be calling the Final Four was a major concern to those who followed college basketball closely. McGuire had retired as the coach at Marquette in 1977, dramatically exiting the coaching stage by winning the national championship after he had announced he was retiring at the age of forty-eight. NBC initially hired him to work out of the production truck, but Packer suggested using a three-man booth for basketball — it had been used previously in football and baseball — and his sharp exchanges with McGuire, aided by Enberg's skills as a smooth traffic cop, quickly made them the game's most identifiable spokesmen.

CBS was aware of that. Enberg and McGuire were both under contract to NBC. Packer's contract was up and CBS grabbed him. Because there were few people at the network who knew very much about college basketball, Packer was given far-ranging authority. NBC still had most conferences under regular-season contracts, so Packer was dispatched to piece together a schedule for the network to televise before the tournament began. Together with Len DeLuca, then a CBS executive, Packer also came up with the idea of turning the entire basketball season into a promotional vehicle for the NCAA Tournament and, specifically, the Final Four. They called the concept "The Road to the Final Four" — the obvious point being that four teams would travel the country to end the season in the Final Four city. That year the city was New Orleans and, on occasion, the announcers would call it "the Road to New Orleans."

Even with a relatively weak regular-season schedule, CBS was able to begin selling the fact that it was now the network of the NCAA Tournament and, more important, the Final Four. There was no way to replace the magic of Enberg-Packer-McGuire, but the "road" concept allowed CBS to establish its own identity. Packer and DeLuca came up with a second idea to promote the fact that the tournament was now on CBS: televising the announcement of the tournament field. Up until then, the names of the teams in the field, where they were going to play, and who they were going to play against had simply been released to the wire services on the Sunday afternoon prior to the start of the tournament. The schools that qualified were called by NCAA staffers and told they had been invited to the tournament and where they were going the first weekend so that plane reservations could be made.

Packer and DeLuca decided to turn the unveiling of the field into a televison show. They asked the basketball committee to allow CBS to come to Kansas City (which was then NCAA headquarters) and announce the field on television once it had been selected and seeded. If nothing else, the network knew that all the teams with a chance to be in the tournament would be glued to their TV sets at the appointed hour. The idea proved golden. Simple as it sounds, it changed college basketball. Instead of being the day the bids went out, the second Sunday in March became Selection Sunday. These days Selection Sunday has become almost a national holiday for basketball fans. Most sports sections around the country count down to Selection Sunday the way kids count down to Christmas. People gather around their TV sets, brackets in hand, ready to fill in the names of what has now become a sixty-five-team field.

Almost from the minute the field is announced, people begin dissecting it, trying to figure out why certain teams were left out, why some were seeded higher than expected, why others are lower. CBS now unveils the brackets during an hour-long show that is not only rife with commercials but in which each regional has a sponsor or, as the network likes to call it in this age of euphemism, a "corporate champion." ESPN, which has evolved in the past twenty-six years into one of the most powerful entities in sports, televises a selection show of its own concurrent with the CBS show. As soon as a bracket goes up, the ESPN panel — led all these years later by Vitale, now the most famous personality in college basketball — begins analyzing the teams and their chances.

CBS got very lucky during its first four years as the network of the Final Four. Each of those seasons produced a championship game that was a classic, each in a different way. In 1982 North Carolina beat Georgetown, 63–62. The winning shot was made by a freshman named Michael Jordan and the game ended memorably when Georgetown's Fred Brown accidentally threw the ball right to North Carolina's James Worthy. The next year

North Carolina State, a huge underdog, beat Houston, 54–52, as the buzzer was sounding on a dunk by Lorenzo Charles, who caught a desperation airball thrown up by teammate Dereck Whittenburg and, in one motion, slammed the ball home for the stunning victory. To this day, the tape of State coach Jim Valvano racing around the court looking for someone to hug is one of the signature moments of the college game. The 1984 final was a match of the two schools that had lost at the buzzer the previous two years: Georgetown and Houston. It did not produce a classic finish, but it was a matchup between the two best centers of the time: Hakeem Olajuwon of Houston and Patrick Ewing of Georgetown. Ewing had a better supporting cast and Georgetown finally got its title for Coach John Thompson. Houston, in spite of three straight appearances in the Final Four with Olajuwon, was never able to do the same for Coach Guy V. Lewis.

And then came 1985, another watershed year for the tournament. Beginning in 1975, the basketball committee — the group of athletic directors and conference commissioners assigned to oversee all aspects of the tournament, including, most notably, team selection and negotiation of the TV contract — had started to expand the field. The tournament had started in 1939 as an eight-team event. It then expanded to sixteen teams and in 1956 to twenty-five teams. That odd number meant that seven conference champions received a bye into the round of sixteen, one of the reasons why UCLA had to play only two games to reach the Final Four in nine of its ten championship seasons under John Wooden.

In 1975 the committee expanded the field to thirty-two teams and, for the first time, allowed more than one team from a conference to be invited, still keeping a cap (at two) on the number that could go from one league. The expansion meant that everyone had to play a first-round game and turned the first weekend into an event, since all the top seeds had to play. The success of the expanded tournament led to more expansion: in 1978 the field was increased to forty teams, creating another round for sixteen teams, with the eight winners joining the other twenty-four teams in what was now the second round. Two years later the field grew to forty-eight and all limits on the number of teams that could be invited from a conference were abandoned. The ACC placed five teams in the field that year. Over the next five years, the committee kept inching up the number of teams — it went to fifty-two teams, then fifty-three. Finally, prior to the 1985 tournament, after much debate, the field was expanded to sixty-four teams. That meant there were no first-round byes and everyone had to play six games to win the national championship. It took four wins to get to the Final Four.

The opening two days of the tournament — still on ESPN in those days, with thirty-two games played in about thirty-six hours — became an annual festival of basketball. Vitale worked in the studio those two days, coming on between games and during halftimes to do analysis and make picks. His sometimes outrageous statements became something basketball fans looked forward to. No one could ever accuse Vitale of not going out on a limb.

The wisdom of expanding to a sixty-four-team field, with the tournament champion having to win six times straight in the ruthless single-elimination model, was proved conclusively in 1985. Because of the expansion, Villanova got into the tournament that year as the number eight seed in what was then called the southeast region. The Wildcats had to play their opening game against Dayton — at Dayton. They barely survived, winning 51–49. But soon they got on a roll, upsetting number two seed Michigan in the second round, then beating Maryland and North Carolina to get to the Final Four. The victory over North Carolina was especially sweet for Coach Rollie Massimino because his team had lost regional finals twice to ACC schools: Duke in 1978 and North Carolina in 1982. In the final seconds of the game, North Carolina coach Dean Smith ordered his players not to foul since the game was out of reach and Massimino was able to stand in front of his bench and soak in the fact that his team was — at last — going to the Final Four.

"Everyone who coaches should have a moment like that," he said later. "To be able to stand on the court those last few seconds and realize it has happened, that you're going to the Final Four, is just an amazing feeling. I have to thank Dean for having the class not to foul. It allowed me to have a few of the sweetest seconds of my entire life."

The next weekend was even sweeter. Villanova beat Memphis State in the semifinals, meaning it got to face Georgetown, the defending national champion, in the final. Outside of the Villanova locker room, there probably weren't half a dozen people who thought Villanova had a chance. The Hoyas were still led by Ewing and he had superb players around him. They had absolutely destroyed St. John's, generally considered the second-best team in the country, in the semifinals and most looked at Monday night as little more than a coronation for Georgetown. The Hoyas were a virtual lock to become the first school since Wooden's retirement to win back-to-back championships.

But the Wildcats had other ideas. They had lost two close games to Georgetown during the regular season and had the advantage of knowing how to play them and knowing they could play with them. "Not only were we not intimidated," Massimino said years later, "we were very confident. We thought we should have beaten them in the regular season and now we were on a roll. We'd won five straight games against good teams. There was no doubt in our mind we could win."

The game was the last one played in college basketball without a shot clock. Before every game, Massimino would write a number on the blackboard for his team that told his players how many points they needed to score to win the game. On Monday, April 1, 1985, the number he wrote on the board was 65. That meant, he believed, if his team scored at least 65 points, it would win the game. He almost never got the number wrong.

Villanova went out and played what is now called by most "the perfect game." In an era when shooting more than 50 percent from the field during a game was considered very good — fantastic against Georgetown's vaunted defense — Villanova shot 79.3 percent. In the second half, slowing the game to their pace, the Wildcats made 9 of 10 shots, the only miss being a tip-in attempt by center Ed Pinckney. They made all their free throws down the stretch and won the game, 66–64, in what is arguably the greatest upset in the history of college basketball. Twenty years later that game is still discussed, written about, and dissected. It has been the subject of documentaries and lengthy magazine pieces, chronicling the ups and (many) downs of those who took part that night.

Gary McLain, the point guard who handled the Georgetown press so well that night, sold a story to *Sports Illustrated* two years after the game saying he had a cocaine habit during that season, often played games high, and was high when the team went to the White House after winning the championship. Massimino, a hero in Philadelphia in 1985, left town a pariah seven years later because he had alienated many people in the wake of the championship.

But nothing could change what had happened that night and what that game had done for college basketball. It clearly established one lasting and unequivocal fact: in an event where one loss ends your season, anything can happen. No game is an absolute certainty, especially in the Final Four. N.C. State over Houston had made the notion that any team can win plausible; Villanova-Georgetown cemented it as fact. The Final Four had become established forever by then as an event, a part of Americana just like the World Series, the Super Bowl, and the Masters golf tournament. It transcends sports. Basketball fans follow the game from November to March. Nonbasketball fans pay attention in March, and almost everyone knows something about the Final Four.

The tournament now has two nicknames: fans and marketers refer to it as "March Madness," another phrase trademarked by the NCAA. To players and coaches it has become "the Dance," just as Major League Baseball is known as "the Show." Everyone wants to dance in March. Sixty-five teams get to dance, but only four — the Final Four — get to the last dance, college basketball's Holy Grail.

Although only four teams get to the last dance, the rest of the college basketball world comes to watch them show off their routines. Throughout the week, there are several hubs of activity. One is the hotel that is headquarters for the National Association of Basketball Coaches (NABC), better known simply as the coaches' hotel. Another is the hotel where the basketball committee and the NCAA's corporate VIPs stay along with the media. Another is wherever CBS is headquartered, and another is the shopping mall where ESPN places its set for the week. The number of people who congregate for a glimpse of Dick Vitale is staggering.

More often than not, the teams stay at hotels that are away from the hoopla. Occasionally a coach keeps his team in the downtown hotel it is assigned to — Boeheim did it in New Orleans in 2003, and his team won — but most of the time coaches want their players someplace where the hotel lobby does not resemble Times Square on New Year's Eve most of the time. "I try to make it clear to my guys that we're going to the Final Four for two reasons," said Connecticut coach Jim Calhoun, undefeated in two trips to the last weekend. "The first is as a reward for getting there, to have a good time, to soak the whole thing in. We get in on Wednesday and we spend two solid days seeing the town, going sightseeing, having fun. By Friday, though, it's time to start dealing with the second reason: winning a championship. They understand that there's time for fun and then time for work. I think not doing both would be a mistake."

A lot of coaches don't see it that way. Bob Knight, who won three championships in five trips to the Final Four while at Indiana, would always bring his team in at the last possible moment, and when they arrived it was strictly business until the moment they left. In fact, Knight may be the last coach not to arrive at a Final Four until Friday. In 1987 he scheduled his team's departure so that it would land in New Orleans in time to go straight to practice and the team's Friday press conference. Except there was a problem: the plane hit headwinds and Knight and his players were late for the press conference. Not that they minded. The Hoosiers won the championship, Knight's third title, when Keith Smart hit a baseline jumper with five seconds left to beat Syracuse, 74–73.

Knight was so thrilled with the victory that he told his players and coaches that the bus for the airport would be leaving at 7:00 A.M. and anyone who was late would be left behind. Two of his assistants, Dan Dakich and Murry Bartow, decided there wasn't much point in going to bed for very long. "We figured we would sleep when we got home," Bartow remembered.

They went out celebrating until the wee hours of the morning. They got back to the room they were sharing and fell into their beds, setting an alarm for 6:30 so they could wake up and catch the bus. But the alarm didn't go off. "One of us woke up at about 6:55," Bartow said. "We were scared to death. We just ran into clothes, stuffed our things into our suitcases, and raced out the door. We got downstairs just in time to see the bus pulling away. Fortunately, we knew, with the one-way streets, the bus had to circle the hotel, so we sprinted to the other side and got there just as the bus pulled up to a red light. We were waving our arms to make sure Coach Knight could see us. The light turned green; the bus hesitated for just a second and then took off. I guess he figured, we were late, he wasn't stopping."

Fortunately, the two bedraggled young coaches were able to hail a cab and get to the airport. They found the gate where Indiana's charter was leaving from and were sitting on the plane when the bus pulled up with the team. Needless to say, there was a good deal of snickering as the players walked by them to their seats. "Coach Knight got on the plane, looked at us, and never said a word," Bartow said. "I think Dan and I were half expecting him to tell us to get off."

The joys of victory.

The place to be for most of the week for those who are not part of one of the four teams playing is the coaches' hotel, even if it is not quite as much fun today as it once was for the coaches.

"Years ago, going to the Final Four was almost like going to a weeklong coaches clinic," Maryland coach Gary Williams said. "You would walk through the lobby and there were coaches everywhere talking basketball. Now, it's a zoo. You can't walk five feet without someone asking you for something."

For the famous coaches, the toughest things are autograph seekers, many of them professional memorabilia collectors, and the radio producers who camp out in the lobby and look to grab the first familiar face they can find. The "radio row" at the Final Four isn't as big as the one at the Super Bowl, where it seems that every one of the 412 all-sports radio stations set up headquarters for the week. But it is still very big, with probably close to a hundred radio stations — some small, some national — trying to round up guests during the week. Not only do the producers try to grab anyone and everyone they can, but they won't hesitate to better-deal a coach if they see an opportunity. In New Orleans a couple of years ago, a producer from a syndicated network had just collared Lefty Driesell, one of three men to have coached four different schools into the NCAA Tournament, and was taking him up an escalator to where his network was set up. Just as they reached the escalator, the producer spotted Arizona coach Lute Olson walking past him.

"Coach Olson," he said, introducing himself, "can we grab you sometime for five minutes?"

Olson looked at his watch. "I can do it right now," he said. "Then I have to go to a meeting."

Olson was completely unaware that the producer had Driesell in hand. "Great," the producer said. Without missing a beat, he turned to Driesell and said, "Coach, can we get back to you later?"

To his everlasting credit, Driesell said, "Absolutely not," and turned and walked away.

"It's not like I need to go on with the guy," Driesell said. "He asked me to do him a favor. I understand Lute's a bigger name than I am now, but you don't treat people that way."

Except sometimes on radio row.

The coaches' lobby is also the hub of most Final Four rumors. March is the time of year when coaches get hired and fired, and there are always jobs open or about to open when the basketball world arrives in the Final Four city. Some of the rumors are crazy. In 2003, after Matt Doherty had been fired as the coach at North Carolina, one lobby rumor had it that if Roy Williams didn't take the job, Dean Smith was going to come back and coach. In 2005 Digger Phelps half jokingly said over dinner to some friends that if DePaul coach Dave Leitao left to take the Virginia job — a rumor that later proved true — he would come back to coach at DePaul after a fifteen-year absence from the profession.

"It's a sleeping giant," Phelps said. "I almost took the job back in '97. I told them then that they should try to get into the Big East. Well, now they're in the Big East. I think the job could be exactly like the Fordham job was when I was there."

Phelps's first head coaching job was at Fordham thirty-four years ago. He was twenty-nine and he led the little school from the Bronx to its greatest season. The Rams went 26–3, upset Notre Dame before a sellout crowd in Madison Square Garden, and reached the Sweet Sixteen of the NCAA Tournament before losing to Villanova. That year — and the win over Notre Dame — springboarded Phelps into the Notre Dame job. Even though he took the Irish to the Final Four and numerous NCAA Tournaments, he never had a year quite as glorious as that first one at Fordham.

Phelps is sixty-three now and lives a very comfortable life as an analyst for ESPN. There is a part of every old coach that wants to coach again. But the likelihood of late-night ruminations, rife with nostalgia about his early days as a coach, leading to actually taking a job was just about nil. Nonetheless, the rumor was all over the lobby the next morning: Leitao to Virginia, Digger to DePaul.

One of the most famous lobby rumors, one that had some truth to it, took place in 1988 when the Final Four was held in Kansas City. UCLA had fired Walt Hazzard as its coach, and all sorts of names were being floated as his successor. On Wednesday evening, while the coaches were checking in to the hotel and registering for the convention, word began to make its way around the lobby: Dick Vitale was reporting on ESPN that Jim Valvano was going to be the next coach at UCLA.

At the time, Valvano was one of the biggest names in coaching. He had won one of the most improbable national championship game upsets in history in 1983, North Carolina State over Houston. Valvano was thirty-seven at the time and had one of the most electric personalities the sport had ever seen. He was smart and he was funny and he could really coach. He became an instant star, hosting TV shows, doing the sports on *CBS Morning News*, flying from coaching a game one day to doing TV analysis at another game the next. In 1985 and 1986 N.C. State made it back to the round of eight, each time falling a step short of another Final Four. In 1988 the Wolfpack had finished second in the ACC but had lost to Duke in the conference tournament semifinals and then been shocked in the first round of the tournament by Murray State.

Valvano was restless. Perhaps the answer was to become the coach of the basketball program that had more tradition than any

other. No one had been able to follow John Wooden since his retirement in 1975 with any consistent success. Maybe Valvano
could be the one to do it.

Vitale had the story right — almost. Valvano had, in fact, interviewed earlier in the week with UCLA's chancellor, Charles
Young, and athletic director, Pete Dalis. It was one of those clan-
destine meetings that academics like to arrange.

"Check in to the hotel under an assumed name," Dalis told
Valvano.

"How about Biff, would that be a good name?" answered Valvano, never one to take things quite as seriously as most people do.

The meeting between Young, Dalis, and Biff actually went
well. Valvano liked Young. It would be hard to say no to UCLA
under any circumstances, even though Valvano knew his family —
wife Pam and three daughters — would be less than thrilled
with the idea of moving to California. Valvano agreed to come
back and visit the campus later in the week after going to Kansas
City, where he had several Final Four obligations. By the time he
reached Kansas City on Thursday morning, half the media covering the Final Four were camped out in the lobby waiting for
him because of Vitale's report.

Valvano was stunned that the story had gotten out so quickly.
He shouldn't have been. Valvano was under contract to Nike at
the time. Nike's basketball guy was Sonny Vaccaro, a Valvano
confidant. Vitale also worked for Nike and was also close to Vaccaro. Biff's trip to L.A. went from Valvano to Vaccaro to Vitale
to the world. Valvano wouldn't comment in the lobby that day,
fueling even more speculation that he was going to UCLA.

"I'll bet anyone here dinner he'll be the coach by the end of
the week," Vitale kept telling people.

He would have lost his bet. Valvano's family put its foot down. What's more, Valvano had a half-million-dollar buyout in the contract he had signed at N.C. State two years earlier.

By Friday there was another rumor in the lobby: Valvano was out, Mike Krzyzewski was in.

That one was really wrong. Krzyzewski had already told UCLA he wasn't interested. Larry Brown, who was coaching Kansas in the Final Four — and to the national championship — was interested in the job. He had already coached UCLA once. He flew to Los Angeles the following week and agreed in principle to take the job. Then he changed his mind and stayed at Kansas — until a month later, when he left to become the coach of the San Antonio Spurs.

No one in the lobby ever mentioned the name of Pepperdine coach Jim Harrick. He got the job.

In 2005 the hottest job on the market was the one at Virginia. Pete Gillen had resigned at the end of the season after seven years that had produced one trip to the NCAA Tournament, in 2001. Everyone in basketball had known all season that Gillen was gone unless Virginia made the NCAA Tournament. Once the Cavaliers lost to Duke in the ACC Tournament quarterfinals to finish their season at 14–15, everyone knew Gillen was out.

All sorts of names had been floated during the season. At the top of Athletic Director Craig Littlepage's list was Kentucky coach Tubby Smith. Clearly, Smith would be an ideal choice: he was a superb coach with a national championship (1998) on his résumé. He was African American, and Littlepage believed it was time for Virginia to seriously consider hiring an African American to coach basketball. He was also expensive: Kentucky was paying him $2.1 million a year. Virginia would probably have to top that. There were rumors that some boosters were willing to come up with the money if that's what it would take to get Smith, but it was also possible that once they came up with the money, Smith would just use the offer to get an extension, and perhaps a raise, at Kentucky.

The family that was putting up the money for the naming rights for Virginia's new arena — the John Paul Jones Arena — had connections to Memphis coach John Calipari. But Calipari, who also made a lot of money, wasn't likely to leave a school in a weakened league (four schools were pulling out of Conference USA to join the Big East) to take over a team that had just finished eleventh in the ACC.

Mike Montgomery, the former Stanford coach who had been a candidate for the Virginia job in 1990, was mentioned. No, Montgomery wasn't walking away from $3 million a year to coach the Golden State Warriors. Notre Dame coach Mike Brey had been considered a candidate early on. Brey had grown up in the Washington, D.C., area, graduated from George Washington University, and been an assistant coach at Duke for eight years. He knew the area and the ACC well. What's more, with the Big East expanding to add Louisville, DePaul, Marquette, Cincinnati, and South Florida, the league — with sixteen teams — would become the most brutal and deep in college basketball. Recruiting against the new schools wouldn't be easy, since no one had ever mistaken any of them for Harvard or Yale when it came to admissions standards. But with Notre Dame struggling for a second straight season to make the NCAA Tournament (the Irish were eventually one of the last teams taken off the board by the basketball committee), Brey's luster had faded a bit by the time Gillen resigned.

Not so Texas coach Rick Barnes, whose team had been in the Final Four in 2003. Barnes had actually taken the Virginia job in

1990 before changing his mind and returning to Providence. Barnes played golf with Fred Barakat, the ACC's associate commissioner, the week before the Final Four when Barakat was in Austin during the regional held there. Barakat asked Barnes if he would be interested in the Virginia job. Barnes was adamant: no, not interested. For one thing, he had what he thought was a potentially great team at Texas for the 2005–'06 season. For another, one of the reasons he had left Clemson after the 1998 season was the constant frustration of trying to compete with Duke and North Carolina. None of that had changed. If anything, the league, now expanded to twelve teams, was tougher than when Barnes had left.

Rumors work in funny ways. By the time the basketball world gathered in St. Louis, a few days after the Barnes-Barakat round of golf, the word was that Barnes and Barakat had played golf and that Barakat had asked Barnes if he would consider the Virginia job. All of which was true. But the rumor left out one thing: Barnes's lack of interest. On Wednesday evening, as coaches started to gather at the Millennium Hotel in the shadow of the Arch, Barnes was the hot name for the Virginia job.

It was going to be a busy week for Littlepage. As a member of the basketball committee — and the already selected chairman for 2006 — he had a full schedule of meetings and parties, not to mention the team practices and the games. As Virginia's athletic director, he was constantly being asked about the status of his search for a new coach. "I told everyone I wasn't going to make any decisions until after I got back from here," he said, sitting in the lobby of his hotel early one morning. "No one wants to believe me. It's a better story if there's something going on."

Of course it was. Who ever heard of a lobby rumor that began: "Hey, did you hear about Virginia? Nothing's happening?"

Which may explain why Littlepage began every conversation with an approaching reporter with a question of his own: "What have you heard?"

He was pretty certain that everyone in town had heard something. He was absolutely right.

3

Getting There

GETTING TO THE FINAL FOUR is easy. Getting into the Final Four is far more difficult. In 2005 the Edward Jones Dome was configured to seat 47,500 people — about 20,000 less than its capacity for St. Louis Rams games. Even with all that empty space, many of the seats sold by the NCAA are so far from the floor that the tickets say "distant view" on them so that those who buy them know what they are getting — or not getting — when they arrive at their seats many miles from the playing floor. No one complains.

Ticket distribution for the Final Four breaks down this way:

- Forty percent of the tickets go to the four participating teams, meaning that in 2005 North Carolina, Illinois, Louisville, and Michigan State each received a little more than 4,700 tickets apiece to give to their biggest boosters.
- Ten percent of the tickets go to the local organizing committee.
- Eight percent of the tickets go to the National Association of Basketball Coaches.
- Eight percent of the tickets go to the Division 1 athletic directors.

- Six percent go to the NCAA.
- Six percent go to CBS, most of those seats going to corporate clients.
- Twenty-two percent go to the general public — meaning that if you were not connected to someone in the groups who controlled the other 78 percent of the tickets, a little more than 10,000 tickets were available, most of them distant view, for each game.

The Final Four actually does better than some other major events when it comes to getting the public into the building. At the Super Bowl each year — with far more tickets available — the public has access to about a thousand tickets. Those tickets cost $500. At the Final Four, tickets downstairs cost $85 and upstairs they cost $65 — a bargain by today's standards. If you really want to get into the games and you aren't a coach, an athletic director, or someone with ties to CBS, the NCAA, or the local organizing committee and if you don't get a ticket through the public lottery, you can still get in: it will just cost you about $2,500. In many cases, those tickets are sold by scalpers and ticket agencies who have connections to the groups that get the tickets. They can be seen on the streets of the Final Four city, cell phones in hand, offering tickets at prices that rise each day leading up to semifinal Saturday, then begin to drop before Monday's game because fans from Saturday's losing teams are willing to sell their tickets at any price.

"If you don't get your price by Saturday, you're in a lot of trouble," one scalper said on Saturday afternoon in St. Louis. He was standing on a street corner, holding four tickets that he said were "prime." They were, in fact, downstairs, about twenty rows up behind one of the baskets. Not exactly where the corporate titans or CBS's best clients would be sitting, but good seats nonetheless. The scalper had been asking for $3,000 a ticket earlier in the week. "I had twelve to begin with," he said. "I sold four at two thousand dollars each and four at three thousand dollars each."

Now it was a little more than three hours before tip-off of the first game and he was getting nervous. "I don't even bother with tickets for Monday," he said. "Most people are smart enough to know there's no need to buy a Monday ticket before the games Saturday because there will be so many tickets floating around Saturday night and Sunday. I keep two on hand, just in case someone gets desperate at the last minute. More often than not, I end up eating them or just going to the game myself. But if I sell all my Saturday tickets, I'm way ahead." His asking price for the last four tickets had dropped considerably: "Give me two grand and all four of them are yours right now," he said.

The money to be made by selling Final Four tickets has become the subject of considerable controversy. The NABC has taken a lot of hits over the years because of coaches scalping tickets. Most are smart enough not to make the sale themselves. You won't see coaches standing on a corner, holding tickets in one hand, a cell phone in the other. But some of the tickets being sold may have belonged to coaches originally.

"The excuse we get a lot is that someone gave his tickets to a friend or a relative and that person did the scalping," said Jim Haney, who has been executive director of the NABC since 1992. "That's why we tell them now that if the tickets fall into the wrong hands, *they* are responsible, no matter how far removed they might be from the actual sale."

The NABC is very sensitive to the issue of ticket scalping and has taken some strong measures in recent years to clean it up. "The ADs get as many tickets as we do, but theirs are distributed very early, so even if someone does sell a ticket, it isn't as likely to be discussed in the public domain," Haney said. "Our tickets are picked up at the Final Four. Our lobby tends to be the hub of activity for much of the week. If something goes on, it will be heard about, talked about, written about. We understand that our image takes a hit when this happens. Every year I've done this job, the one story that's an automatic in the local paper in the Final Four city is on scalping, and a lot of it is about coaches."

Sure enough, on Wednesday morning of Final Four week, the *St. Louis Post-Dispatch* had a story on A-1 of the newspaper about the scramble for tickets, scalping, and the history of coaches as scalpers.

Several years ago the NABC and the NCAA came up with a new system to try to cut down on the scalping they knew was going on early and often, especially among coaches who weren't making the kind of money the famous coaches make today. Under the new system, every ticket is assigned to a specific coach and he is responsible for what happens to those tickets. Coaches have to pick up the tickets themselves. On several occasions in recent years, Harvard coach Frank Sullivan, who didn't want to stay for the weekend, has flown into the Final Four city, picked up his tickets, and then given them to his two assistants so they can see the games. "It seems ridiculous," Sullivan said. "But given what has gone on, I understand it."

If someone's tickets show up in the wrong place — on eBay, in a scalper's hands, in the hands of someone in the arena who brags that he paid $5,000 for them — Haney contacts the coach to tell him he has a problem. The coach is then invited, if he wishes, to write a letter to the basketball committee, explaining what happened. "There's very little slack cut," Haney said. "In

2004 we had forty-five tickets show up in places where they didn't belong. All forty-five coaches involved were told they would not receive tickets for the next five years."

What's more, those tickets were not given to other coaches waiting in line; they were taken out of the coaches' allotment. "When we made this deal with the NCAA, they actually gave us seven hundred more tickets," Haney said. "But it was on the condition that we would lose any tickets that got scalped. We get them back — but only after the coach involved is allowed tickets again."

The most embarrassing moment for the coaches in St. Louis came when a coach was caught scalping a ticket on a street corner and ended up being chased by police — with a TV camera crew recording the entire incident. "The good news is the guy wasn't an NABC member," Haney said with a sigh. "He didn't get his tickets through us. He was a junior college coach from Iowa trying to make some extra money by buying and selling a couple of tickets. But of course the story goes out that a coach was caught on camera scalping tickets and everyone just nods their heads knowingly. Even when we're innocent, we're often judged guilty."

The other way to get into the Final Four is to play or coach your way in. As anyone who has ever done so successfully can tell you, it isn't easy. In 2005 there were 326 teams competing in Division 1 college basketball. Realistically, no more than a hundred have the financing or the tradition it takes to put together a team that can win four games in the NCAA Tournament. If you are a member of the ACC, the Big East, the Big Ten, the Big 12, the Southeastern

Conference, the Pacific-10, Conference USA, the Atlantic 10, or the Mountain West Conference, it is possible, based on the tradition of the league, the finances of the league, and the exposure the league receives on television, to reach the Final Four. There are a handful of schools not from those power conferences — Gonzaga comes to mind right away — that, if everything falls into place, can make a run at the Final Four. Some smaller schools have proven that they can make the Sweet Sixteen: Butler, Valparaiso, and Creighton have reached the second week in recent years. In 2005 Wisconsin-Milwaukee carried the banner of the nonpower schools in the round of sixteen after upsetting Alabama and Boston College, two schools from the power leagues. The dream ended in the round of sixteen against number one Illinois.

The last true nonpower school to make the Final Four was Pennsylvania in 1979. Since then, only one school not currently in one of the nine power conferences has made it to the Final Four: Houston, which appeared three straight years from 1982 to 1984. Back then, Houston was part of the now-defunct Southwest Conference, which included schools such as Texas, Arkansas, and Texas Tech, which are all part of power conferences now. Houston got left out in all the shuffling and is part of the struggling Western Athletic Conference. When Nevada–Las Vegas made three appearances between 1987 and 1991 (winning the title in 1990), it was part of the Big West. It is now a member of the Mountain West and in the thirteenth year of a rebuilding program that started when legendary coach Jerry Tarkanian was forced out while the school was on NCAA probation.

Among those hundred schools, perhaps twenty-five have a legitimate shot in a given year to reach the Final Four. Some schools haven't been in forever. Northwestern hosted the first-ever NCAA finals in 1939 and hasn't been in the tournament since. No one expects Air Force, a member of the Mountain West, to reach the Final Four in the near future. Just getting the school into the tournament in 2004 — for the first time in forty-two years — was enough to earn Joe Scott national Coach of the Year votes. Few people consider schools like South Florida (moving from Conference USA to the Big East in the fall of 2005), Duquesne (Atlantic 10), or Texas A&M likely Final Four teams anytime soon. But that doesn't mean it can't happen for those schools. When John Calipari took the job at Massachusetts in 1988, the school was perhaps the worst Division 1 program in the country. It hadn't tasted anything approaching glory since Julius Erving's departure in 1971, and the best Erving had been able to do was get the team into the NIT. It took Calipari four years to get UMass into the NCAA Tournament and eight years to get into the Final Four. He was able to parlay that success into a gigantic contract to coach the New Jersey Nets in the NBA.

Calipari's success at UMass illustrates why colleges will pay millions of dollars if they believe they have found the right coach. It also helps explain why coaches who win games but get into hot water with the NCAA police can always find work. When Calipari left Massachusetts, soon after its appearance in the Final Four, the school was under investigation for a number of violations, most of them involving star center Marcus Camby. Eventually UMass was forced to "vacate" its Final Four appearance — meaning that, technically, only three teams took part in the 1996 Final Four — and return the money it received from the tournament that year, about $600,000. But that didn't matter. No one cares that UMass's appearance was "vacated." And the money the school made from TV appearances, alumni contributions, and increased admissions applications made the penalty more than worthwhile.

Four years later, when the NBA gig didn't work out, Calipari was a hot commodity because of what he had achieved at Massachusetts and he signed a seven-figure deal to coach at Memphis University. Calipari's not the only coach — by any means — to have a run-in with the NCAA police after winning lots of games and then surface at another school: Eddie Sutton went from Kentucky (which was still on probation for violations on his watch) to Oklahoma State; Jerry Tarkanian went from Long Beach State to Nevada–Las Vegas and then survived several investigations while at Vegas before finally being forced to resign in 1992. He was, naturally, hired soon after at Fresno State. Jim Boeheim not only survived sanctions at Syracuse but went on to win a national championship and be elected to the Basketball Hall of Fame. Norm Ellenberger and Tates Locke both went through major NCAA investigations and coached again. Locke even wrote a book describing how he got caught while at Clemson (the book was titled *Caught in the Net*) and, after a stint in the NBA, returned to be the head coach at Indiana State.

Most coaches who get nailed by the NCAA aren't like Locke. They all claim innocence, either blaming the violations on overzealous assistants, the NCAA's infractions committee, or the media — sometimes all three. Very rarely is a head coach heard to say, "I was in charge, it's my fault." Tarkanian sued the NCAA — successfully — not so much because he was innocent but because the NCAA was incompetent. He is also responsible for perhaps the best line ever to describe NCAA justice. When an air express envelope containing $10,000 fell open while en route from the Kentucky basketball office to the father of a recruit in 1988, Tarkanian said, "The NCAA is so mad at Kentucky, it's going to put Cleveland State on probation for another three years."

Cleveland State, a decided nonpower, had enjoyed a brief spasm of glory in 1986 when it upset Indiana in the first round of the NCAA Tournament and reached the round of sixteen. Soon after, the school was on probation and Coach Kevin Mackey was out of work. Cleveland State doesn't drive TV ratings. Its presence in the round of sixteen, while a remarkable story, certainly didn't put any smiles on CBS faces. Think about it: did CBS want Indiana and Bob Knight playing that year, or Cleveland State and Kevin Mackey? Does CBS — and its corporate partner, the NCAA — want Kentucky on probation and off TV? Of course not. That's why when the big-time schools get caught, the NCAA enforcement committee immediately starts talking about how "cooperative" the school has been while it explains why it has been given only a slap on the wrist. The NCAA even went so far, in 1990, as to postpone a major school's sanctions. Nevada–Las Vegas had just won the national championship and was scheduled to be banned from the next season's tournament for major violations. In one of its more bizarre rulings, the NCAA announced that UNLV would be allowed to participate in the 1991 tournament and then be banned in 1992. Some media pundits (okay, me) began referring to CBS that season as "the official network of the Runnin' Rebels." Watching CBS that season — UNLV was, needless to say, on frequently — one might have confused Vegas with Harvard and Tarkanian with Father Flanagan. To be fair, Tarkanian had some Father Flanagan in him. He reveled in taking players who had been in trouble elsewhere and turning them into productive players in his program. He was probably more honest than 99 percent of college coaches about what he did and why he did it. When he was once asked why he took so many transfers, he answered, "Because their cars are already paid for."

That kind of one-liner and the constant presence of NCAA investigators on his campus obscured just how good a coach Tarkanian was. He took UNLV to four Final Fours, won a national championship, and was one of the better defensive coaches of all time. His good friend John Thompson once said of him, "I really don't care how he gets his players or where he gets them from. What I know for sure is that all of them play very hard on defense on every possession."

Tarkanian's brilliance as a coach is best evidenced by what has happened at UNLV since his departure. The school hasn't been back to the Sweet Sixteen, much less the Final Four, and has gone through six coaches who have an overall record of 232–159. Tarkanian went on to Fresno State, where he rebuilt the program, took it from nowhere to the NCAAs — and then had to leave after a number of players were arrested on various charges and reports surfaced that term papers were being written for players. Of course, if Tark had been sixty when all this happened instead of seventy, you can bet someone else would have hired him. His overall record of 778–202, the sixth-best winning percentage in history, is more than worthy of the Hall of Fame. Don't expect him to be giving his induction speech anytime soon.

Of course, the ideal for a school is a coach who wins big and does so with a clean record. In thirty-six years at North Carolina, Dean Smith won two national championships, went to eleven Final Fours, and graduated most of his players. In twenty-five years at Duke, Mike Krzyzewski has won three national titles, been to ten Final Fours, and graduated most of his players. Bob Knight's numbers can certainly stand up to those two: in twenty-nine years at Indiana, he won three championships, reached five Final Fours, and had most of his players graduate. Knight had other issues: getting arrested in Puerto Rico, throwing chairs, choking players, grabbing students who made the mistake of calling him "Knight," tossing the occasional potted plant over the head of an elderly secretary. Even so, he remains an icon in the sport and had no trouble finding work at Texas Tech after being fired at Indiana.

Krzyzewski and Smith were bitter rivals when they coached against each other. Smith was a godlike figure in North Carolina when Krzyzewski arrived at Duke in 1980. His shadow grew even longer when he won his first national championship in 1982 while Krzyzewski was struggling to a 10–17 record in his second season at Duke. A year later, when Jim Valvano won the national championship at North Carolina State while Duke was going 11–17, Krzyzewski appeared to be completely overwhelmed, surrounded on Tobacco Road by an icon and a rock star. Smith was only fifty-one and had the best program in the sport. Valvano was thirty-seven and was the most popular and in-demand person in the sport. Krzyzewski was 38–47 and had most Duke people screaming for his head.

To his credit, he never panicked and he never lost his sense of humor. During his second season at Duke, he made a recruiting visit to the home of a talented six-foot-ten kid from Oklahoma named Mark Acres. As he made his pitch to Acres and his parents, Krzyzewski quickly became convinced that he wasn't getting through, that what he was selling they weren't buying. Still, he had to go through with the ritual, make the best effort he could, especially since Acres would probably be the best player on his team the day he arrived on campus. Throughout the evening, Acres's mother never once opened her mouth, never asked a question, never made a comment. Finally, Krzyzewski turned to her and asked if there was anything she wanted to know about Duke or if she had any questions at all. Mrs. Acres shook her head and said, "No, I don't need to ask any questions because the only thing that matters is that Mark go to school someplace where he can be close to God."

Krzyzewski paused a moment and then, feeling pretty certain he wasn't getting the kid regardless of how he responded, said, "Well, you know, if Mark comes to Duke, God will be coaching eight miles down the road at Chapel Hill."

The Acres family didn't get the joke. It didn't really matter. Mark went to Oral Roberts.

Other moments during those early years weren't as amusing. Krzyzewski's third season at Duke ended with a humiliating 109–66 loss to Virginia in the ACC Tournament. Duke had a superb freshman class that year: Johnny Dawkins, Mark Alarie, Jay Bilas, David Henderson, and Weldon Williams. The first four would be starters on the 1986 team that would win thirty-seven games and play for the national championship. But as freshmen, they simply weren't ready for the ACC. After the loss to Virginia, all of them wondered if their coach would survive as the pressure on him to compete with North Carolina, eight miles to the south, and North Carolina State, twenty miles east, continued to build.

"I can remember saying to my father, if they fire Coach K, where will I go to school?" Bilas said. "I had picked him far more than the school. If they had fired him, I'm sure I would have left."

Krzyzewski was wondering about his future in the wee hours of the morning after the Virginia loss. Bobby Dwyer, then his top assistant, had put together a small group of people to go out and eat if only to get him out of his room, where his wife,

Mickie, was in tears. Also he wanted to get him away from the hotel and the prying eyes of angry alumni. They ended up in a Denny's in the middle of a driving rainstorm at about 3:00 A.M. It was Johnny Moore, Duke's assistant sports information director, who raised his water glass and said, "Here's to forgetting tonight."

To which Krzyzewski famously answered: "Here's to *never* forgetting tonight."

When Dwyer suggested a little later that there might still be time to get in on the recruitment of Tom Sheehey, then a high school senior who would end up playing at Virginia, Krzyzewski shook his head. "We aren't recruiting Tom Sheehey. We aren't recruiting anyone else this year. We've got [Tommy] Amaker coming in to play the point. If we can't win with Amaker and the freshmen we have now, we *should* be fired."

They won. The next season Duke went 24–10 and got back to the Dance. Two years later the Blue Devils won thirty-seven games and played in the final. Krzyzewski didn't get fired. Duke ended up going to seven of nine Final Fours, including five straight, a string surpassed only by UCLA's eleven in twelve years. In 1991 Krzyzewski won his first title. A year later he won again. Suddenly, he had won more national championships than God, who was still coaching eight miles down the road in Chapel Hill. Smith caught up a year later but by then the battle lines had been drawn. Many of the same Duke people who had screamed at athletic director Tom Butters for not firing Krzyzewski in 1983 were now insisting he was clearly a better coach than Dean Smith. Carolina people certainly didn't want to hear that. One of sport's most intense rivalries became even more intense.

The Krzyzewski-Smith rivalry may have been best summed

up by a scene that took place in the building named for Smith —
the Dean E. Smith Center, aka the Deandome — in 1993. Early
in the game, both Smith and Krzyzewski were up on every call,
clearly wired by the importance of the occasion. Lenny Wirtz, the
veteran referee, finally called them both to midcourt. "Look, guys, I
know it's a big game, but you have to let us make the calls. Don't be
up on every whistle, okay? Give us some space to work."

"Lenny, you don't understand," Krzyzewski said with a smile.
"There are twenty-one thousand people in here and they're all
against me. You three [the officials] are the only ones I can talk to."

Wirtz smiled at the joke. Not Smith. "Lenny, don't let him do
that," he said. "He's trying to get you on his side."

Krzyzewski waved his hand at Smith in disgust and stalked
back to his bench. Turning to his coaches, he said, "If I ever start to
act like him, don't ask any questions, just get a gun and shoot me."

Now it is Duke, and Krzyzewski, who, in the minds of other
coaches, gets all the calls. Even in 2005 en route to winning the
national championship, Roy Williams told Gary Williams in a
private moment that the only reason his team's two games with
Duke (they split) had each gone down to the final play was the
officiating. Gary Williams didn't disagree. To this day, he remains convinced that Duke's 22-point comeback against his
team in the 2001 Final Four was a direct result of the officiating.
For his part, Krzyzewski believes that calls went against his team
down the stretch in 2004 in a Final Four game against Connecticut because the officials were determined to prove that
Duke *didn't* get all the calls.

And Connecticut coach Jim Calhoun, who has won two national titles? He still hasn't completely gotten over the fifth foul
called on Nadev Henefeld in the 1990 regional final against

Duke or the officiating in general in 1998 when his team faced North Carolina in Greensboro in another regional final. "The only good thing about the game in Greensboro," he says now, "is it helped make us the team we became in 1999 [when UConn won the national championship]. Back then, though, it hurt because we were one step short of the Final Four . . . again."

The loss to North Carolina was, in fact, Calhoun and UConn's third trip to a regional final — and their third loss. That Calhoun had Connecticut on the doorstep of the Final Four was, in itself, an amazing story. He had taken the job at Connecticut in 1986 after a very successful career at Northeastern University despite many of his friends and colleagues telling him that the move was career suicide. Connecticut was buried in a Big East dominated at the time by Georgetown, Syracuse, St. John's, and Villanova. Three of the four men coaching at those schools then — Georgetown's John Thompson, Syracuse's Jim Boeheim, and Lou Carnesecca at St. John's — are now in the Hall of Fame. Villanova's Rollie Massimino should probably be there but made some enemies along the way that have kept him out. Consider his record against Carnesecca's: Massimino — 515 career wins; five trips to the Elite Eight; one Final Four; one national championship; Carnesecca — 526 wins, three trips to the Elite Eight, one Final Four. Many would say edge to Massimino; others would call it dead even. But everyone loved Looey Carnesecca. Not everyone loved Massimino.

Calhoun took over at UConn at a time when many alumni were saying the school had to get out of the Big East, find a conference where it could compete. Calhoun believed that conference was the Big East. In 1988 the Huskies showed progress by winning the NIT. But a year later they were in the NIT again, and the grumbling began. It all changed the next season. Connecticut won thirty-one games and the Big East title and came within a buzzer-beating Christian Laettner jump shot of going to the Final Four. Calhoun became a hero at Connecticut, much the same way Gary Williams had become a hero at Maryland after taking the Terrapins from the bottom of the ACC in 1993 to the Sweet Sixteen in 1994. If the round of sixteen was Williams's stumbling block, the round of eight became the wall that Calhoun couldn't get through. And just as Williams began to hear whispers that he was nothing more than a "round of sixteen" coach, Calhoun heard people saying he couldn't take UConn to the promised land of the Final Four.

"Some of it was a little bit frustrating," he said. "I mean, we lose in '90 at the buzzer in overtime on a near-miraculous shot. We lose a great game to UCLA in '95 and they go on and win the tournament. We lost to Carolina in '98 on what was basically a home court for them. But the bottom line was the same: we hadn't gotten there."

Like almost anyone who gets into the coaching business, Calhoun had fantasized as a young coach about taking a team to the Final Four. He had started attending the coaches convention as an up-and-coming young coach in the early 1970s and still remembers the awe he felt when he saw the game's icons in the lobby and around town. "I still remember in 1975, I was in my fourth year at Northeastern, very young, still learning my way around the game," he said. "We were in San Diego. UCLA was playing Kentucky in the final; John Wooden's last game. At some point during the day I went to the hotel's hot tub. When I got up there, Bill Musselman was sitting there. We sat there and just chatted for a few minutes. Now, back then, I thought Bill Musselman was a very big deal. He was the coach at Minnesota, and even though he was controversial, he was very successful. So, I thought sitting in a hot tub and talking to him was kind of cool.

"But then, as I was walking out, I felt someone tugging on my arm. I turned around and it was Adolph Rupp, as in *the* Adolph Rupp. He says to me, 'Boy, are you in basketball?' I said, 'Yes, sir, I am. My name is Jim Calhoun and I'm the coach at Northeastern University.'

"Rupp looks at me and says, 'Well, I have no idea what that is or where that is, but I want to ask you a question.' I said, 'Yes, sir, anything. What is it?'

"And he says, 'Do you think our boys can win tonight?' As if my opinion was somehow going to affect the outcome."

Rupp's boys didn't win. Wooden won his tenth title and walked off into the sunset.

Thirty years later Calhoun is now one of the icons the young coaches stare at in the lobby. His team finally broke through in 1999, not only reaching the Final Four but winning the national championship with a stirring victory over top-ranked Duke in the title game. Five years later Calhoun and Connecticut won a second championship. Now Calhoun has two national titles and more than 700 wins, and was voted into the Hall of Fame in 2005. He was voted in along with longtime rival Jim Boeheim of Syracuse, who first reached the Final Four in 1987 — eleven years after he became a head coach. Sixteen years and two more trips to the Final Four later, Boeheim won a national championship.

Like Calhoun, Boeheim remembers his early days as a young coach standing around the lobby watching the stars go by. "To me, the Final Four back then was like going to a nonstop coaching clinic," he said. "Guys would stand around the lobby all day and all night and talk basketball — I mean the game itself. You could grab someone and ask them to show you how they ran a certain offense or defense and they'd grab a piece of paper and draw it for you. I loved the lobby. Now it's completely different. If you want to sit around and tell stories, you have to go to the sneaker suites because at least there all the hangers-on can't get to you. It's still fun, but it's not the same."

The sneaker suites — which are suites paid for by the various sneaker companies who help fund college basketball generally and big-time coaches specifically — have evolved during the past ten to fifteen years because of the logjam in the lobby. Coaches who are paid by a sneaker company can go to the company's suite and escape the crowds. They can bring guests, and most of the time, a Nike coach will be welcomed in the Reebok or the Adidas suite because those companies know that someday a coach who is with Nike might very well be with them.

Among the truly famous coaches, Boeheim and Calhoun are two of the few regularly seen in the lobby. Most look for back doors or try to put their head down and get to an elevator as quickly as possible. In St. Louis, Mike Krzyzewski had all of his nonofficial meals in his room because he knew there was no way he could go to the coffee shop and eat in peace. Coaches who have an opening on their staff are even more wary of the lobby. Maryland coach Gary Williams skipped the '05 Final Four completely because he had two openings on his staff and knew he would be besieged, not only by coaches looking for work but by friends or representatives of out-of-work coaches campaigning on their behalf.

"It isn't just that you don't want to have to deal with all the people," Williams said. "It's that it is so depressing to have guys come up to you asking for the chance to interview for a job and you know you aren't going to hire them. You feel badly for them and it's really awkward to have to say to them, 'You know, I've got some other guys in mind.' You see the look on their face — because they know what that means — and you feel badly for them." He smiled. "Then there are guys who don't get what you're saying, and that's even worse."

The kind of guy Williams is talking about might be embodied in Tom Abatemarco. It can be argued that Abatemarco has coached at more places than just about anyone in the profession. He has been an assistant at Iona, Maryland, Virginia Tech, North Carolina State (where he helped Jim Valvano win the national championship in 1983), Utah, Colorado, and Cincinnati, and had head coaching stints at Lamar, Drake, and Sacramento State. These days Abatemarco works for the Sacramento Kings, part-time as a coach with their WNBA team, part-time as a marketing person, and part-time as a radio personality. "I'm happy doing what I'm doing right now," he said, sitting in the lobby of the Millennium. "I really don't want to get back into college coaching. Too much work." He paused. "Well, maybe I'd go back for the right job." Another pause. "You know, I really think I could help Gary. He needs someone who can recruit."

Abatemarco could always recruit. He is renowned for his workaholic approach. When Iona was recruiting Jeff Ruland in the mid-1970s, most people gave the small school in suburban New York little chance of getting the six-ten star, given that almost every basketball power in the country was also recruiting him. Abatemarco began staking out Ruland's house. Knowing that recruiting rules prevented him from making contact with Ruland at his home, he began leaving daily messages for him on the windshield of his car.

"Great game last night, Jeff, you really ate that guy up. I'll call you later."

"How's that drop step move you've been working on coming along? You look a lot more comfortable in the post than I've ever seen you."

"Tell your mom that new outfit looked terrific on her."

In recruiting, relentlessness can pay off. Especially if you are relentless and different. Ruland signed with Iona and led the Gaels to back-to-back NCAA Tournaments — putting Jim Valvano in position to get the North Carolina State job after Ruland led the Gaels to 29 victories in his junior year. Abatemarco went with Valvano to N.C. State, where he was part of the national championship and became famous for writing 484 letters (that's not a made-up number) to Chris Washburn. Proving that coaches can get carried away by a recruiting success, Valvano called Washburn's decision to go to N.C. State "the biggest thrill of my coaching career."

This came a year after he had won the national championship.

No one ever had a better Final Four than Jim Valvano and N.C. State in Albuquerque in 1983. N.C. State was, in some ways, the classic Cinderella team. The Wolfpack had struggled after losing their best shooter, Dereck Whittenburg, to a broken foot midway through the season. They finished tied for third in the ACC and went into the ACC Tournament knowing they had to at least reach the final to have a chance to get into the NCAAs. They beat Wake Forest in a close game. Then they upset North Carolina — led by Michael Jordan and Sam Perkins — in overtime and then, in the final, not knowing if they needed to win or not to make the NCAA Tournament, they beat Virginia and national Player of the Year Ralph Sampson. It was a terrific run, and it got the Wolfpack into the tournament as a number six seed in the west regional. They should have lost in the first round to Pepperdine, but the Waves missed free throws late in regulation and State survived in double overtime and advanced. They should have lost in the second round to UNLV, but the Rebels missed free throws late and State survived, by one point, and advanced. The Wolfpack beat Utah relatively easily in the round of sixteen and then shocked Virginia again in the regional final. Tim Mullen — not Sampson — took the last shot of that game with State leading by one. It clanged off the back rim into Sampson's hands. He dunked ferociously — one second after the buzzer sounded.

State had survived and advanced to the Final Four. On Saturday, State played Georgia in what was generally considered the preliminary game prior to the main event between Houston and Louisville, the game that would decide the national championship. Houston had been dubbed "Phi Slama Jama" early in the season by Thomas Bonk of the *Houston Chronicle* and the Cougars lived up to their nickname in the Louisville game. The Cardinals, who had been given the name "Doctors of Dunk" in 1980 when they won the national championship, stayed with them for most of the day, the two teams playing at a pace and with a grace and a high-flying elegance no one in the building could remember seeing in a college basketball game. After Houston had pulled away late to win, Roger Valdiserri, the longtime sports information director at Notre Dame, summed up the way most people felt when he said, "Welcome to basketball in the twenty-first century." He proved to be prophetic.

Sitting in the stands that afternoon with all the other coaches, Mike Krzyzewski felt overwhelmed. This was a few weeks after the 109–66 loss to Virginia. "I sat and watched what those two teams could do and thought to myself, 'How am I ever going to get our program to the point where we can compete with teams like this?' I just couldn't believe basketball could be played above the rim for an entire game that way. Beyond that, I wondered how my team could possibly get to that level. I just wondered if I was in over my head."

Krzyzewski's concerns were long-term. Valvano's were far more immediate. He had forty-eight hours to get his team to that level. Almost no one on the planet thought there was any way State could win the game. Krzyzewski, who knew firsthand how good a coach Valvano was, didn't think it could be done. "Houston looked to me to be playing a different sport than anyone else," he said. Dave Kindred, the distinguished columnist of the *Washington Post*, wrote, "Trees will tap-dance and elephants will drive at Indy before N.C. State wins this game."

By nine o'clock mountain time on Monday night, the trees were dancing and the elephants were warming up their engines. Valvano slowed the game to a walk, and when Houston got the lead late, he went into his fouling act. This was an upset that could not happen today because there is a 35-second shot clock that makes it difficult for coaches to control the tempo the way Valvano did that night. What's more, the "double-bonus" rule, in which all fouls in a half after ten result in two shots, would have worked against State, not only in the championship game but in the Pepperdine game, the UNLV game, and the Virginia game. But that was then, not now, and Valvano squeezed everything he could out of his team and the rules of the game. Houston kept missing one-and-one opportunities and State ended up with the ball in the final minute with the score tied at 52.

If Valvano still had a time-out left, he would have used it because his team was in offensive chaos. Houston was attacking on the perimeter, and with the clock winding down, Whittenburg had to chase down a pass near midcourt. Afraid the clock was about to run out, he turned and launched a shot from thirty-five feet that had absolutely no chance to go in. Suddenly, seemingly from nowhere, Lorenzo Charles, the unheralded sophomore forward who was in the lineup to rebound and play defense while the three seniors — Whittenburg, Sidney Lowe, and Thurl Bailey — did most of the scoring, rose up above everyone clustered around the basket. The ball went right to him a couple of feet short of the rim and in one motion he caught it and dunked it as the buzzer sounded.

It was a scene straight out of *Hoosiers* — except that the movie hadn't been made yet. The entire building went into a state of shock. The Houston players sat on the floor staring into space, not believing they had lost the game and the national title that they thought they had won on Saturday. Valvano simply began running. Later, as part of the speeches he was paid a lot of money to give, he would describe his sprint in great detail. "Dereck Whittenburg had been my designated hugger all season," he said. "But I couldn't find him. He was mobbed. So I'm running around in circles, looking for someone to hug."

Before he was through, Valvano had hugged almost everyone in the state of New Mexico. The victory made him into a media star because he was smart and funny and approachable. Whenever he did clinics as a young coach, Valvano would tell the kids that his dream as a coach was to "cut the last net at the Final Four." When he finished speaking, he would make the campers pick him up on their shoulders so he could cut down one of the nets on the court where he was speaking. Camp directors learned to come prepared with scissors and another net whenever Valvano was the speaker. He was so good, he was worth the inconvenience.

Now he had cut the last net for real. He cowrote a book, *Too Soon to Quit*, in which he explained his philosophy of survive and advance. He hosted TV shows; he did a pilot for a variety show in Hollywood; he coached State on a Saturday and did the color for NBC on a Sunday; he spoke to corporations all over the country; he regularly flew to New York on Sunday night so he could do the sports on the CBS morning show on Monday morning. He was everywhere.

Everywhere except with his basketball team and his family — the two most important things in his life. He had dreamed all his life about winning a national championship. Then, out of nowhere, at the age of thirty-seven, he did it. It wasn't until later that he began to figure out what happened to him in the aftermath of the title. "I had done coaching," he said. "I never dreamed of being Wooden and winning ten; I never dreamed of being Dean [Smith] and contending every single year. I dreamed of winning *one*. I dreamed of that feeling I had that night in Albuquerque. The next thing I knew, I had done it. And I woke up the next morning and it wasn't so much Peggy Lee ["Is That All There Is?"] as 'What do I do next?' There wasn't really one thing I wanted to do, so I tried everything. And I still couldn't find anything that really mattered to me."

Valvano drifted. Because of all the attention he and State had received in the wake of the national championship, there were lots of players who wanted to go to school there. Valvano was now in a position much like Dean Smith in that he was selecting players as much as he was recruiting them. They recruited him. Krzyzewski can still remember the frustration he felt trying to recruit a six-foot-six shooter named Walker Lambiotte. He was convinced Duke was perfect for Lambiotte: he was a good student, Duke's motion offense would get him good shots consistently, and he thought he had connected with the kid. He had. But there was one problem.

"My dad thought V was the coolest guy he'd ever met," Lambiotte said years later. "Don't get me wrong, I liked him too. But once my dad hung out with V, it was sort of a given I would go to State."

That was about all Valvano had to do in recruiting at that point: show up and be cool. Or if the situation called for it, be funny. Or poignant. He put together a video to show to recruits and their families that began with him dribbling a ball from darkness to light and quoting Carl Sandburg on following dreams.

There was, however, a hitch: coaching had become a part-time occupation for Valvano because of all the other things he was trying. He didn't pay close attention to the kind of kids his assistants were bringing to him and he didn't spend that much time with them once they were at N.C. State. The program began to flounder — not so much on the court as off. State was good enough to make it back to the regional finals in both 1985 and 1986, but there were cracks. They became fissures when a book alleging all sorts of wrongdoing in the program came out in 1989. The book was badly flawed, full of mistakes. Even the facts that appeared to be accurate were suspect because the source, a former manager, had been paid for his information. But there was just enough truth and near-truth in the book to cause the NCAA to investigate Valvano's program. Most of what they found had been caused by sloppiness, but it didn't matter. Valvano was responsible. He was forced to resign following the 1990 season.

He was bitter and angry and believed that some in the media, whom he had treated so well through the years, had turned on him. What he failed to understand — or refused to understand — was that he had let his program slide, that he hadn't been paying enough attention. Often during his later years at State, Valvano would sit up late at night in his office, unable to sleep the way most coaches can't sleep after games. He would order a pizza, open a bottle of wine, and tell funny stories until the wee hours of the morning. Then, after almost everyone else had gone to bed, he would sit with his last glass of wine and a cold slice of pizza and say, "I still can't figure out what I want to be when I grow up."

One night Valvano's wife, Pam, finally called him at about 3:00 A.M. and demanded he come home. Valvano got in the car, drove home, changed into pajamas, and went to sleep. An hour later he woke from a restless sleep, realizing he had forgotten to tape his morning radio show. Every morning, Valvano did a five-minute radio bit on one of the local stations. He would tape it before he left the office, picking up a special phone line installed for him and leaving his five-minute spiel on a tape at the station so it would be waiting for the morning show producer when he arrived at 5:00 A.M.

"So I got out of bed, jumped in the car, and drove back to campus. About a block away, I ran a light. There was no one on the road — except for a cop I didn't see. He pulls me over. When he sees that it's me he says, 'Coach, how much have you had to drink?' I'm thinking, I had my last glass of wine more than two hours ago, but I could flunk a Breathalyzer. I mean, who knows with those things? So, I just tell the cop what happened: I was in bed, forgot my radio show and I'm driving back to tape it. He gives me this 'yeah, right' look. And then I remember what I'm wearing. I get out of the car and I say, 'Look, Officer, I'm wearing my PAJAMAS!' He starts laughing, tells me not to run any more lights, and lets me go. I seriously considered wearing pajamas to drive home every night after that."

Valvano could handle almost anything that happened in his life with laughter. Until the book. Until the NCAA came to town. Until he had to resign.

And until he found out he had cancer. Everyone knows the story now: back pains, a trip to the doctor, tests, and a doctor showing him an X-ray that revealed his back to be absolutely covered with cancerous cells. That was in June of 1992. On April 28, 1993, Valvano died. But not before he finally found the next thing he had been looking for since the national championship: cancer. It was cancer that gave his life direction again. Knowing he was going to die, Valvano worked feverishly to set up the V Foundation to fight cancer and to raise money for cancer research, enlisting friends in coaching and in the media. Led publicly by Mike Krzyzewski and Dick Vitale, the foundation has raised more than $50 million since his death.

Valvano was forty-seven when he died, ten years after his glorious run around the court at the Pit on that amazing night in Albuquerque. He is still a part of every Final Four. You can't turn on an NCAA Tournament game without seeing Valvano sprinting around the court; coaches still tell stories about him in the lobby and in the sneaker suites. They talk about the dance contest he won the night before the semifinals in Albuquerque. They retell stories Valvano used to tell.

"Remember the one about the dog?" someone will say. And even though almost everyone in the room has heard it, someone will retell the story about the State alumnus who threatened to kill Valvano's dog after his first season if he didn't beat North Carolina the next year. "But I don't have a dog," Valvano protested.

"No matter," the alum replied.

The next day when Valvano went to the front door to get his newspaper, there was a basket on top of the newspaper. Underneath the blanket, according to Valvano, was the cutest puppy he had ever seen. "And around the puppy's neck," he would say, "was a note. It said, 'Don't get too attached.'"

They've all heard the story. They all know it is probably apocryphal. But they all laugh and drink another toast to V. Who will always be a part of the Final Four.

4

Legends

THERE HAVE BEEN MANY PEOPLE who have achieved legendary status during the sixty-seven-year history of the NCAA Tournament. Players such as Lew Alcindor, Bill Walton, Bill Russell, Christian Laettner, and David Thompson all have a place in the pantheon along with countless others — some, such as Chris Webber and Fred Brown, for reasons they would rather not remember. Adolph Rupp won four titles as a coach, Bob Knight and Mike Krzyzewski have each won three, and Don Haskins won arguably the most important game ever played: the 1966 championship game when his Texas Western team, starting five black players, beat Rupp and Kentucky, three years before Rupp first successfully recruited a black player.

But there is one name that has to stand above all the others, one name that probably defines the sport more than any other: John Wooden. The numbers alone are staggering. His UCLA teams won ten championships in twelve years, including seven in a row from 1967 to 1973. If not for an extraordinary performance by North Carolina State's David Thompson in the semifinals in 1974, UCLA would have won nine straight titles. No other school has ever won more than two in a row, and only one

(Duke, 1991–92) has achieved that feat since Wooden retired in 1975.

"The funny thing is, I really never planned to retire in 1975," Wooden says now. "I thought I would coach for another two or three years, and I think with the players we had in the program and the ones that I had recruited to be freshmen in the fall of 1975, we would have had a good chance to win again, or at the very least contend, during that time."

Wooden retired on the spur of the moment. After losing to N.C. State in 1974, UCLA was not expected to be the power in 1975 that it had been the previous eight years. Bill Walton had graduated, unable to match Alcindor's three national titles because of the loss to State. But UCLA made it back to the Final Four and found itself facing a very good Louisville team in the semifinals. This was a difficult game for Wooden because Louisville was coached by Denny Crum, who had been his top assistant during the glory years in the 1960s when the program had ascended to dominance. Crum had become Louisville's coach in 1971 and had taken the Cardinals to the Final Four in his first season, before losing to UCLA. There was no real tug for Wooden then because getting to the Final Four was a big deal for Crum, and UCLA, led by Walton, was loaded. Now it was different. Crum had put together a superb team, and most people thought the semifinal matchup was a toss-up.

They were right. The game ended up in overtime and Louisville led, 74–73, with twenty seconds to go when a senior guard named Terry Howard was fouled. Howard had grown up in Louisville and had been a hotshot player in high school. He had been a starter for two years at Louisville but as a senior had become the backup point guard. He was a fabulous free throw shooter. As he stepped to the line on that Saturday, he was 28 for

28 from there for the season. If he made both foul shots, it would be almost impossible for UCLA to rally, since there was no three-point shot at the time. Howard missed the front end of the one-and-one. UCLA rebounded and Richard Washington hit a jumper with three seconds to go to win the game, 75–74.

Wooden wasn't sure how to feel. He was, of course, thrilled to win the game. But he knew how crushing the loss was for Crum. "I spent a few moments with Denny and, elated as I felt, I couldn't help but feel awful for him," he said. "As I walked across the court to do the postgame television interview, the thought crossed my mind for the first time. I thought, 'Now's the time to quit.' I'm not exactly sure why I thought it at that moment, but I did. I went into the locker room and I told my team that I was as proud of them as any team I had ever coached, that they had listened well all season and had been a joy to teach. Then I said to them, 'I can't think of a better group to have worked with as the last team I'll ever teach.'

"I'm not sure if they understood right away what I was saying. But then when I went into the press conference and said it, everyone knew what I was saying. I knew it was the right thing because as soon as I said it, I felt satisfied and pleased."

Wooden believed his team would beat Kentucky in the final. "I thought they were very big and they were very good," he said. "But I believed we would give them trouble with our quickness." His analysis proved correct. UCLA beat Kentucky in the championship game and Wooden retired, at the age of sixty-three, with a résumé that will never be equaled. It was important to him that he leave the program in good shape. "We had very good players and I wanted to be sure I didn't leave the cupboard bare for the next coach," he said. "I'm very proud of the fact that we won the league championship the first four years after I retired."

In fact, UCLA went back to the Final Four under Gene Bar-tow the next year — extending its Final Four streak to ten straight years — only to lose to Indiana. The minute the Bruins lost that game, UCLA fans began pining for Wooden's return. Bartow had coached Memphis State into the national champi-onship game in 1973, losing to Walton's 44-point performance in the first championship game played on Monday night, and took UCLA to the Final Four in his first year on the job. But he wasn't Wooden. Tormented by that, Bartow fled the next year when he was offered the chance to start a brand-new program at the University of Alabama at Birmingham. He built a very solid program at UAB and became the first in a long line of coaches who couldn't be Wooden: Gary Cunningham, Larry Brown, Larry Farmer, Walt Hazzard, Jim Harrick, Steve Lavin, and Ben How-land have all sat in Wooden's chair since Bartow's departure. Brown reached the national championship game in 1980 and left a year later to return to coaching in the NBA. Hazzard won the NIT in 1985, his first season on the job, and wanted to hang a banner that said NIT CHAMPIONS in the rafters of Pauley Pavilion along with the ten national championship banners won by Wooden. That idea was swiftly rejected by the school's powers that be.

Harrick did hang a banner, in 1995 winning UCLA's only na-tional title since Wooden's departure. He was gone from the school eighteen months later, after being accused of filing im-proper expense reports. Lavin reached the Sweet Sixteen five times in six years and was considered an utter failure. There is nothing sweet about the round of sixteen at UCLA. Lavin was under fire the entire time he coached there and was booted in 2003 after the Bruins had a miserable season and failed even to reach the tournament. Howland, who had brought great success to Pitt, was hired to replace him and managed to get the Bruins back into the tournament in his second season, although they lost in the first round to Texas Tech.

Wooden is ninety-four now. He has difficulty walking but still attends every UCLA home game, keeps a close eye on the team, and has firm opinions about his old school and about the tournament that he put his signature on in the 1960s and '70s. "I'm very pleased with what Ben has done so far," he said last season. "They've got a very young team, two freshmen starters, four of them playing, and they're getting better with every game. Of course, the difficulty is that times have changed so much. I think if Ben could count on all four of them being here for the next four years, I would feel very confident that we would contend again during that period. But now there are no guarantees for anyone that will be the case.

"I think college basketball and the NCAA Tournament are like almost anything else: bigger doesn't mean better. In many ways, it means not as good. Having said that, I would like to see the tournament format changed so that every Division 1 team gets to participate. It could be done by adding one weekend to the tournament and by shortening the regular season by a week. Maybe that's the Indiana boy in me coming out because for so long that was the way the high school tournament was conducted in Indiana. I think it would be very exciting and I also think it would lead to a more equitable way of dividing up the money. I think I figured out that a team losing in the first round would get fifty-seven thousand dollars. To a lot of those smaller schools, that would be a lot of money. I don't think the power schools and power conferences should control as much of the money as they do."

Wooden says he first began arguing for an open tournament while he was still coaching. The idea has become more in vogue in recent years, especially in the coaching fraternity, because there is so much pressure on coaches to get into the tournament. Of course, the tournament *is* just about open already since thirty of the thirty-one Division 1 conferences have tournaments. Only the Ivy League doesn't. That means, in theory, any team in the other thirty conferences goes into March with a chance to play in and win the NCAA Tournament, since the school that wins the conference tournament gets an automatic bid to the Dance. Almost every year at least one sub-.500 team gets on a roll in its conference tournament and ends up in the field of sixty-five. In 2005 Oakland University (of Michigan) won its conference tournament and took a 13–18 record into the NCAAs.

Opening up the tournament would take away all meaning from the regular season. It would also take away the suspense of Selection Sunday, when everyone in the college basketball world sits around trying to figure out which bubble teams will make the field and which won't. And it would render making the Dance meaningless, since everyone would play in it.

The tournament and the Final Four *have* changed radically since Wooden first took UCLA to the national semifinals in 1962. He won his first title in 1964 in Kansas City at the old Municipal Auditorium, which seated a little more than 10,000 people. "No one even called it 'the Final Four' in those days," Wooden remembered. "In '64, everyone involved in the tournament — all the teams, the coaches, the media — stayed in the same hotel, the Muhlbach, which was right across the street from the arena. It seemed back then as if everyone knew everyone. We were like a little club, everyone who was in college basketball.

"I still remember on the day of the championship game I was in the lobby talking to some people [imagine a coach in the championship game standing around a hotel lobby on game day in 2005] and a coach I had met earlier in the season from Czechoslovakia came up to me. He had been traveling in our country, watching different teams practice to try to learn more about the game. He had watched us and a number of other teams, including Duke, who we were playing that night. He said to me, 'Coach Wooden, I have seen you and I have seen Duke. They are big and they are good. But UCLA, they are a *team*.' He counted on his fingers — 'One, two, three, four, five.' Then he took his five fingers and made a fist. 'Together, your five become one. This is why you win.' I never forgot that."

UCLA's one beat Duke's five, 98–83, that night for Wooden's first title. A year later the Bruins beat Michigan in the championship, led by Gail Goodrich's 42 points. That was the year Bill Bradley led Princeton to the Final Four. The Tigers lost to Michigan in the semifinals but then beat Wichita State in the consolation game with Bradley scoring 58 points — still the record for points scored in a Final Four game. In fact, Bradley — not Goodrich — was selected as the Most Outstanding Player of that year's Final Four. (Austin Carr of Notre Dame holds the record of 61 points scored in a tournament game, in 1970.) Somehow, through time, Bradley's performance has overshadowed Goodrich's. So has Bill Walton's 44-point night in the 1973 championship game, in part because Walton shot a stunning 21 of 22 from the field.

"I always tell Bill that what Gail did was more amazing than what he did," Wooden said, chuckling. "Bill was six foot eleven and was able to take most of his shots close to the basket. Gail was under six feet tall and dominated that game. I get a kick out of teasing Bill about that because I'm probably the only one who will do it."

Wooden continued to attend the Final Four after his retirement, always bringing his wife, Nell, who had been at his side every time he went to the Final Four, with or without his team, dating back to when he first arrived at UCLA. From 1976 to 1984 the Woodens became staples of the lobby scene, usually holding court in a corner as younger coaches would gather around to hear the great man talk. "What I remember about meeting him as a young coach is the way he acted as if you were just as important, if not more important, than he was," Mike Krzyzewski said. "He would look you in the eye, make sure to remember your name, and acted genuinely interested in whatever you were asking or wanted to talk about. I've always tried to remember that as I've gone up the coaching ladder."

Wooden enjoyed spending time with his colleagues, young and old, but he couldn't bring himself to go after the 1984 Final Four in Seattle. The reason: he would have had to go alone. Everyone knew Nell Wooden was extremely sick during that week in Seattle. She and her husband still camped out in the lobby and greeted friends, but Nell was in a wheelchair. "Deep down, I think I knew it would be her last time," John Wooden said. "But I don't think I ever admitted it to myself."

Late one night, after the Woodens had spent several hours talking to friends and coaches and passersby, they said good night to everyone and John Wooden began pushing his wife across the vast lobby of the Seattle Hilton, which was the coaches' headquarters that year. The lobby was still crowded and, as often happens when Wooden crosses a room or a lobby, people stopped what they were doing to watch the great man. At that moment, what they saw was heartbreaking: Wooden pushing his wife's wheelchair, everyone knowing that her time was short.

To this day, no one is certain how it began, but someone started to clap. Then others did the same thing. By the time the Woodens had reached the elevators, everyone in the lobby was turned in their direction, clapping. It was one of those unrehearsed moments that become remarkable ones. Both Woodens turned in the direction of the applause and smiled. Wooden waved his hand in thanks. He knew what the message was, and as touched as he was, it was also very sad. "To be honest, I barely remember it now," he said. "That was a very difficult Final Four for me. No one actually said good-bye, but that's what people were doing."

Nell Wooden died nine months later. When the Final Four was held that spring in Lexington, Kentucky, John Wooden wasn't there, absent for the first time in thirty-six years. "I just couldn't go without Nell," he said. "I had never been to a Final Four without her, and the thought of being there alone was more than I could bear. In the years after that, I just didn't have any enthusiasm to go without her. It would not have been the same."

It wasn't until 1995 that Wooden returned to the Final Four, again in Seattle. It was an offer from Microsoft to come speak and the presence of UCLA — back for the first time in fifteen years — that brought him there. "If UCLA had not been playing, I might have gone up and given the speech and then gone home," he said. "But needless to say, since my school was playing in the games, I wanted to stay and watch them compete."

They competed very well, winning their first national championship in the twenty years since Wooden's retirement. The Bruins' victory in the final was especially impressive since point guard Tyus Edney, their catalyst all season, had been injured in the semifinals and could play only three minutes. Cameron Dollar, his backup, stepped in and played admirably against Arkansas in the championship game and UCLA won its eleventh national title. Wooden was delighted. He did not attend the Final Four in 2005, because he had a commitment to go to a high school all-star game at Notre Dame earlier that week, and trying to do both would have been a little too much for him.

"I enjoy the idea of going back," he said. "But at my age it isn't as easy to do as when I was younger, especially since everywhere you go now is a mob scene. I can honestly say the thing I miss most about not coaching is practice. I always enjoyed that so much because I felt like that was when I was teaching. Four years ago, the McDonald's [high school all-America] game was in Durham and Mike [Krzyzewski] invited me to [Duke's] practice. I really liked his practice. No wasted motion or time. A clear plan about what was to be done that day. I remember sitting there thinking, 'The only thing that would be more fun than watching this practice would be to run it.' They were getting ready to leave the next day for the Final Four and Mike asked me to speak to the team. I told the players that if they worried about the score, they were making a mistake. If they just worked as hard as they could on every possession, they would be fine in the end. That Saturday, they came from twenty-two points down [against Maryland] to win and I felt as if, one way or the other, they had proved that what I was saying was accurate."

Wooden clearly enjoyed his ten championships, but when asked for his most special moments, he doesn't talk about a specific victory or a specific team. "There's no question that the first time you take a team to the Final Four, it is very special," he said. "Even if it wasn't called that the first time we went. There is a great feeling of accomplishment, especially when it takes you as long as it took me [fourteen seasons at UCLA] to get there. And, of course, you always remember the first one.

"But the moments that make me smile the most are a little different. I remember after one of our championships, I think it was the year we beat Jacksonville in the final [1970], a reporter asked Curtis Rowe about the role race played on our team. Curtis looked at him and said, 'Obviously you don't know our coach,' and walked away. The other one I remember very well came the next year when we beat Villanova in the Astrodome. I'd had to discipline Sidney Wicks during the season and it was tough on both of us. Late in the game, when we had things under control, he was fouled. As he was walking to the foul line, he detoured over to the bench, put his arm around me, and said, 'Coach, before it gets crazy, I just want you to know, I really think you're something.' That meant a great deal to me."

No one has meant more to the Final Four than John Wooden.

But what if there hadn't been a Wooden? Who would be considered the greatest college coach of all time? Statistically, Adolph Rupp comes next, with four national titles, but fairly or unfairly, Rupp has been shunted by most people behind three other men who became dominant figures much later than Rupp and, for the most part, after Wooden exited the stage. Alphabetically, the three are Bob Knight, Mike Krzyzewski, and Dean Smith. Knight won three national titles at Indiana (1976, 1981, and 1987) and has been to five Final Fours. Krzyzewski has won three championships at Duke (1991, 1992, and 2001) and reached ten Final Fours. Smith won two titles at North Carolina but reached eleven Final Fours, one fewer than Wooden. Smith has won more games — 879 — than any college coach in history, three more than Rupp and, at the start of the 2005–2006 season, twenty-five more than Knight. Krzyzewski surpassed Smith (sixty-six to sixty-five) in all-time NCAA Tournament victories in 2005, a number that is a tad deceiving because a team can play as many as six tournament games in a year now. During Wooden's heyday, a team like UCLA never played more than four tournament games. Wooden won forty-seven tournament games — forty-one of them (UCLA played five games in 1975) en route to his ten championships.

How you rank the next four after Wooden is purely subjective and, in truth, not that important. All four have very clear legacies, and the three who came after Rupp have clear ties to one another: Krzyzewski played for Knight at Army and got his first job as an assistant coach when he got out of the army working as a graduate assistant coach for Knight in 1974. When he became Duke's coach in 1980, his great rival for seventeen years was the legend working eight miles down the road from him, Dean Smith. The relationship between the three men has always been complicated. Knight and Smith are peers. Smith, who turned seventy-five at the end of February 2006, is almost ten years older than Knight (sixty-five in October 2005), but their head-coaching careers began only four years apart — Smith in 1961 at North Carolina, Knight in 1965 at Army. They met twice in the NCAA Tournament and Knight inflicted two very painful defeats on Smith, beating him in the national championship game in 1981 and then in a stunning upset in the round of sixteen in 1984.

"The one in '84 hurt a lot because we had a great team," Smith said. "We had Michael [Jordan] and Sam [Perkins] and Kenny [Smith] and Matt [Doherty]."

Knight has often said that if that Indiana team had played that North Carolina team ten times, Carolina would have won nine times. But Indiana won the only one that mattered because they didn't play ten times, they played once. Even though the Hoosiers lost a round later to Virginia, that remains one of Knight's most satisfying victories.

The NCAA Tournament committee is always looking for matchups with a little pizzazz on the opening weekend of the tournament, and in 1997 it came up with a made-for-TV dream game. In the first round Smith was going to tie Rupp's record for victories. That meant he would break the record in the second round with a victory. Who would make a better final hurdle than Bob Knight and Indiana? The seedings worked well: North Carolina was a number one seed. Indiana was placed in an eight-nine game against Colorado, the winner to play the Tar Heels. There was one problem: Indiana failed to show up. Colorado blew the Hoosiers out and Knight was so angry and embarrassed that he walked three miles back to his hotel room on a frigid night rather than ride on the bus with his team. Smith got his historic victory against . . . Colorado.

Knight and Smith have always been friendly with each other. They have played golf together through the years, and both say all the right things about each other publicly — and mean most of them. Each respects the other greatly, and they enjoy talking basketball with each other. But the two men could hardly be more different: Smith never curses. Knight always curses. Knight has never smoked and rarely drinks anything stronger than sangria mixed with soda. Smith smoked constantly until 1987, when his doctor ordered him to quit, and likes a good glass of scotch. Smith is happiest away from the public eye; Knight craves it — though he constantly denies that fact. Both were backup players on great teams. Knight was part of a national championship team at Ohio State in 1960 and played on Final Four teams the next two years. Smith played thirty-seven seconds in Kansas's victory in the 1952 national championship game (a fact he later had added to the box score since his name did not appear on the original) and was on the 1953 team that lost in the championship game. Both had to become great coaches to surpass their old teammates — and did.

Krzyzewski was recruited by Knight out of Weber High School in Chicago while Knight was an assistant coach under Tates Locke at West Point. He has often told the story about how uninterested he was in going to Army or into the military until his parents all but shamed him into it, wondering aloud while standing in their kitchen how they could have raised a son who would pass up the chance to go to a great college *and* serve his country. By the time Krzyzewski arrived at Army, Knight was the head coach, since Locke had left to take the job at Miami (Ohio). He was a three-year starter at point guard for Knight and his captain as a senior. Even though Knight made Krzyzewski miserable — as he has done for everyone who has ever played for him — on many occasions Krzyzewski knew how his coach felt about him, especially during his junior year, when his father died midway through the season of a heart attack and Knight flew home with him and stayed several days to make sure he and his mother and older brother were doing all right.

"Under the definition of the term 'tough love' in the dictionary is his picture," Krzyzewski says now, looking back. "He's never been an easy person to deal with, and I don't think he's ever wanted to be an easy person to deal with. But if he's on your side, he's very definitely on your side."

Knight was never close to his father, in large part because he was nearly deaf and it was difficult for the two of them to communicate. Krzyzewski never saw his father very much because he was always working. Each went into the adult world subconsciously searching for a father figure. Knight became close to a number of older coaches who mentored him at an early age: Pete Newell, Henry Iba, Clair Bee, Joe Lapchick, Red Auerbach. Krzyzewski had Knight early in his career and then also became very close to Newell and Iba.

As close as Knight and Krzyzewski were at times, there have frequently been skirmishes between them. Some of the early ones were directly connected to Krzyzewski's choice of girlfriend — later, wife. Mickie Marsh was an airline stewardess (they were still called that in the sixties) when she met Krzyzewski, then a West Point cadet. They started dating and Mickie began coming to games whenever she could. During Mike's senior year, she showed up when Army played at Princeton, a game the Cadets ended up losing in overtime. She and a friend stayed over so that she could spend some time with Mike the next morning before the team bused home. They were eating an early breakfast in the hotel dining room when Knight walked in. Seeing his captain with his girlfriend, just a few hours after a brutal loss, was more than Knight could handle.

"I'm sure he assumed Mickie had spent the night with me — which she hadn't," Krzyzewski said years later. "I knew that was against the rules. But he went crazy, screaming at me about not caring about the team or my teammates. He told me I was off the team and I couldn't ride the bus back to Army, I had to get home by myself."

Krzyzewski managed to get to a bus terminal and back to West Point. During the ride, he was furious with his coach for assuming the worst about him. When he got back he went straight to Knight's office to tell him how unfair he had been and how much he *did* care about his team and his teammates. Knight decided that having to sit in the bus station alone was punishment enough and relented.

Several years later, preparing to leave the army, Krzyzewski went to Bloomington, Indiana, for a job interview with his old coach, who was rapidly becoming an icon at Indiana, having taken the Hoosiers to the Final Four in his second season there. Krzyzewski and Mickie, now his wife, were invited to Knight's house to talk about the job. "It became pretty obvious that Knight wanted to talk to Mike alone," Mickie Krzyzewski said. "But I didn't want to leave the room. I thought Knight was fascinating. He was so smart and so driven. I could see he and Mike had a lot in common, although there were also obvious differences."

Knight kept dropping hints to his wife, Nancy, to clear the room. Mickie kept putting him off. No, she didn't want a tour of the house. No, she didn't want to see the backyard. She was fine sitting right where she was. Finally, Knight, clearly exasperated, stood up, pointed at Mike, and said, "You come with me." He pointed at Mickie and Nancy. "You stay here," he said. He stalked off to the back porch, with Krzyzewski trailing him. When they were outside, Knight turned to his old captain and said, "Mike, I think you have every quality needed to be a head coach — the whole package. But I gotta tell you something. Your wife is a pain in the ass."

Years later Mickie Krzyzewski proudly retold the story.

Krzyzewski got the job at Indiana even though his wife was a pain in the ass, and a year later he became the head coach at Army at the age of twenty-seven. It was Knight who recommended him for the job and played a role in his getting it even though he had not left Army on the best of terms with the brass. Five years later Krzyzewski's name was being mentioned for a number of big-time jobs. One was Iowa State. The other was Duke. Knight had mentioned Krzyzewski to Duke athletic director Tom Butters when Butters called looking for advice, but the person he was really pushing for the Duke job was Bob Weltlich, another of his ex-assistants who was a good deal older than Krzyzewski.

"Iowa State was a couple of weeks ahead of Duke in their process because Duke had gone to the final eight that year," Krzyzewski said. "I went through all the interviews there, and the next thing I know, they're offering me the job. I didn't know what to do. Duke had interviewed me once and Tom [Butters] had said he would be in touch. I knew he had other guys to talk to."

Krzyzewski called Knight and asked him what he thought he should do. Knight was firm. "Mike," he said, "I don't think you can afford to say no to Iowa State."

Krzyzewski was torn. He knew Iowa State was a good job in a good league, a clear step up from Army. But he knew the job he really wanted was Duke. He also suspected that Knight had a little bit of an agenda in telling him to take the Iowa State job. "Weltlich was ahead of me in the pecking order," Krzyzewski said. "He was older. I think Coach wanted him to get the Duke job. He thought it was his turn."

Still confused, Krzyzewski went to Tom Rogers, an army colonel who had once been Knight's officer representative and now served the same role for Krzyzewski. At the military academies, officer representatives (better known as O-reps) work with varsity teams to help with logistics — such as helping players put together schedules or find tutors — and often become close to the coaches they work with. Krzyzewski trusted Rogers implicitly. He asked him what he thought. "I think," Rogers told him, "you need to see this Duke thing through."

Krzyzewski liked that answer. "Which told me it was what I needed to do," he said. "Deep down, that was what I wanted to do. If it hadn't been, I would have just taken Knight's advice."

And the course of basketball history would have changed. Butters has often told the story about how he came to choose Krzyzewski. He had interviewed several more-experienced coaches — including Weltlich — but couldn't get Krzyzewski out of his mind. When he brought him to campus for a second interview, he was convinced he was the right choice. "But how did I justify hiring a coach who had just gone 9–17 at *Army* to coach an ACC team that had just played in the final eight?" he said. "I couldn't bring myself to pull the trigger."

Butters sent Krzyzewski back to the airport. Steve Vacendak, who had played on Final Four teams at Duke in the mid-sixties, now Butters's assistant, came in to ask how the interview had gone. Butters told him that it had gone great, that he was convinced Krzyzewski would be a great coach. "So, you offered him the job?" Vacendak said.

"No, I didn't. I'm afraid of what people will say if we hire him."

Vacendak looked his boss in the eye. "Since when are you afraid of what people are going to say? If you think he's that good, how can you let him get away?"

In a scene straight out of a movie, Butters made a snap decision. "You're right," he said. "Go out to the airport and bring him back here."

Krzyzewski was on a pay phone in the airport, telling Mickie he thought he had done everything right but hadn't gotten the job, when he saw Vacendak approaching. "Tom wants you to come back," he told him, and hustled the stunned young coach into his car. The next day Krzyzewski was introduced as Duke's new coach.

It was Vince Taylor, then a sophomore guard, who summed up the national reaction best: "What the hell is a Krzyzewski?" he asked.

Years later Taylor, now an assistant coach with the Minnesota Timberwolves, laughs about the comment. "It was the first thing that came into my head," he said. "I mean, not only had I never heard of the guy, but there was no way I could pronounce his name." (For the record, it is *je-JEV-skee*.)

The first few years were difficult for the young coach and for the boss who hired him based on a gut feeling. Duke was 38–47 the first three seasons while its two most bitter rivals were winning national championships — North Carolina in 1982 and North Carolina State in 1983. In those days, when Duke fans talked about making the Final Four they were talking about the semifinals of the ACC Tournament — a place Duke didn't go until Krzyzewski's fourth season.

That was the year Duke basketball was reborn, the Blue Devils going 24–10. It was also the winter when Krzyzewski's rivalry with Dean Smith bloomed into a full-blooded two-way vendetta. What started it was the teams' first meeting that season, in Cameron Indoor Stadium. North Carolina, led by Michael Jordan and Sam Perkins, won a taut game decided in the final seconds. At one point during the game, Smith accused the people working the scorer's table of intentionally failing to get the officials' attention to allow his team to substitute. Late in the game a frustrated Krzyzewski drew a technical foul, screaming at the officials about their performance. When it was over, Krzyzewski insisted in his press conference that there was a double standard in the ACC: one set of rules for North Carolina and Smith, another set of rules for everyone else. Smith was furious and said so. Krzyzewski didn't back off until twenty years later.

That was after Smith had retired and Krzyzewski and Duke had become the ACC's dominant — and most hated — program. All the things Carolina had been in the eighties, Duke had become. "And more if you think about it," Smith said. "We won three ACC Tournaments in a row, but never *five*. We were on top in a completely different era, especially in terms of media. No sports talk shows. No Internet. None of the crazy rumors that fly around now when you are everyone's target. At times it was tough for us, but we used it to our advantage, too. I can imagine how difficult it has been for Mike."

It has at times been difficult, Krzyzewski admits that. But being on top has given him a different appreciation for North Carolina and for Smith. "Back then [1984] I was looking at it strictly from my perspective," he said. "I thought my kids were getting the short end and I said so. But there's a tendency to not appreciate sometimes that the other guy is just very good. The reason Carolina won all those close games was because they had a great coach and great players. My guess — now — is that there were very few games that they won because of the officiating. Very few. It is a lot easier for me to see that now that I've been on that side of the fence."

Krzyzewski and Smith will never be close friends, but each can now appreciate the other. Smith even commented late in his career that the program Krzyzewski built probably pushed him to be a better coach. "You make the extra phone call," he said. "You work a little harder. The last thing you want to do is lose to the guy right down the street from you."

The 1984 season was one in which Smith, Krzyzewski, and Knight formed a fascinating triangle. After Krzyzewski's outburst, his team played North Carolina twice more, losing in double overtime in Chapel Hill, then bouncing back a week later to beat the Tar Heels in the ACC Tournament, a victory that probably announced the arrival of Duke and Krzyzewski as important factors in the ACC again. Carolina went on from there to play Indiana in the NCAA Tournament round of sixteen, suffering what might have been the most stunning loss in Smith's thirty-six-year head-coaching career.

The Final Four was in Seattle that year and Smith arrived at a rent-a-car counter only to be told that because he had made his reservation so late, the only car available was a compact. Smith shrugged as he signed the contracts. "I did wait until the last minute," he said. "I was sort of counting on traveling around out here on a bus . . . with my team."

It would be seven more years before Smith would get to go to a Final Four again with his team. By then, Duke and Krzyzewski were in their fifth Final Four in six seasons. But they still hadn't won.

By the time Smith and Krzyzewski arrived at the 1991 Final Four together — Duke to play heavily favored Nevada–Las Vegas, North Carolina to play Kansas — Bob Knight had won three national championships. He had been hired at Indiana in 1971, after six years at Army, when he was still only thirty years old. Two years later the Hoosiers reached the Final Four, losing there to (of course) UCLA and Wooden. In 1975 Knight had a superb team that cruised through the regular season undefeated. But star forward Scott May was injured in February, and even though he came back to play in the tournament, neither he nor Indiana was the same and the Hoosiers lost to Kentucky in the regional final. That was the Kentucky team that went on to lose to UCLA in Wooden's final game.

To say that Knight takes losing hard is like saying that Watergate created some problems for Richard Nixon. Knight rages at defeat, in part because he honestly believes his team should win every game if the players do everything he tells them to. But it also infuriates him to think that people around the country are waking up in the morning and saying, "Hey, look, Knight lost" — even though 99.99 percent of the people alive have far too much going on in their lives to be concerned about how Bob Knight's team is doing other than to note a score. Deep down, Knight believes he knows and understands basketball better than anyone ever has because he learned from the masters of the game — Newell, Lapchick, Bee, Iba, Auerbach — and because his intellect allows him to see things about the game others do not. He might very well be right. But he is never going to match Wooden's ten titles, and that galls him. Having lost to Wooden in the Final Four in 1973, he would have loved nothing more than the opportunity to ruin his farewell by beating him in the championship game in 1975.

He never got the chance.

A year later Indiana went through the regular season undefeated again. This time everyone stayed healthy and the Hoosiers beat Michigan in the national championship game in Philadelphia — in spite of shooting guard Bobby Wilkerson getting hurt in the final — and walked away with a 32–0 record and the national title. No team has gone undefeated since, a source of great pride to Knight. But even as he walked out of the Philadelphia Spectrum that night on top of the college basketball world, Knight could not completely enjoy the accomplishment. He was with his close friend Bob Hammel, then the sports editor of the

Bloomington Herald-Telephone. Hammel became so close to Knight through the years that Indiana's players gave him two nicknames: "the shadow," because Knight was almost never seen without him, especially on road trips, and "Pravda," because he was, for all intents and purposes, the official Bob Knight news agency.

As the two men left the Spectrum that night Hammel was overjoyed for his friend. "You did it," he said. "You went undefeated and you won the national championship!"

Knight's response was almost glum: "Shoulda been two," he said, thinking back to the '75 team that — healthy — was probably better than the one that had just been crowned champions.

Many, if not most, great coaches are that way. The victories are quickly forgotten; the defeats linger. It is part of what makes them great. It also frequently makes them less-than-happy people.

"It took getting sick and not being able to coach to make me understand how lucky I had been," Mike Krzyzewski said, referring to his 1995 season, lost to postoperative back troubles and a complete breakdown that landed him in the hospital in January. "Until then I was always thinking about the next thing. We won national championships and I enjoyed them for a few hours, maybe a few days. Then it was on to the next thing."

Krzyzewski's first national title was completely unexpected. Nevada–Las Vegas had hammered Duke in the national championship game in 1990 and had all its starters back. The Rebels were being fitted for immortality by the time they arrived in Indianapolis a year later with a 34–0 record. Duke was a surprise Final Four team that year, having lost three seniors off the 1990 team. But Krzyzewski had added a superb freshman named Grant Hill to his team, and Christian Laettner and Bobby Hurley had emerged as stars. When Krzyzewski looked at the tape of the game a year earlier, painful as it was, he was convinced his team could win the game.

North Carolina played Kansas in the opening semifinal that afternoon. To some, this was almost an intrasquad game. Roy Williams had worked for Dean Smith for ten years before getting the Kansas job in 1988 and did everything almost exactly the same way Smith did. Kansas's victory was a mild surprise, but the shocking part of the day came when Smith was ejected in the final minute by referee Pete Pavia. Smith was angry with Pavia for giving him a technical foul in the first half and frustrated because his team was about to lose. When one of his players fouled out late, Pavia told Smith he needed a sub.

"How much time do I have?" Smith asked.

"I knew exactly how much time I had, of course," Smith said years later. (By rule he had thirty seconds.) "But I was upset with Pete's approach. I was being sarcastic and Pete decided that was enough."

Pavia, who died of cancer in 1993, said later that he knew Smith was being sarcastic and decided to call him on it. Smith's assistant Bill Guthridge was so upset about what happened that he had to be kept away from Pavia in the hallway under the stands when the game ended.

Krzyzewski, in the locker room, waiting for the game to end, really didn't care that Smith had been tossed or why. "All I knew was that when I realized Kansas had won, I felt this little shudder of relief," he said. "The thought that flashed through my head was 'Okay, even if we don't win, our archrival isn't going to win, either.' It occurred to me that if I had that thought, the players had to have it, too. I walked into the locker room and said, 'Fellas, we all know Carolina just lost. Maybe you feel like that relieves a little bit of pressure. I understand why you feel that way. Now, think about it for another second and then flush it. What just happened doesn't matter. What happens next is what matters.'"

What happened next was one of the great upsets in the history of college basketball. Laettner and Hurley were brilliant and, as Krzyzewski had told his players, UNLV got tight in a close game. The Rebels had been so dominant that they hadn't played a game all year decided in the final minute. Duke had played in close games all season. Hurley made a clutch three-pointer with Vegas up 76–71 and 2:14 left in the game, and Laettner made the two free throws that won the game with twelve seconds left. Vegas superstar Larry Johnson passed up an open three in the last frantic seconds and the game ended with Anderson Hunt hurling a desperation shot at the buzzer that was way off the mark.

As the building went nuts and his players jumped into one another's arms, Krzyzewski ran onto the court, palms down, trying to calm everyone down. "Stop it," he kept saying. "Stop it. We haven't won anything yet!"

"I was angry at that moment," he said years later. "I thought my guys should understand that winning on Saturday isn't the goal. We'd been down that road before — in '86 and in '90 — and lost on Monday. All I wanted to do right then was get in the locker room and tell them in no uncertain terms that we were only halfway to our goal."

Krzyzewski was something of a dervish the next two days. He screamed at Greg Koubek and Marty Clark for wearing newly acquired cowboy hats on the bus to practice on Sunday. He told the team that day that they had better stop acting as if they had won the national championship by beating UNLV on Saturday, or they would surely lose it to Kansas on Monday. "I felt as if I hadn't done enough to get them ready to play against Louisville after we had beaten Kansas in '86," he said. "The loss to Vegas [in 1990] was different. We had no chance to win that game. But '86, if I had been a little more experienced, I think we could have — should have — won. I wasn't going to make the same mistake twice. I knew we were tired mentally and physically, but that didn't matter. We had to find a way to get through forty more minutes."

They did. Krzyzewski rested Laettner at key junctures, Hurley made several huge shots, and Grant Hill made one of the most spectacular dunks in Final Four history early on to set the tone. Duke won, 72–65. Jay Bilas, who had been the starting center on that 1986 team that had lost to Louisville, was an assistant coach at the time. "There's one moment I remember better than anything else that happened that night," he said. "In the final seconds, we got a dunk that wrapped up the game. There might have been fifteen seconds left and Coach K turned away from the court so that he was looking right where I was sitting. He just closed his eyes, clenched his fists, and, almost under his breath, said, 'National championship — *yes!*' I'll never forget that because I was so happy for him."

Duke went on to win the title again a year later, becoming the first — and only — team since Wooden's retirement to win back-to-back titles. In the semifinals, the Blue Devils beat Indiana. Knight took that defeat fairly hard. He and Krzyzewski didn't speak to each other again for almost ten years.

5

Storytellers

EVERY FINAL FOUR WEEK has a rhythm to it, almost like a Shakespearean play in five acts: there is the prologue, early arrivals beginning to trickle into the host city while last-second preparations are still going on, whether they involve putting up WELCOME FINAL FOUR! signs on anything that isn't moving on the city streets, making sure every last banner that *isn't* Final Four–related is taken down in the building where the games will be played, or being certain that the team hotels are overrun with security. Act two usually comes on Wednesday and Thursday, when most of the core participants arrive: teams, coaches for the convention, most media members. Act three is Friday. Fans begin to stream into town, most of them proudly wearing their school's colors so they are easy to identify as they choke the streets looking for parties or pep rallies. Act four is Saturday — game day — when everyone finds creative ways to kill time until the late-afternoon tip-off of the first semifinal reminds everyone why they're here, that there are actually basketball games to be played. And then act five, when the city begins to quiet. By Sunday evening, half the fans are gone and only two teams remain, quietly waiting for Monday night's climactic scene that, in the minds of those involved, will end with all the pathos of *Hamlet*. Someone will lie figuratively bleeding to death onstage while a triumphant army arrives to survey everything that has gone on. Good night, Sweet Prince, indeed.

There are a few people who understand the five acts better than most, because they have lived them over and over for years. In that sense, for them, the Final Four is more like *Groundhog Day* than Shakespeare. Unlike the Bill Murray character, though, they look forward each year to the alarm going off at 6:00 A.M. to start the cycle anew.

Shortly before the Friday afternoon practices began in St. Louis for the 2005 Final Four, Rich Clarkson stood at the baseline of the court inside the Edward Jones Dome, looking around with just a bit of wonderment in his eyes as thousands and thousands of fans poured into the building to watch *practice*. "First Final Four I went to, I think the building seated a little more than ten thousand and they couldn't fill it," he said, laughing. "Of course, that was a few years ago."

Fifty-three years ago, to be precise, when the Final Four, then known only as the National Collegiate Basketball Championship, was played on the campus of the University of Washington in the Hec Edmundson Pavilion. Clarkson was a freshman at the University of Kansas back then, an aspiring young photographer who had persuaded Kansas coach Phog Allen to let him travel with the team that season. "I had to have a roommate on the road," he said. "There were eleven players on the team, so I was assigned to room with the guy generally considered to be the eleventh player."

That eleventh player was Dean Smith, then a Kansas junior. "What I remember about Dean was that the game would start with him sitting on the end of the bench," Clarkson said. "By halftime, he had usually manipulated himself so that he was sitting next to Doc Allen [Allen was an osteopath] and [assistant coach] Dick Harp. I don't think there was anyone on the team back then who wasn't convinced that Dean was going to end up as a coach."

Clarkson had first met Phog Allen as a boy growing up in Lawrence, Kansas. He and his friends frequently played in a series of tunnels that ran underneath the Kansas campus. "One day we heard noises at the end of one of the tunnels and followed it," he said. "We popped out in old Robinson Gym. The team was practicing. We hid out for a little while, but when there was a break, we just walked out into the gym. Doc Allen came over and asked us if we were basketball fans. We said we were. He said, 'In that case, there's someone here watching practice who you should meet.' He walked us over to an older gentleman who was sitting on a chair and said, 'Boys, I'd like you to meet James Naismith.' The inventor of basketball was visiting Doc Allen, his old pupil."

Naismith was not the most famous person Clarkson met as a boy. When he was in junior high school, his two fascinations were aviation and journalism. He combined the two by starting an aviation newspaper. He frequently wrote to famous people in the aviation industry, asking for photos or press releases to put in the newspaper. One of the people he interviewed for the paper — the *Lawrence Aviation News* — was Dr. William Simpson, the chairman of the aeronautical engineering department at Kansas. One afternoon Clarkson got a call from Simpson saying he should come by his office right away. Clarkson showed up and found that Simpson had a visitor.

"Rich, I'd like you to meet Orville Wright," Simpson said.

Clarkson ran home after meeting Wright to write a story for

his newspaper and to tell his parents what had happened. "My father was pretty impressed," he said. "He asked me if I had gotten Orville Wright's autograph. I drew myself up, I think I was eleven or twelve at the time, and I said, 'Dad, a journalist doesn't ask for autographs.' Looking back on it now, I probably should have broken the rule that one time."

It was in high school that Clarkson fell in love with photography, specifically, photojournalism. He went to Kansas intending to become an air force pilot but found out after he had signed up for ROTC that his eyes weren't strong enough to allow him to fly. So, the man whose eyes weren't good enough to fly a plane instead used his eyes to take pictures that have become a part of basketball history. The moment that John Wooden talks about remembering so vividly, when Sidney Wicks put his arm around him to thank him at the end of the 1971 championship game, is one that Wooden can see not only in his mind's eye but in the picture Clarkson gave him of the coach and the once-wayward player.

"I always enjoyed looking for the out-of-the-ordinary picture," Clarkson said. "When I was at Kansas, I divided the game into two parts. In the first half, I would be taking pictures for the AP, the *Kansas City Star,* the *Topeka Capital,* and Acme Pictures. I'd file all of them at halftime. Those were your more routine game shots. Then in the second half I'd just shoot for the *Lawrence Daily World* and I'd look for things that were a little more interesting."

Clarkson made enough money working for all those publications to buy his own camera equipment. When he went to that first Final Four in 1952, he remembers being one of six photographers shooting the championship game. "I think I was the only one who shot the awards ceremony, because everyone else had to leave early to file," he said.

He was back at the Final Four with Kansas in 1953, when it was held in Kansas City. "That was a lot different than Seattle," he said. "Especially with KU playing, it was a very tough ticket. You could feel the excitement in town. I remember [former NCAA executive director] Walter Byers once saying that the best way to guarantee a sellout was to go to Kansas City. Everyone stayed in the Muhlbach and there was a tunnel that went under the street to Municipal Auditorium. It was about a two-hundred-yard walk from the hotel lobby to courtside."

Clarkson didn't get to go back until 1957. Kansas didn't make the last weekend his junior or senior year and then he was in the air force, fulfilling his ROTC commitment, after college. It was while he was in the air force that he began doing freelance work for a relatively new magazine called *Sports Illustrated*. "My first assignment was to shoot Wilt Chamberlain when he was a sophomore at Kansas," he said. "I got him to sit in a folding chair and bend over to tie his shoes to try to give people an idea of just how huge he was. The magazine opened the story with a full page of that photo."

Clarkson was able to get passes to leave the air force base to work for *SI* in return for supplying the base commander with tickets to Kansas games. He returned to the Final Four in 1957, shooting the historic triple-overtime game between Kansas and North Carolina in which the Tar Heels outlasted Kansas and Chamberlain, 54–53. "That was one time when I remember making a conscious effort not to think about the game," he said. "Obviously I was pulling for Kansas, but I couldn't get emotionally involved. When I look around today during a game and see all the security and people watching every move the photographers make, I laugh. I remember in those days I'd just walk right over and shoot the players and coaches in the huddle during time-outs. You could go anywhere you wanted."

Clarkson's first *Sports Illustrated* cover came in 1964, a picture taken during the UCLA-Duke championship game. The cover wasn't supposed to be Clarkson's. It was supposed to be Hy Peskin's. Peskin was *SI'*s star photographer at the time and had made a deal with a camera company to take photos of him taking the cover photo during the championship game. The only problem was that the magazine editors liked what Clarkson filed better and chose one of his photos for the cover.

Clarkson has known all the great coaches of the past fifty years. When Bob Knight wrote his autobiography, he asked Clarkson to shoot the cover. The two men had first met when Clarkson and writer Pat Putnam had been assigned to do a piece during Knight's second year at Indiana. "By the end of the week I was eating dinner at his house," Clarkson said. "In '76, when they went to Philadelphia for the Final Four, Bob let me in the locker room before the game to take pictures. He did it again in '81, when they won the second time."

Clarkson remembers going to a victory dinner with Knight and a group of his friends in 1976. John Havlicek, the Boston Celtics Hall of Famer who had been Knight's college teammate, was in the group. Walking into the restaurant, Havlicek spotted Curry Kirkpatrick, then with *Sports Illustrated,* eating at a table across the room. Knowing that a *Sports Illustrated* photographer was in the Knight group, Havlicek assumed that Knight would be friendly with a writer from the same magazine. What he didn't know was that Kirkpatrick had written a story earlier that year that had enraged Knight. When Havlicek suggested to Knight that they invite Kirkpatrick to join them, Knight said, "You bring that son of a bitch over here and I'll kill him."

Victory never mellowed Bob Knight.

During the nearly ten years that Knight and Mike Krzyzewski

weren't speaking, Clarkson photographed each on several occasions. "Without fail, acting as if they didn't really care, they would both bring up the other one," he said. "As in 'I saw you had a photo of Mike in the magazine last month' or something like that. The fact that they cared about each other was still very apparent."

Clarkson also knew Adolph Rupp, a fellow Kansan, quite well. "First time I was sent by the magazine to shoot him, Kentucky was still playing in the old Memorial Gym," he said. "The benches were at either end of the court. I thought it would be nice to sit in front of the bench, since I wouldn't be on the court, and shoot Rupp from there. The SID said absolutely not. I went to see Rupp in his office. He started screaming: 'I know why you're here, you're just here to make a fool out of me and I'm not going to have it!'

"I said, 'Coach, I'd never want to do that. Why, you helped launch my career as a photographer.'"

Rupp looked at Clarkson as if he had lost his mind. "Do you remember coming to Lawrence to visit your sister one time and you wanted to get your picture taken with Doc Allen? Your sister and my mom were friends, and she called me and asked me to come out and take the picture."

Rupp stared at Clarkson in disbelief for a second. "That was you?" he said. "I remember that. Okay, you can do whatever you want."

Rupp appears in what may be Clarkson's most famous picture. It was shot moments after Kentucky had lost to Texas Western in the 1966 championship game, the so-called *Brown v. Board of Education* final, and it shows Rupp and his players on their bench, clearly in shock over the outcome. "Hard to believe that game was almost forty years ago," he said. "I can still see the look on Rupp's face when I took that picture."

Nowadays, Clarkson, who is seventy-two, is a Final Four institution. St. Louis was his fiftieth, and the NCAA put together a series of his photos to show on the giant message boards in the dome throughout the weekend. "It's a little embarrassing," he said, smiling. "But it's also very nice." Like everyone else who has seen the event grow from small-town sideshow to massive three-ring circus, Clarkson finds it all just a little bit amazing. "If anyone ever tells you they dreamed it would become *this*," he said, gesturing around the dome as more than 30,000 people watched the Friday practices, "they're lying. In some ways it isn't as much fun, because we've lost the intimacy we had years ago. But seeing what it has become is a great thing. I feel proud to have been a small part of it."

Not far from where Clarkson stood setting up camera positions for the next day, Billy Packer sat watching each of the four teams practice. He was seated in the second row, a few feet behind where he would be sitting the next day as the analyst on CBS's telecast of the semifinals. It would be his thirty-first consecutive Final Four — seven with NBC, the last twenty-four with CBS. Packer has been an analyst for so long now that many — if not most — who listen to him have no idea that he was a star on Wake Forest's first (and only) Final Four team in 1962.

"Of course, back then it wasn't even that big a deal to us," he said. "The big deal was winning the ACC Tournament; that was the way you earned your spurs in those days. Once we won the ACCs, they told us there was this other tournament we were going to play in because we won. That was fine with us and we tried to win, but it wasn't the same thing." He smiled. "I remember they gave us watches when it was over. I think half the guys on my team pawned them. First year we went [1961], we lost to St. Joseph's in the regionals. The next year when we won the ACC Tournament again, we were a little more psyched-up for the NCAAs because of what had happened the year before. But I remember when we beat Villanova to win the regional, we didn't celebrate the way we did when we won the ACCs. It just wasn't the same."

Wake Forest ended up playing UCLA in the consolation game that year after losing to Ohio State. (The Bruins had lost to Cincinnati.) "We didn't even know it at the time, but because we won that game, the ACC got a first-round bye the next year — which it kept until the tournament expanded in '75 and everyone had to play a first-round game."

Packer was aware of the NCAA Tournament growing up in Bethlehem, Pennsylvania. His dad coached at Lehigh, and Packer remembers getting out of school early on a fall day in 1954 because La Salle, which had won the 1954 national championship, was coming to town to scrimmage his dad's team. "I remember thinking Tom Gola was an amazing player," he said. "I was thirteen at the time, not even that much of a fan yet, but I was awed by Gola. The next spring, La Salle was back in the Final Four and I listened on the radio because it wasn't on TV. The guy doing the game kept talking about this guy Russell who kept blocking Tom Gola's shots. I'm thinking, 'That's impossible, no one can do that to Gola. Who the hell is this guy Russell?' Think about that, I was a basketball fan, this is the Final Four, and I had never *heard* of Bill Russell."

Russell and his San Francisco team went on to win that year and again the next. Even then Russell wasn't that big a star. He played on the 1956 Olympic team and then joined the Boston Celtics, whom he ended up leading to eleven NBA titles over the next thirteen seasons. "I remember telling Bob Cousy the story about never having heard of Russell before the '55 Final Four," Packer said. "He laughed and said, 'First time I laid eyes on him was in the layup line before his first game.' These days, Russell probably wouldn't have gone to college for more than a year. He'd have been in the NBA."

Packer coached briefly after graduating from Wake Forest, before getting out of basketball and into business. His TV career began soon after that when he was asked to do the ACC Game of the Week. People quickly noticed his ability to break a game down, and he and his partner, the late Jim Thacker, became one of the most popular duos on TV. In 1974 he was asked to do early-round tournament games by TVS, which still shared the TV rights in those days with NBC and the NCAA. A year later Scotty Connell, NBC's executive producer, called Packer the week before the tournament began and said, "We thought you did well last year; you feel like working for us again this year?" Packer said that was fine with him, they agreed he would be paid $750 a game, and he was told to report to Tuscaloosa for the first weekend of the tournament.

"I checked in to the hotel and the clerk said, 'Mr. Gowdy has already checked in.' It had never occurred to me that I'd be working with Curt Gowdy. That was when it first occurred to me that maybe they really liked what I was doing."

Back then Gowdy was *the* name in play-by-play at NBC. If Gowdy did an event, it was a big deal. If you worked with Gowdy, it was really a big deal. In what would prove to be an ironic twist, Packer's first game on NBC was Kentucky-Marquette. Al McGuire, who would become both his broadcast partner and best friend, was Marquette's coach. "Kentucky had [Rick] Robey and [Mike] Phillips," Packer said. "They were both huge. Early in the game Al was up bitching every time they did anything, trying to get them in foul trouble. The officials were calling nothing. Finally, Al just turned to [assistant coach] Hank Raymonds and said, 'You go ahead and coach. This is over.' He was right. He knew if the officials let Robey and Phillips play, there was no way his team could win."

At the end of the first weekend, Connell called again and asked if Packer would go to Portland for the regionals. It was the same way a week later when the Final Four went to San Diego. "That was the first time I had been there since I played in it in '62," he said. "It still didn't strike me as being that big an event."

Packer hasn't missed a Final Four since. In 1978 NBC hired McGuire, who had retired the previous season after leading Marquette to the national championship, and, unsure about what he would bring to the broadcast, initially put him in the truck to help break down replays. By then Dick Enberg was the play-by-play man. After the first game they did together, Packer suggested that McGuire sit with him and Enberg, creating basketball's first three-man booth. "Al was a natural right from the start," Packer said. "He saw things in the game other people didn't and he wasn't afraid to say what he was thinking. I've never been afraid to speak my mind, either. I think that's why we worked well together."

They worked together so well that, with Enberg acting as their moderator, they became the face of college basketball. They were Dick Vitale before there was Dick Vitale. When Enberg-Packer-McGuire came to town to do a game, it was a big deal. "You have to remember that this was still when there wasn't very much college basketball on TV," Packer said. "Even when ESPN did start [in 1979] they weren't in any homes, so our games were still the standard."

The era of the NBC three came to a crashing halt in 1981 when CBS shocked the sports world with its massive $48 million, three-year bid for the tournament rights. Enberg and McGuire were still under contract to NBC, but Packer wasn't. CBS quickly hired him and early on began asking him for ways it could make an impact on the sport, especially since NBC was still doing regular-season games with Enberg and McGuire. "One thing I came up with [along with Len DeLuca] was the idea of the selection show," he said. "That was the whole idea behind the 'Road to the Final Four' concept. To get here, you have to go down a lot of different roads during a long, hard winter, and the teams come from a lot of different places and backgrounds. We wanted to remind people of that by showing them the entire field going into the bracket because the tournament isn't just about the powerhouses, it's about the little guys, too."

Packer has now worked the Final Four with five different play-by-play men: Gowdy, Enberg, Gary Bender, Brent Musburger, and Jim Nantz. He has been the one absolute for CBS since the beginning. There are very few people in basketball who don't respect his knowledge of the game, his work ethic, or his ability to break down what is happening in a game on the fly. And yet he isn't nearly as popular with most fans as Vitale and, to many, is a remote, often difficult person to deal with. Packer makes no apologies for any of this. He has always been outspoken and does not enjoy being around masses of people the way Vitale so clearly does.

As he watched Illinois practice on Friday — with at least two-thirds of the crowd dressed in the school's blue and orange colors — Packer was fuming about a story in the local paper that implied that he and Vitale didn't like each other.

"It's funny how sometimes people try to make a big deal out of Dick and I not being friends," he said. "We haven't spent much time together through the years, but that's because our paths don't cross that much and because, to be honest, when I'm on the road, I don't go out much. I'd rather stay in my room, relax, and prepare. All that means is that Dick and I are different, nothing more, nothing less. He does things one way and it works for him, and I do things another and it works for me. The thing I enjoy the most about this job is preparing and then having a really good game.

"I've learned lessons as I've gotten older. I know now that no one at CBS really wants my input beyond showing up and doing my job. It took a while for me to figure that out. I should have figured it out sooner because I remember Al telling me, 'Billy, the TV people don't want you in their business.' In other words — do your job and shut up."

Packer's not likely to shut up. He still bridles when he hears people talk about Indiana State–Michigan State (Bird vs. Magic) in 1979 being a turning point in the game's history. "It was a bad game," he said, shaking his head in disbelief when the myth was brought up again. "Go back and look at the tape. Bird didn't play well and Michigan State was in control because it had a much better team. Magic had Greg Kelser, Bird didn't have anyone close to that level playing with him. The reason the game is so big in people's minds is because of what Magic and Bird became later, not because of the game itself."

Even so, the game remains the highest-rated college basketball game in history. "There's no question it had the buildup," he said. "Indiana State was undefeated and a lot of people [Packer included] had questioned them during the season because of the conference they played in. Magic was already a big star because of his flair. So people watched. That doesn't mean it was a good game."

Packer is sixty-four now and very comfortable with his role.

He has made lots of money in business and doesn't need to work. But like so many people, he still gets a rush from being courtside, especially for a great game. He readily admits that he still misses McGuire, who died of cancer in 2001 at the age of seventy-two. CBS hired McGuire during the 1990s after his NBC contract ran out, and later hired Enberg. The three were even reunited for a game. "That was a lot of fun," Packer said. "It was almost as if we had never stopped working together."

While Packer is talking about McGuire he looks up to see Enberg approaching. These days Enberg, who looks considerably younger than sixty-eight, does a lot of essays and commentaries for CBS in addition to the play-by-play work he still does. He has also written a one-man play based on the musings of McGuire. He and Packer greet each other with the warmth of men who have shared something special. In this case it isn't just their work; it's their friendship with McGuire.

"We both end a lot of sentences by saying, 'Well, like Al used to say . . . ,'" Enberg said, laughing. Enberg spoke at McGuire's funeral and it was while he was putting together his eulogy that he was struck by the number of wise and funny things McGuire had said to him through the years. That was when the idea came to him to try to write a one-man play. Appropriately, the play was produced and performed in Milwaukee, which is where McGuire made his major mark on the game, as the coach at Marquette. In 1977, on the eve of the national championship game against North Carolina, McGuire talked about retiring to look for "seashells and balloons." Then he walked out of the press conference, got on his motorcycle, and tooled around downtown Atlanta for several hours. It is probable that he is the only coach in history to show up for the national championship game on a motorcycle.

"One of the reasons we got along is because neither one of us was afraid to tell people what we thought," Packer said. "The difference is I make people mad. Al could criticize them and they wouldn't get mad at him. Maybe it was because they knew he was right."

Even after NBC lost the rights to the NCAA Tournament, McGuire continued hosting a one-hour show that would air on Final Four Sunday. It became a tradition that the two coaches in the championship game would show up on Sunday morning to tape an interview with McGuire that would air as part of the show that afternoon. As soon as the interview was over, McGuire would give each coach the same piece of advice: "Tomorrow night, when you walk onto the floor, stop for a minute. Look around, soak it in. Because at that moment, you will be at the pinnacle of your profession, coaching in the one game every coach aspires to coach in. Take it all in, take a deep breath, and then go to work."

The only coach who ever refused to be part of McGuire's Sunday show was John Thompson, not because he had any problem with McGuire but because that was Thompson's way: if everyone else did something one way, he tended to do the opposite. So, in 1985, prior to the Villanova-Georgetown game, McGuire ended the show by interviewing Thompson's towel. Thompson always kept a large white towel draped over his right shoulder during a game, partly because he was superstitious but also because he tended to perspire heavily during games. McGuire took a white towel, draped it over a chair, and asked the towel questions while the credits ran. It might have been his best pre-championship interview ever.

Packer and Enberg both agreed that only Al could have pulled off that trick.

North Carolina was coming out onto the court at that moment and Roy Williams walked over to say hello to everyone from CBS. As various producers and directors gathered around Williams to pay their respects, too, they blocked Packer's view of the court. "For crying out loud," he shouted, "can't you people let a guy get some work done here!"

He was kidding. Sort of.

One person who would agree with Packer's assessment of his relationship with Dick Vitale was Vitale. "Billy's right, we're just different," he said. "He's vanilla and I'm Thirty-one Flavors."

For Vitale, Final Four week was completely different than it was for Packer. For one thing, he wouldn't be calling the games, something he had made peace with years ago, even if he might wish it different. "I learned a long time ago not to worry about things you can't control," he said. "When I was coaching I always dreamed of running one of the big-time programs: a UCLA or North Carolina or Indiana or Duke. But it didn't happen that way for me. I got to coach at Rutgers and Detroit. I made the best of it, and in the end, my life could not have worked out better."

One of the things that is difficult for people to understand about Vitale is that what you see on TV is what you get in real life. The one-eyed bald whack job who overflows with enthusiasm about everything, every single minute he is on the air, is no different from the guy sitting in a room with one other person. Vitale doesn't like things, he *loves* them. It is simply who he is, who he has been, dating back to his coaching career, which peaked when he took the University of Detroit to the Sweet Sixteen in 1977. The Titans lost to Michigan in that game, 86–81, but Vitale still remembers all the details.

"We had three future NBA guys on that team [Terry Duerod, John Long, and Terry Tyler], but they had size on us," he said. "What kills me is we had a six-ten junior college player who had to sit out that year because of a technicality. He was at Robert Morris, and the year he left they became a four-year school. So, instead of being eligible for us that year, he had to sit out! I wore a maize-and-blue jacket for the game in honor of Michigan. Imagine what it meant to our school with the city campus to be in the round of sixteen playing Michigan." (It should be noted here that every Vitale sentence should probably be punctuated with an exclamation point.) "I looked around that night and thought, 'This is what I always wanted to do, this is a long way from East Rutherford High School.[!!!!]'"

Vitale had grown up in New Jersey, gone to Seton Hall, and started his coaching career in local high schools. His first Final Four trip was on a whim. "I had a buddy, Tom Ramsten, a high school coach like me, and there was an all-night diner we'd go to and we'd just sit there and draw up plays," he said. "One year, I think it was 1967, we're sitting there and at four o'clock in the morning we said, let's drive to Louisville — which is where it was that year. We just got in the car and drove. Getting tickets wasn't a problem. We hung out the whole weekend, saw all the famous coaches walking through the lobby, and went to the games. I was awed by the whole thing. I just kept thinking, 'Someday I want to be a part of this.'"

Of course, he never dreamed how he would become part of it. Vitale was hired as an assistant coach by Dick Lloyd at Rutgers in 1971 and played a key role in recruiting the players whom Tom Young took to the Final Four in 1976. "People told me I was crazy," he said, repeating one of his favorite phrases. "I just believed if we worked hard enough, we could be on equal footing with the big-time programs. My buddies would say to me, 'Dick, you're at Rutgers. Calm down. It doesn't happen like that.'"

Vitale wasn't at Rutgers when it did happen for the Scarlet Knights. He was at Detroit, where he had been hired as head coach. "I think I made seventeen thousand dollars my first year," he said. "My whole pitch to the people there was 'Don't accept mediocrity.' We can play with Michigan and Michigan State, we just have to find the right kid for Detroit. I went out and told the guys if they wanted grass, we were in the wrong place. But if they wanted a big city, if they wanted to be watched by the top execs at General Motors and Ford, we were it."

The pitch worked. Detroit got one of the NCAA's thirty-two bids in 1977 by beating Marquette — which would go on to win the national championship — at Marquette on the last day of the regular season. Vitale did a madcap dance at midcourt after the buzzer, one that no doubt would have been replayed about a million times in today's media world. When his team made it to the round of sixteen, Vitale milked the moment for all it was worth. He had photos taken before the game with Curt Gowdy and John Wooden (who were broadcasting the game) and took Michigan to the last minute. It made him a star. The Detroit Pistons, fighting consistent mediocrity and lack of interest at the time, needed a coach — one who might sell a few tickets. Vitale had become a big name in Detroit. They offered him the job and he jumped.

"Most of my friends told me I was crazy to do it," he said. "I remember Jimmy Valvano saying, 'Dick, you're made for college, your enthusiasm won't play in the pros.' I can still hear those words. I have to admit a lot of it was money. I'd gotten up to twenty-five thousand dollars at Detroit being coach and athletic director. This was for four times as much. That was hard to turn down."

Early in his second season with the Pistons, Vitale was fired. The Pistons went 30–52 his first season and were 4–8 on November 8 when he got what he came to call "the ziggy," Vitalese for being fired. Looking back now, he understands it was the best thing that ever happened to him — for a number of reasons. Back then, it hurt. "I felt like a failure," he said. "Maybe that's why I defend coaches so ardently and get in trouble for it now, because I remember how it felt when it happened to me. I still remember, around my neighborhood, people who had been my friends wouldn't even look at me. On Sundays, after mass, we would always have coffee and doughnuts. When I was coaching, there was always a group of people around me wanting to hear stories, wanting to know about our last game or about different players or coaches. Now, I'm standing all alone with my wife. One Sunday I finally walked over to a group and said, 'Hey, can anyone here at least say hello to me? Am I a complete pariah because I got fired? Have I got bubonic plague or something?'"

Vitale's assumption was that he would end up back in college coaching. He had a record of success there that would attract someone. He was only thirty-nine when the Pistons fired him. But a man named Scotty Connell intervened. It can be argued that Connell is the most important person in the history of college basketball announcing. While he was at NBC, he hired Billy Packer and Al McGuire. In 1979 he left NBC to become the first executive producer of college basketball for a new cable network called ESPN. The idea, outlandish at the time, was to broadcast sports twenty-four hours a day. Since there was little college basketball on network TV at the time and there were many games, the sport became an outpost for ESPN, a place where it had a chance to make its mark.

Connell had been the producer for NBC on the night Detroit

lost to Michigan. He had heard Vitale speak, seen his act. He thought his combination of enthusiasm and outrageousness could work for a start-up entity pleading for attention. He called Vitale, newly out of work, and asked if he wanted to try his hand at doing a few games. "I had nothing else to do at the time," Vitale said. "Scotty seemed to think I might be good at it. I figured I'd give it a shot."

That shot changed Vitale's life and the course of college basketball history. "Putting aside all the great things that have happened to me, I am convinced of one thing absolutely," Vitale said. "If I had gone back into coaching, I would have been dead by fifty. I mean that. Almost for sure, my marriage would not have lasted. I still remember my second year at Detroit, I managed to convince Michigan to come in and play in our Christmas tournament. This was huge for us. First round, they played Western Michigan while we played Eastern Michigan. We were going to play them in the finals and it was going to be a big deal. Except we lost at the buzzer. I still remember that Christmas. It was miserable. I just sat and watched tape and didn't talk to anyone. I don't know how my wife put up with it. If I'd gone back into coaching, even if I hadn't been dead, there's no way my marriage would have survived, no matter how patient she was."

Vitale made his ESPN debut on December 5, 1979, doing color on a game between Wisconsin and DePaul. His partner that night was a man named Joe Boyle, who was by trade a hockey play-by-play man. In fact, that was the only college basketball game he ever did for the network, making him the answer to a trivia question: Who worked with Dick Vitale on his first night as a broadcaster?

Vitale quickly became a cult figure at ESPN. The network wasn't in that many homes at the time, but it began acquiring games that people wanted to watch. Then it made a deal with the NCAA to televise early-round games of the tournament. Rather than attach Vitale to one tournament site, Connell made the decision to put him in the studio so he could be on all the time, talking at halftime and between games about what was going on. Vitale's outrageous comments and predictions became a part of the tournament to basketball fans, most famously when he promised to stand on his head if Austin Peay beat Illinois in a first-round game in 1987 — then did after Austin Peay pulled off the upset.

"It worked out well, though," he said, laughing. "Austin Peay asked me to come out and speak at their banquet that year. I actually made money on the deal."

Vitale was soon making a lot of money in a lot of places. As ESPN grew, so did his popularity. He began doing commercials, speaking for huge fees (up to $50,000 and more nowadays), and endorsing everything from pizza to sneakers. College students in particular loved him, especially when he came to their place to do a game and engaged in pregame shooting contests or allowed himself to be passed up through the stands. Much to the horror of many basketball purists, he became the number one face and voice of college basketball. To those who enjoyed Packer's steady, solid analysis, Vitale's screaming endorsement of anything and everyone he met was anathema to their ears. Vitale doesn't so much break down a game as surround it — he talks about his family, every coach, most of the players, numerous fans, writers, people he met overseas during the summer, the hockey lockout, and every restaurant he has ever set foot in. If you don't know Vitale, it is easy to think he is simply sucking up to people. It really isn't true: he simply likes almost everyone he meets.

"I've had times where people who have ripped me have come

up to say something and I greet them and I'm friendly to them," he said. "My wife will say, 'That guy ripped you, why are you nice to him?' I say, 'Why not? The guy is doing a job; he has an opinion. I may not like it, but so what? Life is too short to make enemies. Making friends is a lot more fun.'"

That approach, and his genuine enthusiasm and willingness to try almost anything, has made Vitale the most famous person in college basketball — period. Some can't stand listening to him, many more clearly love him, but all know him. He has been criticized, sometimes justifiably, for defending any and all coaches. He doesn't apologize for it. "Whenever I watch a losing coach, it reminds me of why I'm lucky I never got back into coaching," he said. "The worst thing is that phony postgame handshake. I wish they'd cut that out. If guys really want to do it, fine, but most of the time you lose you just want to get out of there. Whenever a guy gets fired, I bleed for him. For one thing, I know it is almost impossible for a guy who gets fired from a big-time job to get back to that level and how hard it is going to be going back down a level or two. I'm lucky I never had to do it."

Vitale's Final Four weekend is filled to the brim. He makes appearances for corporations, gives speeches, does several-times-a-day bits from ESPN's set (complete with screaming, adoring fans in the background), and probably signs more autographs than every other coach in town combined. In 2005 he had hernia surgery in early March and there was some question about whether he would be well enough to make it to his twenty-first consecutive Final Four. "Some people told me, 'Don't do it, Dick, you can miss one year,'" he said. "I said, 'Are you kidding? Miss the Final Four! Miss my favorite weekend of the year? No way, baby!'"

It should be thus forevermore.

6

Partying

BY THURSDAY AFTERNOON, the events surrounding the Final Four are well under way. The teams are in town and off practicing at secret locations. They are required to show up at the arena on Friday for a practice that is open to the public, but even that won't be real. All will schedule their real workouts away from the arena and then spend their fifty required minutes on the court getting accustomed to the shooting backgrounds, having dunk contests, and perhaps scrimmaging a little bit.

It didn't used to be that way. Only in the past dozen years have teams taken to scheduling an extra practice on Friday. "I remember when we were in Seattle in 1984, our workout in the Kingdome was very much the real deal," said Terry Holland, who twice took Virginia to the Final Four and was later chairman of the basketball committee. "We were the last team to practice that day and they were having some kind of cookout inside the dome that night. When they started turning on the grills, the place was just filled with smoke. Our kids were coughing, having trouble breathing. I started screaming at [basketball committee member] Dick Shrider that this was ridiculous; how were we supposed to practice for a Final Four game when we couldn't breathe?"

That's not likely to be a problem nowadays. And if someone did schedule a cookout inside one of the domes, the coach whose team couldn't breathe would probably just see it as a convenient excuse to get his team away from the required appearance a little bit early. One thing coaches really don't like about the Final Four is being forced to do everything the NCAA demands. Most are used to being unquestioned dictators in their worlds, and all of a sudden, on the most important weekend of their lives, they are being told what to do.

"I remember my first one, in 1982, they made us go to this meeting," said John Thompson, the former Georgetown coach who made three Final Fours (and reached the final each time) and won the national championship in 1984. "First of all, I didn't like being told that I had to go to a meeting. Then we get in there and they're telling us, 'You will wear this pin on the bench,' and, 'When you are introduced, you will walk down and shake hands with the other coach,' and on and on like that. I'm sitting there thinking, 'Let's just play the damn games and stop all this nonsense.'"

Nonsense is part of the Final Four, whether it is the lengthy Friday afternoon meeting Thompson was referring to that remains mandatory for head coaches — all coaches, no assistants may attend in their place — or the hijinks in the coaches' lobby or all the various official parties throughout the week. On Thursday night the NCAA throws something called the "salute" dinner, which is appropriate since it is the NCAA saluting itself. The salute dinner is also mandatory for the coaches, who are each asked to get up and speak briefly. It is one of those good news/bad news jokes: On the one hand, you are thrilled to be one of the four guys still coaching. On the other hand, because you are coaching, you have a lot better things to do than stand up in front of several hundred people and tell them how glad you are to be there.

South Carolina coach Dave Odom, who has been to the final eight (at Wake Forest) but never the Final Four, may have spoken for all coaches as he walked out of the dinner one year: "My dream is to go to that dinner some year because they force me to go," he said.

Everywhere you turn during Final Four week there are parties. The U.S. Basketball Writers Association, for whom the Final Four is a convention much the way it is for the coaches, has its annual dinner for board members, past presidents, and USBWA Hall of Fame members on Thursday night, too. The main reason it is held on Thursday is that the writers all know there is no way they will be invited to the salute dinner — which is fine with most of them. CBS throws all sorts of parties as well. There's a Wednesday night dinner thrown by the public relations staff; then a Friday night party, usually in a bar, for anyone who has ever coached; and then the big Sunday night dinner for CBS execs and members of the basketball committee. The coaches association has its official dinner on Sunday night but now also has a Sunday breakfast for all its past presidents and is planning to add in 2006 a predinner event for any coach who has ever taken a team to the Final Four.

And on and on. The best party of the 2005 Final Four had absolutely nothing to do with ex-presidents or Hall of Famers or salutes or CBS or the basketball committee. It was put together by Frank Sullivan, the longtime coach at Harvard, in honor of his buddy Tom Brennan, who was retiring at the age of fifty-five after nineteen years as the head coach at the University of Vermont. Sullivan invited about a hundred people to a bar far removed from downtown St. Louis — "It was the best I could do for the money I had," he said — and close to three hundred people showed up. Brennan had told Sullivan that there was absolutely no way he was going to speak and then spoke emotionally for fifteen minutes.

Brennan is one of college basketball's true Runyonesque characters. He was an assistant coach early in his career under Rollie Massimino at Villanova and later coached at Yale for four years before taking the job at Vermont in 1986. During his first three seasons there he was 14–68 — and didn't get fired. "How many schools in the country would not fire you with a record like that?" Brennan said. "When I say the people at Vermont took me in, I mean it; they really took me in."

Brennan survived at Vermont in part because the school is never going to hire and fire the way big-time schools do, but also because he became one of the most popular people on campus before he became a winner. Most coaches have to win to be popular; Brennan was an exception. He built a solid program and also became a radio talk show host. On a whim, a local radio station asked him in 1991 if he wanted to do the sports for a week or two while their regular sports host was away. Brennan figured what the heck and did it for yucks. The chemistry he quickly developed with the show's host, Steve Cormier, was so good that Cormier asked him if he would be interested in cohosting the show. Fourteen years later *Corm and the Coach* was syndicated throughout the state and got higher ratings than either Howard Stern or Don Imus in the morning drive.

Brennan is a natural behind the microphone. He's smart, well read, and quick-witted. He has as many opinions on who should be governor of Vermont as he does on who should start for the Catamounts at point guard. In the spring of 2000 he had recruited a very good point guard from Rhode Island named

T. J. Sorrentine, a hard-nosed little player with great range who he thought would give his program a boost. That same spring he also signed a local kid named Taylor Coppenrath. "His main asset," Brennan said, "was that he was six-nine. I thought if we redshirted him a year, worked with him, he could help us down the line."

Vermont lost eleven straight games the next season while Coppenrath was sitting out, and Brennan was tempted to play him because by then he had an inkling the kid might be a little better than just someone who could help down the line. A year later, with Sorrentine at point guard and Coppenrath starting as a redshirt freshman at center, Vermont won the regular-season title in the America East Conference and was 21–7 before crashing in the first round of the conference tournament. "I thought maybe I'd blown my best chance to ever make a postseason tournament," Brennan said. "I mean any postseason tournament. We would have walked to the NIT if they had taken us."

Sadly, the NIT would rather have an eighth-place team from the ACC or the Big East than a regular-season champion from a one-bid league whose players and coaches would be willing to walk to New York for a chance to play. The Catamounts stayed home. Then Sorrentine broke his wrist in preseason that fall and had to be medically redshirted.

But the dream didn't die. Coppenrath was emerging as a star. During his freshman season he had scored 33 points in a game at Binghamton. Brennan was beside himself. "Taylor," he said, "you remind me of Larry Bird. You can be Bird!"

Coppenrath, who is the classic strong, silent type, shook his head at Brennan and said, "Coach, don't be ridiculous."

Three nights later he scored 3 points at Albany. "Hey, Taylor," Brennan said, "Bird never got held to three, you know."

He had cooled it with the Bird talk after that, but Coppenrath kept getting better. In March of 2002, after finishing second behind Boston University during the regular season, the Catamounts made it to the championship game, to be played at BU. After the semifinals, BU coach Dennis Wolff congratulated Brennan on the win and told him he looked forward to seeing him in six days in Boston (the America East final is played six days after the semifinals to accommodate — surprise — ESPN) and had one request: "No calls this week."

Brennan laughed. One of his favorite tricks in his guise as talk show host was to call opposing coaches on the air very early in the morning and wake them up. "Anyone else but Tom, you would have to kill the guy," Wolff said over the din of the Brennan farewell party. "From Tom you accept it and laugh it off."

Brennan called Wolff that week. Then on Saturday his team went into Boston and beat Wolff's team on a last-second jumper by a kid named David Hehn, who grew up in Canada but somehow became a basketball player instead of a hockey player. For the first time in history, Vermont was in the Dance. The entire state went nuts. Getting snowed in in Denver en route to Salt Lake City for the first round couldn't dampen the joy, nor could a one-sided loss to Arizona. "Hey, I did my job," Brennan said. "I won the press conference."

A year later, even though Coppenrath missed three weeks with an injury late in the season, Vermont won the conference tournament again — Coppenrath coming back to play in the final and scoring 43 points. It was that night, during the victory celebration at his house, that Brennan decided to quit. "I looked around and I saw how happy everyone was," he said. "I knew it couldn't possibly get better than this. Taylor and T.J. and the other rising seniors [five in all] had one more year and I wanted to coach them and go out with them. I felt completely satisfied. I don't think you can be a good coach if you're satisfied. It was time to go."

He made the announcement before the season began in the fall. By then, he and Coppenrath and Vermont were getting more national publicity than most highly ranked teams: a feature in *Sports Illustrated,* an ESPN camera crew trailing them for days at a time, a *USA Today* cover story. "No one loves Tommy Brennan more than me," Brennan said at one point, "and *I'm* getting sick of me."

Along with the attention and the yucks came pressure. Vermont was now supposed to be good. It was supposed to dominate the league. A close loss in the opener at Kansas actually left Brennan frustrated. "The officials got us," he said. Then he caught himself. "Whoever thought the day would come when I'd be upset about losing a close game at Kansas. Wow."

There were some off nights and a couple of disappointing losses early, but the Catamounts did dominate the league. The toughest weekend for Brennan was the first two rounds of the conference tournament, held in Binghamton. Because Vermont was the top seed, the championship game would be played in Burlington, in 3,200-seat Patrick Gym, a building that had once been all but empty for home games and was now sold out every night. "I knew if we got back to Patrick, we weren't losing there," Brennan said. "But it made me nervous to think we might stumble before we got there. When we won our semi, I was more relieved than I'd ever been after a win. And exhausted. I was so tired I let Lynn [his wife] drive home. I never do that."

He was right about playing in Patrick. Vermont blew out Northeastern. Midway through the second half, the chants began: "Thank-you, Bren-nan." The crowd was saying good-bye and thank you. Brennan cried on the bench. The next morning Dennis Wolff called to congratulate him. "I'm proud of you," he said. "But what was all that crying about?"

"We were up thirty," Brennan said. "I had nothing else to do."

There was a great sense of anticipation later that afternoon when the team gathered for the NCAA tournament selection show. Because it had played a tough nonconference schedule, Vermont had been in the top thirty in the vaunted RPI (Ratings Percentage Index) rankings all season. The RPI is supposed to rank teams based not only on record but on whom they have played and where they have played them. The members of the basketball committee reference the RPI all the time, insisting it is only part of how they seed the field — except when they want to back up something they've done. Then they cite the RPI. Based on the RPI, Vermont should have been seeded somewhere between seventh and tenth in its regional. Everyone waited to see where the team would fall in the draw, and then it popped on the screen: number four (in the so-called Austin regional) Syracuse against number thirteen Vermont — a Friday game in Worcester, Massachusetts.

"Number thirteen!" Brennan screamed. "How in the world can we be a number thirteen?"

Easy. They weren't from a power conference. The basketball committee takes care of power teams first and foremost. Of course, Syracuse and Coach Jim Boeheim, certainly a power team from a power conference, weren't thrilled, either. "First of all, I knew they were good," Boeheim said later. "Second, playing in Worcester, I knew half the state would be there."

Brennan told his team that week that the days of going to the NCAA Tournament and making videos and soaking it in were over. This was the last chance for the five seniors and for him.

They would go down to Worcester to win. On Tuesday, Brennan had Boeheim on the radio show.

"I really like to look at tape right after a game," Boeheim said. "I can't sleep anyway, and that way you look at it while it's still fresh in your mind. How about you, T.B., do you do that?"

"Yeah, I look at tape after games sometimes," Brennan answered. "If there's tape of the game on in the bar where I'm drinking, I'll look at it."

As it turned out, Boeheim wasn't far wrong about half the state of Vermont showing up. Maybe it was two-thirds. A lot of people thought that Syracuse, which had closed the season hot, had a chance to get to St. Louis. The Orange never got out of Worcester. Jesse Agel, Brennan's longtime assistant coach, came up with a game plan that slowed the pace, taking advantage of the fact that Syracuse rarely attacks defensively out of its 2–3 zone defense. The game rocked back and forth through regulation and into overtime, with Worcester's DCU Center in an absolute uproar. With a little more than a minute left in overtime and Vermont clinging to a 56–55 lead, Sorrentine stood thirty feet from the basket, dribbling down the shot clock. Brennan waved him over near the bench and, over the din, yelled, "Run red, TJ!"

"Red" was an end-of-the-shot-clock play in which Sorrentine would try to penetrate, bringing the defense to him, and then slide the ball to Coppenrath. Sorrentine shook his head. "It's okay, Coach," he said. "I got it."

Even in what might have been the most tense moment of his coaching life, Brennan couldn't help but laugh. "Not the first time he's overruled me," he said later. "And with good reason, I might add."

Sorrentine waited until the shot clock was under ten seconds then shouted, "Run the play," for the benefit of the Syracuse defenders, who backpedaled just a tad, expecting Sorrentine to make some kind of move to the basket. Instead, he took one dribble and let fly from 27 feet. "I didn't realize I was that far out," he said later, smiling. "But when it left my hand it felt good."

It *was* good. And even though there was still work to do in the final minute, Sorrentine's shot was the dagger in Syracuse's heart. Gerry McNamara, who had made seven three-point shots in the national championship game as a freshman in 2003, missed the last shot, an off-balance three that went wide, and Vermont had pulled the upset, 60–57. It was one of those games and moments that bring people back to the NCAA Tournament year after year. For Vermont this was the national championship. Brennan had been wrong a year earlier: it *could* get better — and it had. "I just hope I can make it back here for the game Sunday," Brennan joked in the postgame bedlam. "I'm going to do some partying tonight." He shook his head in disbelief. "Never, never did I dream a moment like this." He stopped and pinched himself. "Just wanted to be sure I wasn't dreaming it now.

"Boy, would I love to be Coppenrath and Sorrentine right now. Young, single, and . . . them."

Within the hour, an equally stunning upset would take place in Indianapolis: Bucknell, another school that had never won an NCAA Tournament game, representing a league (the Patriot) that had never won an NCAA Tournament game, shocked third-seeded Kansas. Pat Flannery, the coach of the Bison, who had graduated from the school in 1980, had dealt with heart problems in 2004 and had been forced to leave the team for two games in 2005 because of stress. The victory over Kansas was his moment to pinch himself. There would be no parties for him in St. Louis (he wasn't retiring), but everywhere he turned there were congratulations. "It was as if everyone in my profession suddenly knew who I was," he said. "What a great feeling."

Both teams lost very respectably in the second round: Vermont to a Michigan State team that would make it to the Final Four; Bucknell to Wisconsin. Those games almost didn't matter. The Vermont and Bucknell teams of 2005 will gather for years to come to replay a memorable season — and one night each will remember forever.

"The best thing," Brennan said at his farewell, "is that so many people have enjoyed it. When we got home, it was as if everyone in the entire state couldn't stop smiling. There's this tremendous feeling of 'We really did something special,' and —"

He was interrupted by a loud voice calling his name. "Hey, Brennan!"

Stalking through the crowd came Roland Vincent Massimino, who knows something about improbable wins, having coached Villanova's miracle in 1985. The night before, Brennan and Sullivan and a number of Massimino's former assistants had stayed up late regaling one another with stories about the old days. This was Massimino's first Final Four since 1985. He had been through a lot since then: leaving Villanova in 1992 for Nevada–Las Vegas after alienating a lot of people at the school, being forced out at UNLV, and then going on to seven unsuccessful years at Cleveland State. He was seventy-two now, living in Florida again but — amazingly — planning to coach one more time. He had agreed to coach a start-up program at a tiny NAIA school in West Palm Beach. "My wife and I went to see some Division 2 games this season," Massimino said. "She says to me, 'Rollie, these teams aren't very good.' I said, 'Sweetheart, these guys are four levels up from where I'm about to coach.'"

Massimino is one of those people who needs to coach the way

most people need to breathe. He also needs to give people a hard time. It is his way. The night before, his ex-assistants had finally had a chance to get even. Sometime about two o'clock in the morning, Massimino had claimed he needed to go home, that he was tired. Jay Wright, who is now Villanova's head coach but, like Brennan and Sullivan, once suffered working for Massimino, stopped him. "You aren't going anywhere," he said. "You killed us for years. Tonight we get to kill you."

Massimino stayed. "You were such a pain to work for," Brennan told him. "You made us miserable."

"And how'd it work out?" Massimino shot back. "Did you become a pretty good coach or not?"

In a twist of fate, the stroke of midnight had marked exactly twenty years since the night that Massimino's Villanova team had stunned Georgetown, the seemingly unbeatable defending national champion, 66–64, in what is still considered the greatest championship game upset of all time — more remarkable even than NC State over Houston.

"Upset! Upset! I still get angry when I hear that," Massimino had said the night before. "We played 'em twice in the regular season and should have beaten 'em both times! If we hadn't won that game, I'd a killed my guys. They knew they could do it and they knew how to do it. That's why we did it."

Shooting a stunning 79 percent for the game — including 9 of 10 in the second half — didn't hurt, either. "Look at the shots we got," Massimino said. "We took shots we could make in our sleep all night."

Now, after all the battles and the controversy, Massimino had come home. Villanova, at Wright's behest, had thrown a twenty-year anniversary party for Massimino and the team in January and a banner honoring Massimino had been raised to the rafters in the Pavilion, Villanova's home court. Now he was finally back at the Final Four and loving every second of it. He thrashed his way through people and made it to Brennan, who assumed he had come to say good-bye and give him one more hug before leaving.

He was right . . . sort of. "CNN just called," he reported to Brennan. "They want me to come on in an hour."

"Okay, I understand," Brennan said. "It's great that you came. . . ."

Massimino was waving his arms to indicate that Brennan didn't understand what he was saying. "I need your tie," he said. "I can't go on TV without a tie. Gimme the tie."

Once an assistant, always an assistant. Brennan dutifully pulled the tie off and handed it to Massimino, who then rewarded him with a hug and a kiss on the cheek. "You know I love you," he said softly.

"I love you, too, Coach," Brennan said.

Massimino stalked away.

"I really like that tie," Brennan said. "And I'll never see it again."

It was dark by the time the party for Brennan began to break up. The city was now teeming with people. In addition to the teams, the coaches, and the media, fans had come pouring into downtown — all looking for a good time. Radio row at the coaches' hotel was chockablock with celebrities, some moving from one show to another — especially if they had something to promote. Dick Vitale had finished his on-air duties for the night and was at a corporate gig that featured a Dick Vitale sound-alike contest. In the coaches' lobby, one could see such current coaching stars as Jim Boeheim and Jim Calhoun talking to people while ex-stars like John Thompson, Jerry Tarkanian, and Lefty Driesell also made the rounds. Billy Tubbs, who had coached Oklahoma into the national championship game in 1988, wandered into the bar and spotted several old friends. Tubbs had retired from Oklahoma, then unretired to come back as athletic director at Lamar University and, a year earlier, had fired his coach — Mike Deane — and hired himself to replace Deane.

"I did a nationwide search for the best possible replacement," he said. "The search found me."

When Tubbs was coaching at Oklahoma, he was famous for two things: running up scores on weak teams and his absolute dead-on Jack Nicholson sound-alike voice. One year, after the Sooners had beaten a completely overmatched opponent by 90 points, someone asked Tubbs what he said to the other coach during the postgame handshake after a 90-point blowout. "I said, Can you come back next year?" Tubbs said.

Rarely did someone get in the last line on Tubbs. An exception was Rick Brewer, the longtime sports information director at North Carolina, who for many years was the moderator of the Final Four press conferences. In fact, Brewer was the last moderator to actually refer to the players as "players" rather than "student-athletes," as the NCAA handbook insists they be called. During the Sunday press conference in 1988 prior to the championship game between Kansas and Oklahoma, someone asked Tubbs if he thought perhaps God wanted Kansas to win the title, given that the Jayhawks had been a sixth seed in their bracket and were now in the final.

Sounding exactly like Nicholson, Tubbs said, "What number does God wear?"

Without missing a beat, Brewer said, "Twenty-three," cracking up everyone in the room — including Tubbs — because at that point in his career most people believed that Michael Jordan *was* God.

Brewer's exchanges with Duke coach Mike Krzyzewski in years that Duke made the Final Four were also frequently memorable.

"Coach, what do you like best about coaching at Duke?" someone once asked.

"Well, it *is* ten miles from the University of North Carolina," Brewer said, in his best nasal Dean Smith–like voice.

"And I like it there anyway," Krzyzewski said quickly.

Brewer, who most people believe was there when UNC first opened its doors in 1789, does an absolutely perfect imitation of Smith. Once, someone made the mistake of telling Smith just how good Brewer's imitation was. Surprised, even though his nasal Kansas twang has been mimicked throughout the ACC forever, Smith turned to Brewer and said, "Rick, do *you* do me?"

Flustered for once, Brewer finally threw up his hands and said, "Coach, *everybody* does you."

Another oft-imitated ex-coach was stalking the lobby late Friday evening, one of the easiest people to identify in all of sports: John Thompson, the Hall of Fame Georgetown coach turned radio talk show host. Thompson is six foot ten and must weigh 350 pounds. When he was coaching, he often said that he believed he intimidated people because "I'm big, I'm black, and I'm loud."

Make that very loud. Thompson became a coaching icon by taking a small Jesuit school from nowhere to the national championship. When he was hired in 1972 — he was a high school coach at the time — the university president, Reverend Robert Henle, told him that if he could take Georgetown to the NIT once every two or three years, everyone at the school would be very happy. In his third season Thompson and Georgetown reached the NCAA Tournament. In 1980 the Hoyas came within seconds of reaching the Final Four before losing to Iowa in the east regional final. A year later Patrick Ewing enrolled, and the Hoyas played in the national championship game three of his four years there.

But it was hardly seashells and balloons being around Georgetown's program. Thompson was, by his own admission, paranoid and secretive. His teams practiced behind doors chained shut to keep people out. When the team traveled, even the athletic director didn't know where it was staying. Thompson's very close relationship with Sonny Vaccaro, then the guru of Nike basketball, which paid the coach very big money, led to accusations that Vaccaro was funneling players to him. Thompson and Georgetown played a ludicrously easy nonconference schedule, except for the occasional game put on by Thompson's friend Russ Potts, a former athletic director turned promoter. To say there were whispers among coaches about exactly how Potts got Thompson to play some of those games is an understatement.

Thompson was frequently confrontational. When someone asked him at the 1982 Final Four how he felt about being the first African American to coach in the event, he went off. "I resent the hell out of that question," he said. "Because the implication is that I am the first black man capable of coaching a team to the Final Four, and that's far from the truth. I'm just the first one given the opportunity to do so."

That was the trouble with Thompson: on the one hand, he made you crazy with all his rules and his paranoia and his assistant coaches' prowling the locker room after games just in case someone asked a player a "nonbasketball question." He once complained to a reporter who had asked two players what they planned to do when they finished playing basketball. "Are you implying," he thundered, "that because they are black they won't know what to do when they aren't playing basketball anymore?"

On the other hand, he was as smart and as interesting as anyone in the game. His opinions were as big as he was, and when he chose to share them, not listening was a mistake. After Ewing graduated (and he did graduate), Georgetown continued to be very competitive, but not as good as with Ewing. The Hoyas made the round of eight in 1987, 1989, and 1996 but haven't made the Final Four since. Thompson was selected to coach the U.S. Olympic team in 1988 but did a poor job of picking players (too many defenders, not enough shooters), and when the United States lost to the Soviet Union in the semifinals and settled for a bronze medal, some of the spark went out of Thompson. He continued coaching until halfway through the season in 1999, when he abruptly resigned, talking about going through a divorce and being tired but never fully explaining his sudden departure. Longtime assistant coach Craig Esherick took over and the program nosedived, not even making it into the Big East Tournament in 2004. Two weeks after saying there was no way Esherick would be fired, the president of Georgetown fired him, eventually hiring Thompson's son John Thompson III to try to bring the program back to the kind of glory days it had seen under his father.

In the meantime, Thompson was reborn as a radio talk show host in Washington. Because of who he was (he had been elected to the Hall of Fame in 1998), he could get almost anyone in sports on his show. Those who knew him could see the changes in him. Old enemies became friends. Thompson and Morgan Wootten, the great high school coach, whom Thompson hadn't spoken to for more than twenty years, dating to his days in the high school ranks, became almost cuddly when talking to each other on the air.

"The media exaggerated the hell out of our rivalry, didn't they, Morgan?" Thompson would say.

"Boy, they sure did, John."

Once, when asked why he had never recruited any of the great players Wootten had at DeMatha, Thompson said: "There are some people on earth you can live apart from."

Thompson readily admitted that being out of coaching had changed his outlook on life and on people. "It's almost as if you spent your whole life working in a flower garden but never noticed there were any flowers," he said. "I know how corny that sounds, but it's true. When I was coaching, it was all about the competition, about trying to win, about trying to get an edge and making sure no one got an edge on you. I *was* paranoid — except when there were people who were actually out to get me.

"When I first got the Georgetown job, I was obsessed with knocking down barriers. When Father Henle told me the NIT was fine, part of me understood that, because when I was at Providence in the sixties, the NIT was still a big deal. Twice we turned down the NCAA to go to the NIT. But that was a different time. I told Father Henle if the NCAA was the place to be, that was where we would be. When I first started coming to the Final Four in the seventies, I often thought about wanting to coach in it, but back then I was still learning. I can remember sitting in the lobby and listening to Big House Gaines [the legendary coach at Winston-Salem State] telling stories, and feeling as if I was in a life seminar. Now I sit with him and I see these young coaches walk by without even noticing him, and I want to grab them and say, 'Boy, do you know who this is? Do you know this is a Hall of Fame coach?'

"I remember when we got to New Orleans in '82, being shocked when I walked out on the court for Friday practice. I was used to closed practice, I mean no one in the gym. Now there are people roaring and yelling and screaming. It helped me understand the significance of the event and the moment. But that didn't mean I had time to sit around and think about it or talk about it. And then I had these people running at me, telling me to go to meetings and wear pins and the like. I did not deal with that well."

The '82 championship game between North Carolina and Georgetown is one of the most remembered games ever played: it was Dean Smith, still seeking his first championship, taking on his star pupil, Thompson. The two men had become friends when Thompson was a high school coach, and Thompson had been an assistant coach for Smith during the 1976 Olympics. Now Thompson and his team, led by Ewing, were the last roadblock between Smith and a championship.

"I remember not wanting to let myself get caught up in the friendship during the game," Thompson said. "I didn't want to look down at him. Early in the game, Patrick went to the foul line and I heard Dean saying to the referee, 'Now, it's okay with me if he goes over ten seconds. You don't have to call that.' I felt better when I heard that because I thought, 'Okay, he's playing one of his mind games, that means he wants to kick my butt, so it's okay for me to try to kick his.'"

Ewing was a notoriously deliberate free throw shooter, frequently timed by observers as going well over the ten-second time limit. No one in basketball can ever remember a ten-second violation being called on a free throw shooter. It was never called on Ewing. Thompson recognized his mentor's putting the thought into the heads of the officials early, and it helped him forget friendship until the game was over.

That game ended famously: Michael Jordan making the winning jump shot that announced his arrival as a superstar and Georgetown's Fred Brown getting confused on the ensuing possession and throwing the ball directly to North Carolina's James Worthy to deny the Hoyas a chance to win the game. Thompson hugged and consoled Brown on the court when it was over, and he was put on a pedestal by many for reacting that way — a pedestal he still laughs about.

"I'm glad I did what I did," he said. "But I could just as easily have said, 'Fred, what the f—— were you thinking about out there,' and it would not have changed one bit the way I felt about Fred or the way he felt about me. God knows I've jumped players for mistakes. As it was, something inside me told me there was no sense jumping him, because the game was over, the season was over. So I consoled him — as I probably would have done in the locker room later if I had jumped him. That's the way coaching is. What I did was not a great act of humanitarianism, the way it has been made out to be. It was an instinctive coaching act that could easily have been different."

Georgetown won the national championship two years later, and Brown was the first player to come to the bench to hug Thompson when the victory over Houston was assured. As disappointing as the loss to Villanova was a year later, Thompson felt a sense of completion after the '84 title. "I wanted to prove I could do it," he said. "I wanted to prove *we* [African Americans] could do it. Once that barrier was down, the hunger was still there, but it wasn't quite the same.

"Now, not coaching, I'm completely different. I see more things and enjoy more things. I can be relaxed around people. I like going to games now and talking to people, old friends and even old enemies. I like being here [at the Final Four] because I still like the games and I like seeing my friends, especially now, because I have a lot more of them than when I was coaching."

As Thompson spoke, Gene Keady walked by. He had just completed his twenty-fifth — and final — season at Purdue, the school more or less forcing him into retirement when his once-proud program slipped. Keady had been a remarkably consistent winner at Purdue and had twice taken teams to the final eight. But he never reached the Final Four, a fact that will probably keep him out of the Hall of Fame. Thompson and Keady exchanged warm greetings and small talk before Keady moved on.

"I feel a certain emptiness when I see Gene," Thompson said softly. "The man is a much better coach than a lot of guys who have been to the Final Four or even won national championships. But the way our profession works, they judge you on things like that. It's not fair, but it's a fact of the lives we've chosen to lead."

Just outside the entrance to the hotel sat another coach who had been close to the Final Four on multiple occasions without ever getting to coach on the last weekend: Lefty Driesell. Driesell reached the round of eight four times — twice at Davidson — and then twice more at Maryland. Driesell coached four places during a forty-year college coaching career: Davidson, Maryland, James Madison, and Georgia State. In all four places he inherited floundering programs and took them to heights they had never been to before. He is one of only four men in history (Eddie Sutton, Jim Harrick, and Rick Pitino are the others) to coach four different schools into the NCAA Tournament. In all, he won 786 games before retiring at midseason — much like Thompson — in 2003 because, at seventy-one, he felt burned out.

Now, at seventy-three, he looked ready to coach again as he smoked a cigar just outside the hotel entrance while passersby stopped to shake his hand and tell him how much they missed seeing him on the sidelines. "Someone offers me a million dollars, I'll come back," he said. "But I ain't taking any job where I have to go stay in motels by the side of the road in the middle of nowhere. I'm done with that."

Driesell is honest enough to admit it bothers him that he's not in the Hall of Fame. "Last time I was on the ballot, they didn't even have my résumé right," he said. "They left Georgia State off it completely. You think that makes me feel good about my chances?"

Driesell belongs in the Hall of Fame even though he didn't reach the Final Four. There is recent precedent: Temple coach John Chaney was elected because he had a superb record even without a Final Four trip and because there was a sense that his contributions to the game went beyond wins and losses.

The same is true of Driesell. He helped make the ACC in the 1970s by building a program at Maryland that made the league relevant outside the state of North Carolina. He was involved in some of the great games in the history of the sport, most notably the classic 1974 ACC Tournament final against North Carolina State. Maryland was led by Tom McMillen, Len Elmore, and John Lucas; State by the incomparable David Thompson, seven-foot-four Tom Burleson, and five-six Monty Towe. With no shot clock and no three-point shot, the game was tied at 86 at the end of regulation. State finally won, 103–100, in overtime and Lucas sat on the scorer's table and cried during the awards ceremony after missing a late free throw. That scene caused the ACC to excuse the runner-up from future awards ceremonies, a wise move later copied by the NCAA.

After the game Driesell walked out of the Greensboro Coliseum and climbed onto the State bus just before it pulled out. "I just wanna tell y'all I'm proud of you," he said. "I have a great team and they played great and you guys beat us. Now you *better* go out and win the national championship."

State coach Norman Sloan said years later that Driesell's getting on the bus might have been the classiest move he ever witnessed as a coach. The Wolfpack did win the title that year, upsetting UCLA and Bill Walton in the national semifinals in double overtime.

Sadly, Driesell left Maryland under a cloud in 1986, forced out in the wake of the cocaine-induced death of Len Bias, who died the morning after he was chosen by the Boston Celtics with the second pick in the NBA draft. It took Maryland years to recover from the Bias tragedy, and Driesell's career was never the same, even though he coached successfully at James Madison and Georgia State. In 2001 he put together a team at Georgia State, a commuter school in downtown Atlanta, that won thirty games, including an upset of Wisconsin in the first round of the NCAA Tournament. When someone asked him after the game about coaching at a "mid-major" school, his answer was classic Driesell: "Mid-major?" he repeated. "I ain't never been mid anything. Ask Wisconsin if we're a mid-major."

That was his last hurrah. Georgia State lost in the second round to his old school, Maryland, and hasn't been back on the national map since. Driesell has been a Hall of Fame finalist but still isn't in, despite all the victories at all the different places and all the color he brought to the game. There will always be people who will blame him for Bias's death and people who won't let him forget the famous "UCLA of the East" line he delivered in 1969 when he was introduced as Maryland's new coach.

"We will be the UCLA of the East," he declared, thus setting the bar impossibly high for himself and his program. Maryland had great success in Driesell's seventeen seasons there, but no one was going to come close to matching Wooden, ever. The line was hung around Driesell's neck like an albatross every time the Terrapins lost in March, as they inevitably did. Driesell, with his country Virginia accent, inspired love in some and ridicule in others. He was as entertaining as anyone in the game, never afraid to speak his mind to anyone at any time.

In 1982, after his Maryland team had lost four starters — including Buck Williams and Albert King, both taken in the top ten picks in the NBA draft — he took a young team into North Carolina to play the Tar Heels, who were led by James Worthy, Sam Perkins, and a freshman named Michael Jordan. To make the situation even more impossible, Driesell's best player, center Charles Pittman, was injured. "If I was smart like Dean, I'd tell y'all we ain't got no chance," Driesell said the day before the game. "But I ain't that smart. I think we're going to go in there and whip 'em."

Remarkably, they almost did, losing in the final minute when Worthy stole the ball from point guard Reggie Jackson with Maryland leading by one and trying to kill the clock. When Dean Smith was asked how a depleted Maryland team could walk into Chapel Hill and come within seconds of a stunning upset, he shrugged and said, "You can always play one great game without a key player."

Smith has made this comment thousands of times, about both his team and opponents. He believes a team will rise to the occasion for one game after a critical injury. But when the comment was repeated to Driesell, he took it as an insult, that Smith was refusing to give his team credit for a gutsy effort. "Dean's got

Perkins, Jordan, and Worthy," he said. "I got a bunch of freshmen and I come in here and almost whip him, and that's all he can say? That ain't right."

At season's end, Maryland had struggled to get into the NIT; North Carolina had won the national championship. That spring, at the ACC meetings, Smith showed up for the coaches meeting with newspaper clippings from the Maryland game in Chapel Hill. Highlighted in yellow were Driesell's comments. "Lefty, I'm very disappointed you would say all this . . . ," Smith began.

Driesell exploded, telling Smith he had a lot of nerve complaining about something like that when he had just won the national title and he (Driesell) had been through an awful season. Still angry, Driesell wrote Smith a note when he returned home, telling him he would not shake hands with him — win or lose — after they played the following season. Smith, every bit as stubborn as Driesell, wrote back that he would always shake hands with an opposing coach following a game.

Naturally, the game in Chapel Hill the next year went to the final play. In an absolutely brilliant coaching move, Driesell put his son, Chuck, a little-used benchwarmer, in the game at the finish and called a play for him rather than for leading scorer Adrian Branch or Bias, then a freshman. The play worked perfectly. Chuck Driesell was wide-open under the basket. No mortal on the court had any chance to get near him before he laid the ball in for the winning basket. Unfortunately for Maryland, Carolina was playing four mortals and Michael Jordan. From the top of the key, Jordan flew in behind Driesell and deflected the ball away at the last possible second as the buzzer sounded.

The Carolina players sprinted off the court. Driesell sprinted after the officials, demanding a call: a foul, goaltending, ball out-of-bounds to Maryland — *something*. Smith sprinted after Driesell to shake his hand. When Driesell turned and saw Smith coming at him, hand extended, he didn't see good sportsmanship; he saw taunting. He slapped at Smith's extended hand. A step behind Smith, his longtime lieutenant and close friend Bill Guthridge saw Driesell swing his hand at Smith's hand and lost *his* temper. He put his head down and rushed at Driesell. Behind Driesell, one of his assistants, Mel Cartwright, saw Guthridge coming and turned to pick up a chair.

The only reason there wasn't a full-scale riot was that Rick Brewer, UNC's sports information director, tackled Guthridge before he could get to Driesell, wrestling him away long enough to allow others to intervene. Who knows what would have happened if Brewer hadn't stepped in.

Now, twenty-two years later, it is all different. Smith has spoken up on Driesell's behalf to try to get him into the Hall of Fame. Guthridge, who succeeded Smith as Carolina's coach in 1997, talks fondly about the good old days when Lefty was at Maryland. All three will tell you with absolute straight faces that their rivalry was largely a media creation. However, in 2001, after his thirty-win season at Georgia State, a friend suggested to Driesell in the coaches' lobby at the Final Four that he might surpass Smith as the all-time winningest coach if he could hang on for about four more seasons.

"Never happen," Driesell said.

"Why not?"

"'Cause if I ever got close, Dean would come back."

7

March to the Arch

THE FOUR TEAMS WHO MADE IT to St. Louis in 2005 had varied Final Four histories, ranging from North Carolina's three national championships to Illinois's zero, without so much as an appearance in the championship game. The Illini had reached the Final Four in 1989 under Coach Lou Henson, only to lose on a basket just before the buzzer to fellow Big Ten school Michigan, which went on to win the title on Monday. Not long after that trip to the last weekend, the Illini found themselves under investigation by the NCAA.

The other three schools had more memories and happier ones. North Carolina was in its fifteenth Final Four. It had won the national championship in 1957 under Frank McGuire and in 1982 and 1993 under Dean Smith. The Tar Heels had been in the Final Four four times since that third championship but hadn't advanced beyond Saturday. Carolina had been in three of the most memorable championship games ever played: in '57 they had beaten Kansas and Wilt Chamberlain in triple overtime; in '82 Michael Jordan had hit what proved to be the winning shot against Georgetown; and in '93 Michigan had been denied a chance to tie the game in the final seconds when Chris Webber called a time-out his team didn't have.

Michigan State, Carolina's opponent in the second of Saturday's semifinals, had won two national championships. The first, in 1979, had been the Magic vs. Larry game — the highest-rated game in the television history of the tournament, even if Billy Packer insists that the game wasn't any good. The second had come in 2000 in the middle of a three-year run when Coach Tom Izzo took the Spartans to the Final Four three straight times: losing to Duke in the '99 semifinals, beating Wisconsin and Florida for the title in 2000, losing to Arizona in the semis a year later. The Spartans were now back, having come through the Austin regional as a fifth seed by upsetting Duke in the regional semis, then beating Kentucky in an extraordinary double-overtime game in the final.

Finally there was Louisville. The Cardinals also had plenty of Final Four history. Between 1972 and 1986 they had reached it six times under Denny Crum, winning titles in 1980 and 1986. But they had not been back since their 1986 victory, even though the MOP of that Final Four had been Pervis Ellison, then a freshman. The Cardinals didn't even make the tournament a year later and had been deep into the event only once in the ensuing eighteen seasons, in 1997, when they were crushed by North Carolina in the east regional final. Crum, in spite of his Hall of Fame credentials, had been more or less forced into retirement after the 2001 season, and the school had ardently and successfully pursued Rick Pitino as their coach.

This was an interesting choice, given that Pitino had been the King of Kentucky from 1989 to 1997, rebuilding the tarnished University of Kentucky program after an NCAA investigation and probation to regain the status that most Kentucky fans considered a birthright: perennial national contender. The Wildcats had reached at least the round of eight in five of Pitino's last six seasons, had gone to three Final Fours and two title games, and had been national champions in 1996. Pitino left in 1997 after his team lost a classic national championship game to Arizona in overtime, lured by money ($10 million a year) and absolute power to take over the Boston Celtics.

When Pitino took over the Celtics, it looked as if the team would end up with the number one pick in that year's NBA draft, and everyone knew that pick would be Tim Duncan, the precocious six-foot-ten Wake Forest center. Except that the Celtics, even with the most Ping-Pong balls in the lottery, didn't get the number one pick, the San Antonio Spurs did. Things might have been different if the Ping-Pong balls had bounced differently, but Pitino ended up failing miserably in Boston, making one personnel mistake after another. That failure did not taint him as a college coach, however, and when he resigned from the Celtics early in 2001, it seemed as if half the colleges in the country were lined up to hire him.

Pitino finally chose Louisville, a decision that sent shock waves through the state of Kentucky. UK fans had been willing to forgive Pitino for leaving for the Celtics. After all, the no-madic coach — he had gone from Boston University to the New York Knicks [as an assistant] to Providence College to the Knicks as head coach and then to Kentucky, all in a ten-year stretch — had stayed at Kentucky for eight seasons and brought glory back to the school. Leaving for the NBA was forgivable. But coaching another college? No, unacceptable. And coaching at Louisville, the in-state archrival of the Wildcats? Pitino became Judas and Benedict Arnold rolled into one.

That didn't really bother Pitino. He was coaching at a place with basketball history, knowing he would be able to recruit good players and rebuild the program. Within two years the Cardinals were back in the top twenty-five in the polls and back in the NCAA Tournament. But even with high-seeded teams, they had not advanced beyond the second round. The 2005 team appeared to be Pitino's best, led by Francisco Garcia and Taquan Dean, both outstanding shooters. What's more, Garcia was a superb lock-up defender. Louisville finished the regular season on a roll, and some thought they might be a number one seed. The committee somehow made them a number four seed but helped them out by placing them in the same regional with the weakest of the number one seeds — Washington. Louisville beat Washington easily in the round of sixteen, then produced a memorable comeback against West Virginia, which had gone from not in the field going into the Big East Tournament to upsets of Wake Forest (in double overtime) and Texas Tech to reach the final of the Albuquerque regional. Louisville overcame a superb shooting performance by the Mountaineers to win in overtime, meaning Pitino had coached three different schools (Providence, Kentucky, and Louisville) to the Final Four — the first coach in history to do so.

Clearly, Pitino was a coach headed for the Hall of Fame. In fact, the case could easily be made that three of the four coaches in St. Louis — Pitino, Izzo, and Roy Williams — already had Hall of Fame credentials. They had been to a combined fourteen Final Fours and five championship games, and Pitino and Izzo each had a national title. Bruce Weber had been at Illinois for only two years. And yet, to many, his team was the favorite. The Illini bused into St. Louis under cover of darkness late Wednesday night.

As the bus made its way from Champaign-Urbana across Illinois, fans were everywhere — standing by the side of the road, hanging good-luck signs from overpasses, waving at the players as the bus whizzed by them. Even when a drenching thunderstorm hit the middle of the state, people stood outside to watch the bus go by. No one had enjoyed a more remarkable season than the Illini. When Weber had been hired two years earlier to replace Bill Self after Self left for Kansas, many Illinois fans were skeptical about the hire. Weber had been a longtime assistant to Gene Keady at Purdue and had not gotten his first chance to be a head coach until he was forty-two years old. He had been very successful in four years at Southern Illinois, but there was a tendency among fans of the giant state school to look down at Southern Illinois as if it were a minor league franchise of some kind. Even though Weber took the Salukis to the Sweet Sixteen in 2002, people wondered why the school hadn't hired a "big time" coach to replace Self.

The first season hadn't been easy. At one point Weber showed up for a game dressed in black because he wanted people to understand that Self was "dead and gone" at Illinois. The team came together late in the season and made it to the Sweet Sixteen before losing to Duke. With four starters back, the following season began with high hopes, especially because there appeared to be a route to the Final Four that wouldn't involve getting on a single airplane if the Illini could be a high seed: first weekend in Indianapolis, second in Chicago, and then the Final Four in St. Louis, about a three-hour drive from campus.

"The phrase 'March to the Arch' [the official motto of the St. Louis organizing committee] has been stuck in my head all season," Weber said.

Illinois lost only once in the regular season, on a buzzer-beating three-point shot at Ohio State in the regular-season finale. That loss comforted Bob Knight and the members of the 1976 Indiana team, since no one has gone undefeated since Indiana in 1976. Indiana coaches, players, and fans everywhere take great pride in that fact. In 1991 Nevada–Las Vegas made it to the Final Four with a record of 34–0. When the Rebels, the defending champions, were upset in the semifinals by Duke, Quinn Buckner, who had been Indiana's captain in 1976, went on a local TV show and said gleefully, "There's a lot of teams that have won one title in a row. Not a lot of them have gone undefeated, though, have they?"

If Illinois had been the team to match Indiana's feat, it would have been especially painful for Knight and Indiana fans. Not only were the two teams from the same conference, not only did the two states border each other, but Knight and Illinois coach Lou Henson had feuded openly throughout the 1980s. Knight had done everything but come out and publicly accuse Henson of being a cheat (he whispered it to anyone who would listen), and Henson had called Knight a bully. There had been games that had ended without handshakes, and Knight had once famously said that he didn't believe Henson could "coach lions to eat red meat." Knight was among those Illinois people held responsible for the investigation that had landed Illinois on probation in the early 1990s. Knight had no problem with their thinking that.

Illinois wasn't going to go undefeated. In his coaching exile in Lubbock, Texas, Knight no doubt raised a glass of sangria in tribute to Ohio State — his alma mater — on the night the Buckeyes beat the Illini. Illinois had gone on to win the Big Ten Tournament and three NCAA games before running into a buzz saw in a hot Arizona team in the regional final in Chicago, which was, for all intents and purposes, an Illinois home game. Arizona appeared completely unbothered by the thousands in blue and orange for thirty-six minutes, leading by 15 points with four minutes to play. It looked as if the "March to the Arch" was going to end one step shy of the goal. Somehow Illinois rallied, burying numerous three-point shots, while Arizona completely lost its composure. Illinois outscored Arizona 20–5 in those frantic final minutes. The miracle comeback completely convinced Illinois fans that theirs was a team of destiny — that this was, at least, their year.

Of course, every year all four teams arrive at the Final Four convinced they are that year's team of destiny. All of them have won at least four games in a row and, almost always, all have had a narrow escape along the way. North Carolina had needed a fortuitous call in the final minute against Villanova to ensure its victory in the Sweet Sixteen and had gone to the final minute before escaping a hard-nosed Wisconsin team. Michigan State had blown a lead against Kentucky, the game being tied by a miracle three-pointer just before the buzzer that required close to ten minutes for TV replay to confirm it was good, and then had come from behind to win in double overtime. And Louisville had been down 22 in the first half against West Virginia before it had rallied to win in overtime.

Four teams marched to the Arch convinced they were going to march out with the trophy in their hands. Only one of them could be right.

Through the years, the Final Four has become a gathering place not just for coaches but for players, many of whom have left the basketball world to go on to other things. But they still love the game and the feeling of the event they played in when they were young and convinced they would play forever.

Among the ex-players making the trip to St. Louis, perhaps no one was happier to see his alma mater reach the final weekend again than Terry Howard. "I've lived in Louisville my whole life," he said. "Grew up more of a UK [Kentucky] fan because my mom and dad were UK fans, but I always liked Louisville. I've had two [of five] children go to Louisville and, of course, it's my school. The only thing better for me than having Louisville in the Final Four would be to have Louisville and UK both there."

That had almost happened in 2005, Kentucky losing in double overtime in the regional final to Michigan State. The only time it actually happened was in 1975, Terry Howard's senior year at Louisville. Howard had been a star as a high school senior, a sweet-shooting point guard with the kind of quickness with the ball that brought recruiters running. "Pretty much every basketball school in the country offered me a scholarship," Howard said. "Except for UCLA. Coach Wooden said I could come as a freshman and walk on and then he'd find me a scholarship as a sophomore. I really didn't want to do that."

Howard eventually narrowed his list to Kansas, Alabama, Maryland, Kentucky, and Louisville. He was tempted by Maryland coach Lefty Driesell because he liked the idea of being part of "the UCLA of the East." He also liked Alabama coach C. M. Newton a lot. And, as one might expect, he was in awe of Kentucky coach Adolph Rupp. "For a long time I thought that I would go to Kentucky," he said. "I even made a verbal commitment to Coach Rupp on the telephone. But I couldn't really get away from Pete Maravich. He was my hero. I wanted to be like him. I didn't think I'd be able to do that at Kentucky."

Maravich was a senior at LSU in 1970, the same year that

Howard was a senior at Westport High School. Maravich had become a legend playing for his father, averaging an astounding 44 points a game, racing down the court on every possession, long floppy hair flying, socks drooping, and either shooting the ball or making some kind of spectacular pass — frequently behind his back or between his legs. "I just loved watching Pete play," Howard said. "Anytime they played anywhere close to us, we went to see them. I liked putting the ball behind my back and between my legs. I had a feeling Coach Rupp wouldn't approve of that sort of thing."

There was another factor: race. "The Southeastern Conference was still, for the most part, all-white," Howard said. "My senior year I think there was one black playing in the league, Wendell Hudson at Alabama. I spent my summers playing over at Shawnee High School against all the black kids in town. I was friends with a lot of them and I enjoyed the style of play — up and down — a lot more than the SEC, which was walk-it-up basketball most of the time. I knew Coach Rupp had started to recruit blacks because I played against Tom Payne [Rupp's first black recruit] and he was a year ahead of me in high school. But Louisville had black players and it was in the Missouri Valley Conference, which was far more integrated. I thought I would enjoy that style of play a lot more."

When Howard called Rupp and his top assistant, Joe B. Hall, to tell them he had changed his mind and was going to go to Louisville, they were stunned. "They just couldn't understand the idea of going to U of L over UK," he said. "I could see why they felt that way."

Freshmen weren't eligible to play on the varsity in the fall of 1970, so Howard played on the freshman team. At the end of that season, Louisville hired Denny Crum, who had been

Wooden's top assistant at UCLA, to take over the program. Howard went into his sophomore season expecting big things — the Cardinals were a talented, veteran team — but never got to play because he came down with viral meningitis. Louisville ended up in the Final Four that year, playing (and losing to) UCLA in Los Angeles. Howard didn't even get to make the trip because he was hit with appendicitis on the day the team left.

It was all different the next year. He was healthy and started as a redshirt sophomore along with three other sophomores and a junior. "We were young, but we were talented," he said. "We kept getting better as the season went on."

Early in that season Louisville played in the Rainbow Classic in Hawaii. The Cardinals reached the final and played North Carolina. Late in a close game, Dean Smith went to his four-corner offense, spreading the floor and letting guards George Karl and Steve Previs handle the ball, running the clock down (there was no shot clock) and either getting fouled or getting an open layup on seemingly every possession.

"We got home and put in the four corners the first day we were back," Howard remembered. "I was the point guard and I was our best foul shooter. That meant the last few minutes of the game, the ball was going to be in my hands. I loved it."

Louisville was an NIT team in 1973 (there were still only twenty-five NCAA bids back then) and reached the round of sixteen in 1974. At the start of the '74–'75 season, *Sports Illustrated* picked the Cardinals number one because they were both experienced and deep. The only problem for Howard was that he had become part of the team's depth — going from two-year starter to the bench. "Denny always believed that if two guys were close, he played the younger guy," Howard said. "Phil Bond was a sophomore and he was very good. Denny came to me before the season and told me I was still going to get my minutes and I would be in at the end of the game and that it really didn't matter. But it did matter. I'd been a starter for two years, it was my last year — I wanted to start. But I certainly couldn't argue with the results."

Howard remains close to Crum thirty years later. His oldest son, Todd, played for Crum before hurting his knee and is now the top assistant coach at IUPUI, the city school in Indianapolis cosponsored by Indiana and Purdue. "I loved playing for Denny," he said. "He was amazing. He never used [profane] language even in the heat of the battle and I never saw him anything but cool at the end of a tight game. I remember he liked to say, 'Fellas, if you do this, I can't guarantee we'll win, but if you *don't* do it, I guarantee you we won't win.'"

Howard shook off the disappointment of not starting and became an invaluable third guard, taking over the offense and the basketball whenever a game was close in the final minutes. The reason was simple: he never missed a free throw. "I wanted the ball at the end and I wanted people to foul me," he said. "Denny had a thing where we all had to make ten free throws in a row at the end of practice before we'd leave. Sometimes I'd shoot them left-handed because I knew I wasn't going to miss with either hand. Almost every free throw I shot that year was at the end of a close game when I knew I had to make the shot for us to win.'"

Louisville rolled through the NCAA Tournament that year, reaching the midwest regional final against Maryland. That Maryland team may have been Lefty Driesell's best: it had dominated the ACC during the regular season and was led by John Lucas, who would be the first pick in the NBA draft a year later, and stars Brad Davis, Steve Sheppard, and Mo Howard. Louisville crushed the Terrapins, 96–82, leading from start to finish. "We were primed for that game because we knew how good Maryland was," Howard said. "I was ready for it because Lefty had recruited me and, even though I liked him, I wanted to beat him. Of course, I didn't have to make any crucial free throws because there weren't any to make at the end of the game."

The victory put Louisville into the Final Four, played in San Diego that year. The Cardinals would play UCLA — the team they had lost to in 1972 — while Syracuse played Kentucky in the other game. "Having UK there made it all the better, especially since we had never gotten to play against them. We were convinced that we were going to play them in the final."

Rupp had refused to schedule Louisville. Joe B. Hall, who succeeded him in 1973, had followed his lead. It was not until 1983, when the Kentucky state legislature voted to require the two schools to play each other, that they began playing annually during the regular season. As luck would have it, the teams met in the NCAA Tournament in the spring of 1983, with Louisville winning the game in overtime. This was ten years earlier, and the Cardinals wanted to play Kentucky almost as much as they wanted to beat UCLA.

"We were convinced we would beat UCLA," Howard said. "We thought we were better than they were."

UCLA had finally had its seven-year string of titles ended in 1974 when North Carolina State, led by David Thompson, beat the Bruins in the semifinals, aided by the fact that the Final Four that year was in Greensboro, about sixty miles from N.C. State's campus. Bill Walton had graduated, and even though UCLA was back in the Final Four, led by Richard Washington, David Meyers, and Marques Johnson, the Bruins didn't carry the aura they had in the past.

Both Kentucky and Louisville flew to San Diego a day earlier than usual back then (Wednesday) in order to get acclimated to the time change. Both coaches asked the NCAA to find a place to practice on Thursday since the San Diego Sports Arena, the Final Four site, wasn't available until Friday. "We showed up Thursday afternoon to practice at some high school, and as we're getting off the bus, we see another bus pull up," Howard said. "It was Kentucky. Somehow, the NCAA people had gotten confused and thought we were Kentucky, or Kentucky was Louisville. Anyway, they'd booked us both for the same place at the same time. They didn't realize we were two different teams."

One can only imagine if two teams, not to mention archrivals, ever had the same thing occur today at a Final Four. Imagine Mike Krzyzewski and Roy Williams getting off their buses and seeing each other. Or Jim Calhoun and Gary Williams. Blood might be spilled. In 1975 Joe Hall and Denny Crum flipped a coin. Kentucky won the toss and practiced first while Louisville sat around and watched. "Yup, we watched," Howard said. "And when they were done, their coaches stayed and watched us. I guess you could say it was a different time."

On Saturday, Kentucky beat Syracuse easily in the first game. Then UCLA and Louisville played what those who were there remember as one of the great NCAA Tournament games ever played. It was back and forth the entire afternoon. They ended up in overtime. As always, Howard was in for the endgame, handling the ball for the Cardinals. With the clock under thirty seconds in overtime, Louisville led by one and the ball was in Howard's hands. "For some reason, as loud as it was, I could hear Coach Wooden yelling at his players, 'Don't foul Howard! Don't foul Howard!' He was actually up off the bench because he didn't want them to foul me."

But with the clock winding down and Howard not wanting to relinquish the ball, UCLA finally fouled. There were twenty seconds left. Howard looked over and saw Wooden clap his free hand against the ever-present rolled-up program he held in his left hand. "I was completely confident," Howard said. "This is what I did."

At that moment, Howard had attempted 28 free throws during the season and had made all 28. It was a one-and-one, meaning he had to make the first shot to get the second. The three-point shot was still twelve years away from being voted into existence, so if Howard made both shots, UCLA would need to score twice: one possession would not be enough. "It didn't feel any different than any other free throw I'd shot all season," Howard said. "I remember walking to the line. Pete Trgovich was to my right. Marques Johnson or Richard Washington walked past me and said something about not making it, but I'd heard that a million times; it was standard stuff.

"The one thing that surprised me was that Coach Wooden didn't call time-out to try to freeze me. I thought he would. Maybe he outthought me by not calling it because, to be honest, I was expecting it. But I went up there and did everything exactly the way I always did. The shot felt good out of my hand. Nothing felt different."

But the shot was different: it spun out of the basket. Teammates later told Howard that they thought the ball had actually gone into the basket before it popped out. "I've never watched it," Howard admitted. "It comes on just about every year, Final Four time; someone shows it as one of the great games, but I've never sat down and watched it. Doubt if I ever will."

Of course, the game wasn't over at that point. In fact, Louisville still led by one. UCLA came down the court and ran the clock down, and Washington hit a difficult 10-foot baseline jumper with three seconds to go. That was the ball game. Howard doesn't remember very much about the immediate aftermath. "I just remember the locker room was very quiet," he said. "There just wasn't much for anyone to say. My wife [Rhonda] was eight months pregnant with our second son at the time, so we just went out to eat. We saw a lot of Kentucky fans in the restaurant. To tell you the truth, they couldn't have been nicer. When we got back to the room, there were a lot of messages. I remember C. M. Newton had called, and some of the folks from NBC had called, too. The messages were the same: keep your head up, you had a great career — that kind of thing.

"I think that was the hardest part, knowing I wouldn't get another chance."

Louisville did have one game left to play — the consolation game against Syracuse. "We had a shootaround on Sunday and I just felt like I had to make some free throws," Howard said. "I made eighty-seven straight. Of course, the next night we won pretty easily and I didn't have to shoot any. The last free throw of my career was a miss."

Howard still has a box full of letters that he received after the game. Virtually all of them were encouraging. The one that meant the most to him came from John Wooden. "He reminded me that he always said that a game isn't decided by one player or one play," he said. "It was our team that was in a position to win and our team that lost. Richard Washington had to hit a tough shot to beat us. It was great of him to write."

He paused. "I still wish I'd made the shot."

Howard had a brief fling as a pro. He actually got to go to training camp with his hero, Pete Maravich, because he was signed as a free agent by the New Orleans Jazz. He played in two exhibition games with the Jazz, got cut, had a quick shot in Philadelphia — "Two days," he said — and then played in South America before going to work, first in real estate, then in sporting goods, and now back in real estate development.

"I can honestly tell you there's not a day that goes by that the free throw doesn't come up in some way," he said. "I was in a meeting today and someone mentioned I had played at Louisville. The guy we were meeting with looked at me and said, 'You aren't the guy who . . . ?'

"I said, 'Missed the free throw against UCLA. Yup, that was me.' It's the easiest way to handle it. That way, people don't feel awkward. Sometimes they'll just say, 'You played in the Final Four, right?' And I just nod and say I was on the '75 team. If they ask me more, I tell them.

"I've never gotten to the point where I can't talk about it or won't talk about it. I understand why people bring it up. I'm honored to have played on that team and in that game and to think that Denny wanted me to have the ball in that situation. Sometimes it's tough. I've seen it listed among the ten worst moments in Final Four history. A couple of years ago someone did a story on Gary Anderson, the kicker up in Minnesota, and me, because he had missed a field goal in the conference championship game after not missing all season. They called them the two most surprising misses in history or something."

Anderson's kick came in 1999 with the Vikings leading the Atlanta Falcons, 17–10, and less than two minutes to play. It was a relatively easy kick, 37 yards, and Anderson hadn't missed all year. But he missed the kick. The Falcons drove the length of the field for a tying touchdown and won in overtime to go to the Super Bowl. There was a difference between Anderson and Howard: Anderson got to kick again. He kicked in the NFL for four more years and, in his final season at the age of forty-four, kicked a game-winning 46-yard field goal for the Tennessee Titans in the final seconds of a playoff game against the Baltimore Ravens.

Not surprisingly, Howard identifies with others who have had inglorious Final Four moments: Georgetown's Fred Brown; Syracuse's Derrick Coleman (who missed two late free throws with his team leading Indiana in 1987); Chris Webber. "Even with those guys there's a difference," he said. "Fred Brown got to come back two years later and win. Coleman and Webber have both had long pro careers. I just had to go on with my life."

He's done it quite well: five children (his daughter is now a manager at Louisville), a successful business, and a love of basketball that keeps him playing in rec leagues even today at fifty-two. Every year he makes the trip to the Final Four, where people still point fingers at him and say, "Are you the guy . . . ?"

"The one I remember the most was maybe a year or so after I graduated," he said. "Of course, now I look quite a bit different than thirty years ago. Back then, it seemed like everywhere I went people would point or whisper or say something. I was working in real estate and I was out somewhere working sales around a lake, quite a few miles out in the country. I went into a place to get something to eat. It was one of those places with a bunch of old boys sitting around a stove. When I walked in, their mouths dropped open. I'd seen it before, so I just said, 'Yes, I'm the guy.' One of them looked at me and said, 'You know, it's really too bad about that shot. I guess it just spinded out.'"

It spinded out. Thirty years later Terry Howard — and many, many others — haven't forgotten.

8

Refs

ON FRIDAY MORNING Hank Nichols walked briskly through the lobby of the Renaissance Hotel en route to a meeting. By now, many fans were staking out the Renaissance, which was directly across the street from the Edward Jones Dome, knowing that many of the sport's famous names were bound to show up at some point since this was the hotel where the NCAA basketball committee was staying, meaning that many of the weekend's meetings would be held in the building.

No one stopped Nichols for an autograph. As he stepped outside and lit a Merit cigarette, a line of autograph seekers who had just besieged Jim Boeheim moments earlier didn't even glance at Nichols. Which was exactly the way he wanted it.

To those in college basketball, he is one of the most familiar and important people in the game. But as the Friday morning scene proved, very few of the general public could pick him out of a lineup. In real life, he is Dr. Henry Nichols, distinguished professor of business administration at Villanova University. In his basketball life, he is Hank Nichols, longtime referee and, for the past seventeen years, the guru of all NCAA basketball officials. "When I was offered the job, I told my father about it,"

Nichols said. "He did some officiating years ago and he said to me, 'Henry, they want you to try to straighten out the officiating? That's perfect — you'll have a job for life, because it will never happen.'"

That was in 1988, and in 2005 Nichols would be the first to admit that his officials — everyone in the game refers to the referees as "Hank's guys" — are far from perfect. "But we've come a long way," Nichols said. "I know fans don't appreciate that, but we have. Guys are trained better today, they learn, they go to schools, and we get on 'em when they screw up. When I first started working, all I had were [old-time refs] Jim Hernjak and Steve Honzo saying to me, 'Kid, you don't want to make that call.'"

Nichols, who is sixty-six now, grew up in Morganton, North Carolina, the town best known as the home of Senator Sam Ervin Jr., the man who presided over the Senate Watergate hearings. He and his older brother, Bob, were both good athletes, both basketball players. "Bob was four years older than me," Nichols said. "After he graduated from high school, he ended up going to a prep school for a year and we played against each other one night, guarded each other, in fact. My dad refereed the game. Bob fouled out. For years he claimed that was proof that Dad favored me because I was the baby."

The baby ended up at Villanova and, after graduating in 1959, spent a couple of years in the marines because of an ROTC commitment before briefly playing minor league baseball in the Cincinnati Reds' farm system. When he realized he wasn't going to make it to the big leagues, he followed Bob to Buffalo and became a coach and teacher at DeSales High School. "In the winter of '65 Bob and I were both looking for ways to make some money on the side and he said, 'Hey, let's take the refs' test, we'd be good at it.' I'm sure the fact that my dad had done it influenced him. But we did and I started working high school games, making maybe five or ten bucks a game. But I liked it and when I went 2–17 one year at DeSales, I realized I was probably better at reffing than at coaching."

By 1969 Nichols was working college games, assigned out of the ECAC, which at the time ruled college basketball on the East Coast. He had gone back to school by then to get both his master's and his PhD, in educational administration and counseling. He had met Hubie Brown when Brown was coaching at Niagara. When Brown went to Duke as an assistant coach for Bucky Waters, he invited Nichols to work a scrimmage between Duke and Jacksonville. "Jacksonville had Artis Gilmore, Pembrook Burrows III, and Rex Morgan," Nichols remembered. "They were the best team I'd ever seen." (They went on to play in the national championship game in 1970.) Out of that experience came the chance to work games at Duke's summer camp, which led to a recommendation to ACC officiating supervisor Norval Neve. By the early '70s, Nichols was working in both the ACC and the ECAC and rising rapidly. He had a good feel for the game and the players and made it clear who was in charge. Nichols was famous among players for almost never calling a charge. Often when a player would try to take one, Nichols would call the block and then just look down at the player who had tried to take the charge as if to say, "Not happening tonight, son."

Nichols worked his first ACC championship game in 1974, the famous North Carolina State–Maryland game. Late in the game several players began jostling with one another just prior to an inbounds play. Showing his understanding for what he was a part of at that moment, Nichols jumped in between the players, pointed his finger at everyone involved, and said, "Stop it right now. You will not do that in *this* game."

A year later he was assigned to his first Final Four and got to work the championship game. According to Nichols, he got lucky that night — thanks to his partner, Bob Wortman. "It's probably fair to say I was a little hopped up," he said. "It was my first final *and* it was John Wooden's last game. Early in the game [UCLA star] David Meyers slammed the ball down in frustration over a call and I teed him up. Wooden couldn't believe it. He got up and started to argue with me. I'm not sure what would have happened, but I think if we had gotten into it, I might have ended up teeing him up, too. That wouldn't have been good, to tee John Wooden up in his last game. Fortunately for me, Bob Wortman got to Wooden before I did and got him calmed down. I'll always be grateful to him for that."

Nichols eventually worked ten Final Fours and six championship games and became one of the most respected officials in the game. Throughout the time that he was a referee, Nichols continued to teach at Villanova. In 1987 Dave Gavitt, who had been the chairman of the basketball committee, came to him with an idea. "Dave was like a lot of people in the game who thought we needed to make officiating more consistent," Nichols said. "It was too regionalized, too different from league to league. A foul in the ACC wasn't a foul in the Big Ten. We needed more good officials and we needed it to be more consistent. He wanted me to supervise officiating across the country and help pick the guys who would work the tournament. The timing was good. I was forty-eight. I enjoyed working the games, but the travel was wearing me out. And there were times when I had people calling me a c—— and I'd say to myself, 'I'm an educator. I don't need to be talked to this way.' The offer was really a godsend, perfect timing."

Nichols continued to work selected games the first four years on the job so he could meet younger officials and give some of them an up-close look at how he worked and what he expected. The last game he worked was late in 1990: James Madison against Old Dominion, with Lefty Driesell coaching JMU. He went out with Lefty's voice ringing in his ears.

Every year, Nichols begins the season by doing seminars — they used to be in person, but now they're done by video — for both coaches and officials. Both are told what calls are going to be emphasized during the season: It might be calling three seconds more often, or hand-checking. Coaches might be warned that officials are going to give them less rope before giving them a technical foul. Of course, in the end, everyone winds up refereeing the way they're most comfortable. "You put it out there, you try to get the guys to be consistent, but you know they're going to ref the way they want to ref," Nichols said. "I can't blame them; that's probably what I would have done, too."

What coaches ask for constantly and what Nichols tries to give them is consistency. "I know what makes coaches crazy more than anything is when a charge on one play isn't a charge on the next," Nichols said. "Or if guys change the way they officiate late in the game. A foul should be a foul — first minute or last. That doesn't mean it always happens that way."

Nichols's biggest job each year is choosing ninety-six officials to work the NCAA Tournament. The process begins in February, when each conference nominates officials it believes should be selected to work the tournament. In many cases, if not most, Nichols is familiar with the officials and he tries, through watching games on television and going to them in person, to keep abreast of how officials are working during the season. "Referees are like players," he said. "Some get better, some lose a step. Sometimes a good official has a bad year. Sometimes a guy you didn't think was very good shows improvement. I try, as best I can, to know how a guy is reffing *now*. But there's no doubt some of it is on reputation and on the word of the supervisors."

Occasionally if Nichols isn't familiar with someone's work, he will call the supervisor to ask about him. There are also times, he says, when he makes a mistake and underrates an official. "There was a guy named Steve Olson," he said. "He was nominated one year and I left him out. Just didn't think he was good enough. Then I saw him several times the next year and he was very much good enough. I had just missed on him. When I saw him that season, I told him, 'I made a mistake last year leaving you out.'"

Like most good officials, Nichols always told coaches when he realized he had blown a call. "One year I had LSU-Kentucky in the regionals," he said. "There was a block/charge and I called it for Kentucky, and as soon as I had signaled the foul I knew I'd gotten it wrong. A minute later Dale Brown called time and said, 'Hank, can I talk to you?' I knew what it was about. I said, 'Send your captain.' He didn't bother. Next time by the bench I said what I always said in those situations: 'I owe you one, but I'll never pay.'"

Which was his way of saying he was sorry while letting the coach know he didn't believe in make-up calls. A make-up call is perhaps the worst thing an official can do because it usually means he has now made two bad calls instead of one.

Once Nichols has the nominations from the conferences, he puts together a list of who he thinks should work the tournament and takes it with him to Indianapolis when the basketball committee meets to select the field. He usually meets with the committee on Thursday morning to show the members his list and, in some cases, explain why certain officials are on the list and some aren't. He then meets again during the weekend with the officials subcommittee, which in 2005 consisted of Southern University athletic director Floyd Kerr, George Mason athletic director Tom O'Connor, Princeton athletic director Gary Walters, and Mid-Continent Conference commissioner John LeCrone.

"Occasionally they or the staff might catch a conflict problem," he said. "They might, just as an example, remind me that Duke Edsall [an ACC official who has worked the Final Four in the past] is the brother of Randy Edsall, the Connecticut football coach. I know most of them already, but every once in a while when I start assigning games, they'll catch one."

Nichols does not begin assigning games until he has the bracket, which is usually about 3:30 on Sunday afternoon. He is paid to know the game, so there are certain first-round games he looks at as potentially more difficult than others and tries to make sure to have at least one or two experienced officials on that game. In 2005 he sensed that Vermont-Syracuse would be a difficult game and put Verne Harris, who has worked the last two national championship games, on that crew.

"You try to mix it up, regardless," he said. "You want the younger guys with veterans. Some games, like that one, you say, 'Okay, let's make sure we've got one of our best guys there.'"

Twelve officials go to each site. Only six, plus a standby, remain for the second round. Which six will remain is decided before the first round, in part because Nichols doesn't want officials competing to get noticed so they can advance and in part because it is easier logistically to tell officials in advance how long they will be staying at a site. But not working the second round does not mean an official can't advance to the round of sixteen.

"We like to tell guys that not getting a second-round game doesn't mean they can't advance. We just have to make decisions Sunday and then it is up to them to ref their way into the second week. It happens sometimes, just as sometimes guys we expect to advance don't work as well and don't advance."

Nichols knows that every time he selects one referee, he disappoints another. "This is not a science," he said. "It's an art and sometimes you choose the wrong colors. All we can do is make our best guess as to who will do the best job."

Once Nichols has gone through the bracket on Sunday afternoon and put together teams of three referees per game, he presents it to the committee and staff for a last look to make sure he hasn't missed anything. Then, at about the same time the bracket is going up, staff members begin calling officials to tell them they've been selected and where they are going. "Then it's up to us to make our travel plans," said Reggie Greenwood, a veteran referee who had consistently been selected for the tournament prior to 2005 but had never made the Final Four. In 2005 he made it. Why? "Because he reffed better," Nichols said. "He's worked at it and gotten better. He deserved it."

Once the tournament begins, the officials are graded by Nichols, who travels to as many sites as he can; by evaluators who are assigned to sites; and by the committee members at each site. They all fill out a form on each official in which they are asked to "strongly recommend" him for advancement, "recommend," or "not recommend." It is rare for someone who is not "strongly recommended" by all or most of the evaluators to advance. The exceptions usually come when Nichols has seen a game and believes the official has done better than the evaluators rated him or thinks there may be a particular reason why he didn't grade as well as others.

From a field of ninety-six the first week, the list is narrowed to thirty-six the second week — nine at each site — everyone working one game. As with the first weekend, being assigned a round-of-sixteen game as opposed to a round-of-eight game does not mean you can't advance to the Final Four. Who advances is decided early Monday morning after a teleconference involving Nichols, the committee, and the staff. The same process takes place during the second week with ten officials — nine to work the games plus a standby — selected for the Final Four. Every official who has worked gets a call on Monday morning.

"They either tell you, 'Thanks very much for all your hard work,' or, 'We'd like you to go to . . . ,' wherever it is you're going," said Tim Higgins, who has been a college referee for twenty-six years and has worked twelve Final Fours. "It's a tough call when they just give you the thank-you, but you understand. When I get that call, I always just resolve myself to work a little harder next year."

Higgins got that call in 2005 after the regionals. He thought he had done good work but he also understood that Nichols can't just pick the same nine guys for the Final Four every year. "Hank's got to do a juggling act," Higgins said. "We all understand that."

In fact, Nichols readily admits that he has to be aware of geography, of who works for what conference, and experience. "I like to bring in at least one new guy every year," he said. "It's important to extend the Final Four pool so that as guys get older, there are younger guys to step in." In 2005 Reggie Greenwood and Mike Shouse were the new guys. Shouse worked Illinois-Louisville; Greenwood had Michigan State–North Carolina.

The standby official in 2005 was Larry Rose, meaning he sat at the scorer's table through all three games for two reasons: to be ready to jump on the court if one of the officials was injured and to keep track of the game to prevent his partners from making a mistake.

"It's the hardest job in officiating," Rose said. "For one thing, you are so close to working the Final Four, but you aren't actually out there. We're all competitors, we all want to feel like we're part of the game. For another, you have to stay in the game mentally because if you don't, you will miss something and embarrass your buddies."

During the North Carolina–Michigan State game, Greenwood, Bob Donato, and Randy McCall got confused about who was supposed to shoot a free throw. Rose, paying close attention, noticed that they put the wrong shooter on the line for the Spartans. "Soon as I saw it, I said to the scorer, 'Hit the horn,'" Rose said. "He said, 'What, what?' I said, 'Hit the horn!' He wouldn't do it. So the kid shoots the first shot. Fortunately, the error is still correctable at that point because no time has gone off the clock, so I stood up and started waving my arms. That's when they saw me and we got it fixed."

Needless to say, the other three officials were grateful to Rose. "They know the game is going to be evaluated, and if someone [probably Nichols] sees that the wrong shooter took free throws, that will hurt them in the future," he said. "They were ready to kiss me when they got back to the locker room. I told them a handshake would be fine."

Rose has worked six Final Fours. He is a high school vice principal in southwestern Virginia not far from where he grew up. He was a good enough baseball player to be offered a partial scholarship to what was then Hampton Institute (now Hampton University). To pay for the nonscholarship part of his tuition, he had to have a work-study job. "I was assigned to referee intra- mural basketball games for work-study," he said. "Right from the beginning I enjoyed it. I felt like I was part of the action even when I wasn't actually playing in the game."

He continued officiating after college, working his way up from high school to the Central Collegiate Athletic Association before being hired by Fred Barakat to work in the ACC in 1982. "Fred started me out slowly," he said. "I was like a lot of young officials who needed to be brought along. I worked a lot of games with Lenny Wirtz early on, which was a blessing."

Wirtz is a legendary figure among ACC people: coaches, players, officials, and fans. Short, hyper, and intense, Wirtz was once the commissioner of the Ladies Professional Golf Associa- tion Tour. "He was the best because he was the most consistent official who ever lived," Tim Higgins said. "We all say we treat every game the same. Lenny actually did it."

Fans hated Wirtz because he was less likely to be influenced by a home crowd than most officials. Dean Smith was frequently frustrated by Wirtz because he would shake off his protestations with a laugh and keep working. "Lenny and I have been together for twenty-five years," Smith said one night. "I think we're entitled to a divorce." When Rick Barnes was coaching at Clemson, he decided one night to get thrown out of a game that he knew his team wasn't going to win in order to make a point. He screamed at Wirtz. He cursed at him. He came on the court and pointed his finger in Wirtz's face. "Rick," Wirtz said, "do what you want, say what you want. I know what you're doing and I'm not throw- ing you out."

Rose learned from Wirtz and worked his way up through the ACC officiating hierarchy. In 1990 he was selected for his first

Final Four — as the standby. "Fred told me later that Hank told him I deserved to work," he said. "But the ACC had two teams [Duke and Georgia Tech] there, so I couldn't work any of the games. Back then I was just thrilled to be there, to be considered one of the top ten guys."

Three years later he got the call saying he had been selected to work. He did the Michigan-Kentucky game in the Superdome — a game that went into overtime — and came home feeling as if he had climbed the mountain. "People look at you differently when you have been a Final Four ref," he said. "It becomes part of your résumé. I remember I worked at the Portsmouth Invitational [a postseason camp for college seniors that is scouted by the NBA] and before my first game the announcer said, 'And let's welcome back from working the Final Four, Larry Rose!' That was a great feeling."

Like most officials, Rose gets along with the majority of the coaches he works with (referees almost always say they work "for" coaches). "I remember I had Kentucky-Stanford in '98 [national semifinals], and Tubby Smith, who almost never says anything, jumped up on a call and said, 'What kind of a bullshit call was that?'" Rose said. "Then he realized I was standing almost right next to him. He said, 'Larry, I'm so sorry, I didn't mean it.' I said, 'Sure you did, Tubby, but I'm not teeing you up for *that* in a Final Four game.' I think he was shocked because I was laughing. You have to give coaches some rope under that kind of pressure."

One night at Maryland, Rose almost tripped over Gary Williams while running down the court because Williams was a couple of feet inbounds, screaming instructions at his players. "I said, 'Gary, get out of my way so I can work the game.' He said, 'Hey, Larry, that's my court you're working on.' I said, 'Right now, Gary, it's *my* court.' He just laughed."

Nichols always counsels his officials before a Final Four game on how to deal with the coaches. He reminds them that, just as for them, this is the biggest stage in the game for the coaches. "He's almost like a coach when he talks to us," Rose said. "He talks about how the teams play, what to look for, and reminds us to try to understand how hyper the coaches may be, especially early. The first part of the game is critical for everyone. I've always found that once I get the first call out of the way and get it right, I calm down and I'm okay."

Rose has now worked in the last sixteen NCAA Tournaments and has always made it at least to the regionals. But he has never worked a championship game. "I know part of it is that the ACC almost always has a team there," he said. "It's a little bit of a catch-22. Being in the ACC has made me the referee that I am and allowed me to handle pressure. I would never have made it to the Final Four at all if I hadn't worked in the ACC all these years. But because the league is so strong, it makes it harder for me to get the final. I'd like to think one day I will."

Tim Higgins got the final the very first year he made it to the Final Four, 1988. "I was floored, completely shocked," he said. "I was still in shock that I was there at all and then Hank announces in the meeting that I'm the ref on the final." (The officials in every game are designated as the referee, umpire 1, and umpire 2 — the ref being the ultimate authority in any disputes.)

The officials' meeting on Final Four weekend is held on Saturday morning. Until a few years ago all nine officials who were working would meet with Nichols and he would begin by announcing the assignments for the weekend. That has now changed. The three who work on Monday night don't fly in until late Sunday or early Monday. That takes some of the tension out of the Saturday meeting because the seven officials (including the standby) in the room all know their assignments before they arrive.

"It's good for a lot of reasons," Higgins said. "For one thing, whether guys admit it or not, it's a letdown to be in the room and find out you've got a semi instead of the final. We all want the final, just like players and coaches want to be in the final. For another, there's just no good that comes from getting in on Friday and then having nothing to do until Monday. It just makes you more tense about it all. The funny thing is, when I work a Final Four game with someone who is doing it for the first time, I always say, 'Treat it like just another game.' Which is silly because it isn't just another game. The minute you walk out there it feels different because it *is* different."

Higgins began officiating in 1972 after getting out of the army, "to get some beer money." He started working high school games in New Jersey — where he had grown up and gone to college at Fairleigh Dickinson — and got his big break when the Big East came into existence in 1979. Twenty-six years later he and Jim Burr, another perennial Final Four ref, are the only two men who worked the first year of the league's existence who are still working.

"I always tell people this is the best part-time job in America," he said. "For one thing, it forces you to stay in shape. For another thing, I really enjoy the friendships. For another, in terms of business, there's nothing I could do that could be better. Guys I deal with see me working on television all the time. It's invaluable."

Higgins owns his own business selling commercial building supplies and has offices in both Manhattan and Brooklyn. He has worked every NCAA Tournament since 1985. He still remembers being shocked when Nichols announced that he would be working the 1988 final. "There was a moment of shock, then a

John Wooden (with trophy) and the 1971 UCLA Bruins,
perhaps his most difficult and gratifying team. (© ASUCLA Photography)

Mike Krzyzewski. He always brings his team to the Final Four, one way or another. (© Duke University Photography)

The committee at work. Very serious stuff. (Courtesy NCAA)

Jim Valvano. They still tell his stories long into the night. (© ESPN)

Endless enthusiasm. Dick Vitale (right) speaks . . . and speaks . . .
(© ESPN)

Tom Brennan. No one enjoyed the Final Four more.

(© Sally McCay/ University of Vermont)

Bill Bradley. The Final Four's first Rhodes Scholar. (© Rich Clarkson / Sports Illustrated)

Clay Buckley. The last of the Buckley dynasty, he finally got the family the ultimate victory. (© Duke University Photography)

Wes Miller. Savoring every moment . . . on and off the court. (© Jeffrey A. Camarati / UNC Athletic Communications)

Sean May. Complete satisfaction: the MOP Award and the first hug by Roy Williams. (© Jeffrey A. Camarati / UNC Athletic Communications)

Three champions: Dean Smith, Michael Jordan, and Roy Williams.
(© Jeffrey A. Camarati / UNC Athletic Communications)

Roy Williams. The final net was his, at long last. (© Jeffrey A. Camarati / UNC Athletic Communications)

moment of being thrilled," he said. "And then I thought, 'Oh boy, Tim, you better not screw this up.'"

One of the reasons Higgins has succeeded is that he has a self-deprecating way of working a game. He is not one of those officials who has to prove he is in charge. He looks and sounds like Barney Rubble, as opposed to some of his colleagues, who want to be Fred Flintstone and give all the orders. "I always tell coaches that I don't tee them up, they tee themselves up," he said. "I don't do it unless there's no choice."

Higgins had the chance early in his career to work with — and learn from — Nichols. "He was great at defusing bad situations," Higgins said. "One night he and I and a guy named Dave Pollock have Georgetown-Syracuse in the [Carrier] Dome. This was back when that was one of *the* games every year. I called a bad foul against Syracuse, really a terrible call, putting [Patrick] Ewing on the line for two shots. The place was going crazy. They're throwing things, screaming profanities. [Jim] Boeheim is angry; [John] Thompson is angry. I mean, it's chaos. Hank goes down to talk to the two coaches. I'm standing there with Pollock and I said, 'Should we go help?' and he just says to me, 'Timmy, let the big dog eat. Hank's got it under control.'"

In 1990 Higgins was assigned to work the Final Four in Denver. He and his wife, Kathy, took a drive to the Air Force Academy to spend the day with an old friend who was teaching there. They toured the campus and finally walked into the chapel. "We sat down for about a minute and the guy behind me turns to his wife and says, 'Oh no, not f—— Higgins!' I mean, I hear that all the time on the court, but not usually in church!"

Nichols and the tournament committee take great pains to keep the names of the Final Four officials secret until the minute they walk on the floor. One reason for this is that certain officials have reputations for working games a certain way — calling more fouls, fewer fouls — and the NCAA doesn't want gamblers to know who is working in advance. It is also a matter of principle: the officials are supposed to be faceless — even though, as Higgins's story about the Air Force Academy clearly illustrates, they aren't — so the NCAA doesn't want their names in the newspaper or on TV in advance of the games. Of course, by Thursday anyone who wants to find out who the officials are can. One reporter and Nichols have an annual ritual whereby the reporter names all the officials for Nichols and Nichols just shakes his head and says, "Next year, you won't find out."

Higgins takes it a step further. "In 1992 they literally tried to sneak us into Minneapolis in the middle of the night," he said. "They took us out a side door of the airport and through a back door of the hotel. I gave the front desk clerk my name and he said, 'Oh yes, Mr. Higgins,' and handed me *twenty-three* phone messages, most of them from people I knew looking for tickets. Some secret."

The officials are given first-class treatment throughout the tournament, perhaps in part because they aren't paid very much. The first weekend they are paid $700 a game; the second, $850; and the third, $1,000. "You make the Final Four, you lose money," Larry Rose said. "They don't pay for your wife or if you want to bring children or anyone else. So, if it's a big deal to you — which it is — you probably lose money on the whole thing." In fact, the official who makes the most money at the Final Four is the standby. The nine officials who work the games get paid for one game; the standby gets paid for three.

"It is nice when they take you to and from the games with a police escort," Higgins said, laughing. "Sometimes I think, 'How cool a thing is this, me getting a police escort.' In Tampa a few years ago we told our escort we wanted him to find a restaurant for us after the game where there would be no fans, because we really didn't want to rehash the game with people who were either very happy or very sad. We get dressed and the cops take us to a biker bar. Wasn't a soul in there without a tattoo. But no one bothered us."

Higgins didn't make a thirteenth Final Four in 2005. He worked the Louisville–West Virginia regional final and hoped to get the call but didn't. "I'm really okay with it," he said. "Disappointed, of course. But look, I've been to twelve. I think there are fifty referees out there — I mean it, fifty — who are worthy of working the Final Four who have never been to one. I sat home and watched on TV and rooted for all the guys to do well because they're my friends. If they do well, we all do well. I really think how the guys do in the Final Four sets the tone for all of us for next season because the whole basketball world is watching and all of us are being judged on how the guys who are there are doing."

The single most famous call in Final Four history was John Clougherty's foul call in overtime that put Michigan's Rumeal Robinson at the line with Seton Hall, up by one and 1.8 seconds to play in the 1989 final. Robinson made both shots and Michigan won the game. What made the call controversial was that Robinson passed the ball and yet Clougherty called the foul when there was clearly no advantage gained because of the contact. Officials are counseled over and over not to anticipate plays (Clougherty thought Robinson was going to shoot when he saw the contact) and not to put someone at the line unless the contact creates a disadvantage for the player who has been hit. Clougherty, one of the best officials of the past twenty-five years, who worked eleven Final Fours, will always be remembered most for one call.

Recently, there hasn't been one call that outraged people, but there was one game that is still argued about and discussed: Duke-Connecticut in the 2004 semifinals. It was a matchup of two Hall of Fame coaches, Mike Krzyzewski and Jim Calhoun, who both have reputations for working the officials. Krzyzewski's approach to officials was best described years ago by an ACC ref who said, "Mike's like a football coach. If you take a possession away from him, you better have a damn good reason why you did it." Larry Rose, who likes Calhoun, says of him, "If you let him, he will talk to you all night."

Nichols always advises his officials to be sure not to "referee the coaches." What he means is that they can't react every time a coach complains about a call, because the best ones — and in the Final Four you are almost always dealing with top-of-the-line coaches — will see that they can get you to react and just keep after you. That's what happened in the Duke-UConn game. After UConn center Emeka Okafor picked up two quick fouls, Calhoun was up screaming. For the next few minutes, UConn got every call. When *his* centers got in foul trouble, Krzyzewski began barking. Sure enough, the calls turned the other way. By halftime Nichols was so exasperated, he did something he had never done in seventeen years as the supervisor: he went into the locker room to talk to his officials.

"I just told them they had to take control of the game," he said. "They were letting the coaches control the game. They had to make their calls and stick by them and forget the coaches. I reminded them that they had whistles around their necks for a reason. They did better the second half."

That is Nichols's story and he's sticking to it. The consensus was that the officials ruined what should have been a great game. Even Calhoun, whose team won, said afterward, "It would have been nice to have been able to see what these two teams could do if they'd been allowed to play."

Nichols shrugs when the subject comes up and insists it wasn't all that bad. The three officials — Ted Hillary, Olandis Poole, and David Hall — were nowhere to be found at the 2005 Final Four.

Hank Nichols was there. Because, just as his father predicted, he was still working on trying to get the officials straightened out. "We've come a long way," he said. "But there's always work to be done."

9

Players

WHILE THE COACHES ARE A CONSTANT at the Final Four, coming back year after year to trade stories and talk about the old days, a player's involvement in the event is far shorter. The absolute maximum number of times a player can participate in a Final Four is, of course, four. Technically, if a player redshirts, he could be on the bench (though not eligible to play) for a fifth year. But that's it. The list of players who have been to four Final Fours isn't very long: Clay Buckley, Greg Koubek, Christian Laettner, and Brian Davis. All went to Duke during the period from 1988 through 1992, when Duke reached five straight Final Fours. When UCLA went to ten straight, from 1967 to 1976, freshmen were not eligible to play. (The freshman class of 1973 was the first to be eligible, but none of them played in that year's Final Four.) Cincinnati also went to five straight Final Fours in the 1960s, before freshmen could play.

Most players dream of being in one Final Four. Only a handful get to play in more than one. Most arrive at a Final Four understanding that chances are good they will never play in another, especially these days, when so many players jump to the pros prior to their senior year.

"It's actually something you don't want to think about when you're there," said Jay Bilas, whose one and only Final Four was in 1986 as a Duke senior. "There's enough pressure as is, without thinking to yourself, 'Okay, this is it. I'll never get this chance again.' But the thought is definitely there. That's why I never feel all that bad for the coaches when they lose. They can have other chances; they can spend twenty-five or thirty years trying to get back again, and often do. It isn't true of the players."

Bilas is forty now, a very popular and well-compensated television analyst who also has a law degree and works during the off-season in a law firm in Charlotte. He's married with two children, and his adult life has been, by just about any standard, a complete success.

And he still hasn't gotten over losing the 1986 national championship game to Louisville. "It's the difference between being remembered and being forgotten," he said. "We won thirty-seven games that season, and people were writing and saying we were one of the best teams of all time. Now when I see lists of the best teams of the last twenty years, we aren't even in the top ten. That's for one reason: we lost. It doesn't change the bond you had with your teammates or take away the good memories of the fun times, but it leaves you with a little hole that you know can't be filled. I can still hear Bob Knight speaking to our team the day before the final, saying, 'Boys, don't hold anything back in this game, because no one remembers the team that loses.'

"In 1991 I was an assistant coach when we won the national championship. Tommy Amaker [the point guard on the '86 team] was there, too. The night we won, Johnny Dawkins, who was still playing in the NBA at the time, called Tommy and me and said, 'Does this make up for '86?' And we both said the same thing: 'Nothing can ever make up for '86.' I don't want to be overly melodramatic. We've all gone and lived productive lives and we still have a great time when we get together, but it's still there — whether we talk about it or not.

"I remember in '91 when the game was over, I stood on the court and watched our players celebrate. I was happy for them because it occurred to me that whenever they got together in the future, they would have this memory rather than the empty one we had after our last game. But that's what makes the Final Four what it is. Everyone watching understands what's at stake for the players, because most of them get only the one chance."

Greg Anthony got two chances. Unlike Bilas, he got to celebrate, got to be part of a national championship team in 1990, when Nevada–Las Vegas hammered Duke, 103–73, in the championship game. Most people virtually conceded the national title to UNLV the next year, and the Rebels arrived in Indianapolis 34–0 and seemingly primed to be the first team since Wooden's retirement to win back-to-back titles. Except they never got back to the final. They were stunned by Duke, 79–77, in the semifinals. When Anthony, who went on to play in the NBA and now works for ESPN, thinks about his college career, he thinks first about the title lost, not the title won.

"I guess it's human nature to think that way," he said. "When we won, it seemed too easy because we won the final by thirty. So losing the next year never really crossed our minds. When we did lose, it was a complete shock. I'm not sure I'm completely over that shock yet."

Many players who have been on teams that have lost in the Final Four remember being in a kind of shock, which meant they didn't understand right away how long the loss would linger. "I remember getting back to my hotel room and thinking,

'Gee, it's too bad we lost, but I'll have a couple more chances before my career is over,'" said Jeff Capel, who was a Duke freshman in 1994 when Scotty Thurman hit a late three-point shot to give Arkansas the championship, denying Duke a third title in four years. "At that point in time, you went to Duke, you just figured the Final Four was part of your schedule every year."

Capel did make it back to the Final Four in 1997 as a senior — to play in an all-star game held that weekend. During his last three seasons, Duke won one NCAA Tournament game and didn't reach the round of sixteen. "Being the son of a coach, I think I have an understanding that nothing is guaranteed — even things you once thought were," he said. "But when you're young, even if you think you understand that, you don't."

Capel is now a very young coach — he was hired as the head coach at Virginia Commonwealth when he was twenty-seven and took the school to the NCAAs in his second season. But he understands that even success doesn't mean you'll get to coach forever. His father — Jeff Capel Jr. — had great success at Old Dominion, winning (among other games) one of the great first-round games ever played, when his team (as a number fourteen seed) upset Villanova in three overtimes in 1993. When the school stopped going to the postseason, Old Dominion started looking for a new coach.

"It was very tough to see my dad go through that," Capel said. "I had come to the Final Four with him a couple of times, and the saddest thing to me was to see the coaches in the lobby who were looking for work or had just been fired. I never dreamed that would happen to him. I love what I'm doing now and it is great fun to be here and see people, but I'm very conscious of how quickly things can change — whether you're playing or coaching."

* * *

There weren't any members of the Buckley family in St. Louis. That was surprising only because over a period of four decades, from the '60s to the '90s, a Buckley played in at least one Final Four. In fact, Jay Buckley, his brother Bruce, and his son, Clay, played in a total of seven Final Fours, beginning with Jay's appearance in 1963 as a Duke junior and ending in 1991, when Clay was the co-captain of Duke's first national championship team.

"It took a long time for the family to get one, but we finally did," Jay Buckley said. "I think we were all beginning to wonder if it was going to happen."

How many families can claim to have three different members who not only played college basketball but made their final appearance in the national championship game? That's what the Buckleys did. Jay Buckley's last college game was the 1964 title game: Duke's loss to UCLA. Bruce, thirteen years younger than Jay, played his last college game for North Carolina in 1977, when the Tar Heels lost the final to Marquette. It was Clay who finally got it right in 1991 when Duke beat Kansas in his last game.

"Of course, it took us four tries," Clay said, alluding to the fact that the four Duke teams he played on all reached the Final Four. "Looking back, it's amazing to think that we did that. Every good team's goal at the start of a season is the Final Four. We actually lived up to it. But if we hadn't won in '91 and I had finished my career without a championship, I'm honestly not sure I would be able to watch the Final Four right now. To be that close and to never win would have been very difficult."

His father and uncle say they have no such trouble. Regrets — they have a few. But they still watch. "I was lucky to, in effect, have a second chance with Clay," Jay Buckley said. "It was certainly different, being a father and watching, but it was a great feeling, especially that last night in Indianapolis when they beat Kansas."

Jay was the best of the three Final Four Buckleys, a six-ten center from Bladensburg, Maryland, who was recruited by everyone in the country when he was a senior at Bladensburg High School in 1960. He was a good enough player to attract the attention of Red Auerbach. The great Celtics coach lived in Washington and kept a close eye on most players from the D.C. area. When Buckley was a senior, Auerbach tried to persuade him to go to Harvard. "In those days they still had the territorial draft in the NBA," Buckley said. "If I'd have gone to Harvard, I would have been in the Celtics' territory and they would have had first shot at me when I graduated. I was flattered and my grades were good enough. But in the end [then assistant coach] Bucky Waters convinced me that [then coach] Vic Bubas was building a powerhouse. I wanted to be a part of it."

He was, playing alongside three-time All-American Art Heyman and future NBA star Jeff Mullins. The Duke class of '64 has the distinction of never having lost a game to North Carolina (7–0 in three years of eligibility) and reached the Final Four in both 1963 and 1964. "Of course, back then winning the ACC Tournament was such a big deal because you had to win to get into the tournament, so in a very real way, you had to win *seven* games in a row to win a national championship — three in the ACC Tournament and then four in the NCAAs," he said. "I remember the Final Four being back-to-back nights and the feeling of exhaustion you had when it was over."

Buckley scored 25 points against Michigan in the semifinals in 1964, and he and his teammates honestly thought they were going to win the national championship the next night. "I really think watching UCLA play Kansas State in the second semi was a mistake," Buckley said. "It wasn't a very good game. Neither team played well. We looked at UCLA and they weren't very tall, they weren't powerful. We just thought they were a team from California that probably wouldn't do all that well in the ACC."

Duke led the game early, but UCLA's quickness and shooting wore the Blue Devils out, and the Bruins won going away, 98–83, for John Wooden's first championship. "Of course, now the loss doesn't look as bad, given what Wooden went on to accomplish," Buckley said. "It stung back then, though. I can't say it doesn't still sting a little bit today." Jay Buckley was drafted by the Los Angeles Lakers, but he had been offered a fellowship in physics at Johns Hopkins. "The fellowship was worth more than the Lakers offered," he said. He went on to get a PhD and become an astrophysicist. A *true* "student-athlete."

Like his older brother, Bruce played at Bladensburg High School. He was eight years old when Jay played his last college game and still remembers not seeing his brother's great game against Michigan. "My sister was in a play at school," he said. "I went with my mom. I don't think the game was even on TV where we were. We got home and people were phoning to tell us what Jay had done. In those days you didn't even think about actually going. My dad had died when Jay was a freshman. My mom was a librarian with six kids. We weren't likely to go caravaning around the country to watch Jay play."

If Bucky Waters was responsible for Jay going to Duke, he was also responsible — at least in part — for Bruce not going to

Duke. By the time Bruce was a high school senior in 1973, Waters was completing his fourth season as Duke's head coach. The Blue Devils had gone 12–14 and rumors were rife he was going to be fired. "I just felt like it was an unstable situation there," Bruce said. "Carolina, with Dean, was anything but unstable. I thought I would fit in there."

He was right on both counts: Waters resigned in September of what would have been Bruce's freshman season, and the Duke program fell into chaos. The athletic director, Carl James, actually tried to hire Adolph Rupp, who had just been forced into retirement at Kentucky. Rupp was ready to take the job — a press conference had even been scheduled — when the director of his business operations died suddenly and he had to stay in Lexington. Duke ended up promoting Neill McGeachy to interim coach and it wasn't until 1978, a year after Buckley graduated, that Bill Foster got the program back on the map.

Bruce Buckley was never a starter at North Carolina, but he played consistent minutes off the bench and was a contributor throughout his career. As a senior, he spelled Mike O'Koren, then a heralded freshman, at the small forward spot. Carolina was an NCAA Tournament team in 1975, losing to Syracuse in the round of sixteen, and 1976, losing to Alabama in the first round. Finally, in Buckley's senior year, the Tar Heels got on a roll. "We just kept winning close games," Buckley remembered. "In the ACC final against Virginia, Phil [Ford] fouled out and John [Kuester] had to run the four corners the last few minutes and he did a great job. Then we had to come from behind in the first round of the tournament against Purdue and then from way behind against Notre Dame."

Ford was hurt late in the Notre Dame game, hyperextending his right elbow when he took a hard fall running the four corners.

It was probably the four corners as much as any one thing that eventually led to the shot clock in college basketball. "Even as players, we had mixed emotions about it," Buckley said. "It wasn't exactly a fun way to play, but it was certainly a very effective way to play."

North Carolina played Kentucky in the east regional final with three future pros injured: Ford, with a hurt elbow; Walter Davis, with an injured finger; and Tom LaGarde, who had torn an Achilles tendon and was on the bench in street clothes. Ford and Davis both played. The Tar Heels won, to reach Smith's fifth Final Four. Then they beat UNLV in the semifinals, with O'Koren scoring 31 points. That was the second game of the semifinal doubleheader. In the opener, Marquette's Jerome Whitehead scored at the buzzer to beat UNC-Charlotte. "I remember when we went down there, people were saying we were going to play Charlotte in the final," Buckley said. "We didn't want that, because they were the in-state rival and they would have had so much to prove since we never played them. The funny thing is, we were standing in the tunnel, waiting for the game to end. There were no Telscreens in those days. We couldn't even see the scoreboard. We just heard this huge roar, and a minute later the guy says, 'Okay, you can go out now.' We ran out to warm up and we didn't even know who had won the game."

Carolina fell behind again in the championship game but rallied to tie with twelve minutes left. Buckley was on the court when the Tar Heels made their run. When they got the ball back with the score tied, Smith signaled for the four corners. Buckley isn't sure if he noticed O'Koren reporting to the scorer's table to come back in or if he learned later that he was there. "I know he was getting ready to come back in for me," he said.

Carolina was running the four corners at that stage not to kill the clock but to try to lure Marquette out of its zone. "I was just trying to change sides of the court to go set a screen," Buckley remembered. "I wasn't running a backdoor cut or anything. But [Steve] Krafcisin saw me open and passed me the ball. I was right near the basket and there was no one around me, so I just went up and shot. To tell the truth, I was kind of surprised to get the ball and to find myself open. Except I wasn't quite as open as I seemed to be. Someone came flying at me. I wasn't sure if it was Whitehead or [Bo] Ellis, but he blocked the shot."

It was Ellis, who made a spectacular play and started a fast break the other way. Marquette took the lead and Carolina never caught up. "Obviously, I wish things had happened differently," Buckley said. "My life was never tied up in basketball. I wasn't all that emotional about playing my last college game, although I do remember that waiting from Saturday to Monday was terrible. It was as if I could feel the energy draining from my legs each hour that went by. I was planning to go to law school and move on. But, of course, I wish I'd seen Ellis or maybe passed or maybe that Steve hadn't passed me the ball when I wasn't really looking for it. I know that play didn't decide the game, because there was a lot of time left, but I think about it sometimes. What I really remember, though, is the locker room after the game. That's such an emotional moment. I remember the seniors each getting up and giving a little speech after the last game the three years prior, and now suddenly it was my turn. I didn't say much, but I know there was a lot of hugging and crying."

One person pulling hard for Carolina that night was Duke graduate Jay Buckley. He had been disappointed when his brother decided to go to Carolina, but he understood. "Duke was in flux," he said. "Plus, Dean was great to our entire family, especially my mom. It was tough to argue with the decision." He laughed. "I never hated Carolina the way some Duke people do. I think part of it is that I never lost to them, but I also think there's an understanding among players that if someone is a rival, it's because you respect them. If you don't respect them, where's the rivalry? Even when I was playing, if an ACC team was playing outside the league, I pulled for the ACC team. I still do — even Maryland, which can be hard sometimes because living here [in suburban Washington, not far from the Maryland campus], surrounded by Maryland fans who hate Duke, it can be tough at times."

The brothers have an agreement now that whenever Duke plays Carolina, the loser calls the winner after the game to offer congratulations. They chat about the game, and that's pretty much the end of it. "I remember a couple of years after I graduated, Carolina beat a pretty good Duke team by about twenty and I called Jay and gave it to him pretty good," Bruce said. "Well, the next week in the ACC Tournament, Duke turned around and won by twenty and I got the same phone call. We decided after that to tone it down a little bit."

When Jay's son, Clay, grew to be a six-foot-nine prospect, there wasn't much doubt where he would go to college. By then, Duke was well beyond the troubles of the early 1970s, not only stabilized by Mike Krzyzewski but turned into a national power. "I wasn't pressured to go to Duke — I was brainwashed," Clay said. "My dad always took me down to reunions and to games. I got my first recruiting letter from Coach K when I was in the seventh grade. But I never hated Carolina. For one thing, I always heard about how great Coach Smith had been to my uncle and to my grandmother. For another, whenever I've encountered people from there, they've been people I've liked."

In fact, when Clay first went to Duke's basketball camp as a six-five eighth-grader, he found himself on the same plane with a group of kids who were obviously basketball players. "Are you guys going to the camp?" he asked. Sure are, they said, you just come with us when we get off the plane. Clay followed the other kids and found himself getting on a bus. "I was confused because I thought my dad had said that one of the coaches from the camp was going to meet me," he said. "But these guys were older, they knew what they were doing, so I got on the bus."

They arrived at what was clearly a college campus, but not one that looked familiar to Buckley. He suspected something was wrong as he lined up to register, then knew something was wrong when he saw kids who had already registered coming out the door wearing brand-new T-shirts that read, CAROLINA BAS-KETBALL CAMP.

"I got out of line and ducked inside, wondering how in the world I could get myself over to Duke," he said. "The first person I saw was [then Carolina assistant] Eddie Fogler. He recognized me and said, 'Clay, I think you're in the wrong place.'" (Even when players are in the eighth grade, coaches know these things.) "He couldn't have been nicer. He got me to a phone, where I called my parents and they made arrangements to get me picked up."

Buckley did receive one recruiting letter from Dean Smith. "It said, 'I know you're inclined to go to Duke, but if you change your mind and want to go to a *real* school, you know where to find us.'"

Like his uncle, Clay was never a starter, and when he did play, he was a dirty-work guy. "It's amazing the number of screens you can set in the motion offense," he said, laughing. "The funny thing is, I play old-man's basketball [rec league] now, and I'm great at trailing the fast break and shooting the three-pointer. Coach K would be amazed if he saw me."

Buckley is now a successful executive at AOL, but he still loves basketball. "I never thought of myself as an NBA player," he said. "I went to college to be as good a college player as I could possibly be, and even though I was never a star, I loved my college experience. I have to admit there would be an emptiness if we hadn't won in '91. My sophomore year, when we lost to Seton Hall in Seattle, I think there was a feeling that maybe we'd missed our best chance. Danny [Ferry] was graduating, and none of us knew how good Christian [Laettner] was going to become. Even my senior year when we started to play really well, we knew we were going to have to go through Vegas to win, and they had just killed us the year before."

Most Duke people talk now about how confident they were going into the UNLV game. Buckley says they may not have been quite as confident as they sound now. "I think Coach K did a great job of convincing us we could play with them," he said. "But there was still doubt; there had to be. They were 34–0 and no one had really challenged them all year. But I still remember early in the second half seeing some of their guys yelling at one another on the court, and we all kind of looked at each other because Coach K had said, 'When it's close, they're going to start bickering with one another. They're going to get frustrated.' Which is exactly what happened."

North Carolina was in that Final Four and had just lost to Kansas in the game in which Pete Pavia ejected Dean Smith. The Carolina fans, their team eliminated, many of them angry with the Duke fans for taunting Smith as he left, were pulling zealously for UNLV. One exception was Bruce Buckley. "Oh, I definitely wanted Duke to win," he said. "For one thing, I respect what Krzyzewski's built there. For another, I wanted to see Clay win. I didn't want it to end for him the way it did for Jay and for me."

It didn't. It ended with a 72–65 victory over Kansas. Clay Buckley didn't score in the game. That really didn't matter. He can remember vividly everything about that night — including the look in his father's eyes. "It's funny," he said. "I know Jay [Bilas] always says he looks at the losers after the championship game because he knows they're feeling what he felt back in '86. I always look at the winners. I try to look into their eyes to see if they really understand what they just did and how much it is going to mean to them down the road, or if they're just into chest pounding and making sure people are looking at them. I'm not sure these days what the answer is — different with different guys, I guess — but I'd love to go and tell them to savor that moment, really savor it, because they're part of a very lucky few who get to have it."

Even in a family that played in seven Final Fours, that moment came only once.

Making the Final Four is special for everyone, but never the same for a coach as it is for a player. Some of it has to do with age, some of it with the camaraderie of being part of a team instead of coaching one. For one assistant coach, Michigan State's Doug Wojcik, being in the Final Four had great meaning — because he had just missed making it as a player and wondered if he would ever have another chance to get there.

Wojcik came out of Wheeling, West Virginia, in 1982, just wanting to play college basketball somewhere — anywhere. "I wasn't exactly highly recruited," he said. "I had a friend named Mike Sonnefeld who had gone to Navy, and he encouraged me to try to go there. But Navy wasn't all that interested in me. Years later I saw my recruiting file: they thought of me as a marginal prospect at best."

Encouraged by Sonnefeld and his high school coach, Skip Prosser (who had attended the Merchant Marine Academy), Wojcik kept after Navy until Jim Leary, one of the assistant coaches, told him the school might be willing to send him to the academy's prep school for a year. "That was actually great for me because I was very skinny and needed a year to fill out."

Even filled out, Wojcik wasn't slated to play much at Navy until another point guard, Willie Jett, flunked out of school. He became friends as a plebe with another skinny freshman named David Robinson. "David was only six-seven that year and he really didn't know how to play," Wojcik said. "But you could see he had amazing athletic ability."

A year later Robinson had grown six inches. He was seven-one and was rapidly becoming the kind of player that you *never* see at a military academy. Wojcik had become the starting point guard. The Mids made the tournament that season (1985) and faced LSU in a first-round game in Dayton, Ohio. No one from LSU knew what league Navy played in. The players said they had heard something about Navy having "a big center," but that was about all they knew. Navy won, 78–55. The game was summed up by a moment in the second half when LSU coach Dale Brown jumped up to tell one of his players, "You take number ten and tell Mike to take Wojcik."

Wojcik *was* number ten.

A year later the Mids were back in the tournament and were sent to Syracuse to play Tulsa in the first round, the winner to play Syracuse *at* Syracuse in the second round. Most people were already anticipating a Syracuse-Indiana game in the Sweet Sixteen. It never came close to happening. Cleveland State shocked Indiana in the first round, and Navy beat both Tulsa and Syracuse — Syracuse by a dozen (the game wasn't that close in reality) in a game Jim Boeheim still says was one of the most stunning losses of his coaching career. Navy then beat Cleveland State in the round of sixteen and found itself one step away from the Final Four. The opponent was Duke.

This was not the Duke that has now become the target for most college basketball programs. This was not the Mike Krzyzewski who has now become the Coach K of American Express fame (or infamy, depending on your point of view). But it was Krzyzewski's first great Duke team, led by Johnny Dawkins, Mark Alarie, David Henderson, and Jay Bilas. "All I know," Wojcik said, "is they were much too good for us."

Perhaps the 71–50 final margin had something to do with the pregame pep talk Krzyzewski, Army class of 1969, gave his team. After telling his players how much he respected Navy and how remarkable it was for a Navy basketball team to be in the Elite Eight, he told them that if they did not *kill* Navy, he would never speak to them again. They took him seriously. The moment Wojcik, and most who saw the game, remembers most vividly came midway through the second half when Wojcik stepped into the lane to try to stop a driving Dawkins and Dawkins simply jumped *over* him and dunked the ball. "I can still see his feet in my face," Wojcik said almost twenty years later. It was at that point that the Duke students began chanting, "Abandon ship," in the direction of the Navy bench.

Robinson and Wojcik still had one more year left. But Vernon Butler and Kylor Whitaker, both outstanding shooters, had graduated. Coach Paul Evans left to take the job at Pittsburgh. The Mids — with Robinson on the cover of *Sports Illustrated*'s preseason basketball issue — made it back to the tournament but lost in the first round to Michigan in spite of Robinson's 50 points.

The season still had memorable moments. Robinson and Wojcik played their final home game in Halsey Field House against Army in front of a standing-room-only crowd, Midshipmen almost literally hanging from the rafters to watch. Army had a great guard named Kevin Houston, a shooter with amazing range. This was the first year of the three-point shot, and Houston took full advantage, torching Wojcik and Navy for 38 points. "By then, Kevin and I had become friends," Wojcik said. "There's always a bond between guys from Army and Navy. I was pleading with him during the game, 'Please stop it, my entire family is here, all my friends. It's my last home game.'" Houston never stopped shooting, but Navy managed to rally late to win in overtime.

Wojcik knew he wanted to follow in Prosser's footsteps and coach when he graduated, but he had a five-year commitment to the navy. He served on the USS *William Simms* (the *Billy Simms* to everyone on board) and then came back to the academy as an assistant coach in 1992. After the graduation of Robinson and Wojcik and Evans's departure, Navy basketball had fallen into disarray. Working for Don DeVoe, Wojcik was part of the rebuilding. Navy went to three NCAA Tournaments between 1994 and 1998, and everyone agreed that the dogged recruiting of Wojcik and fellow assistant Emmett Davis was a key reason for the turnaround. When Dino Gaudio was the coach at Army, he frequently told Wojcik that he would gladly recommend him for any job in the country — if only to get him away from Navy. "It seemed like any place we went to recruit, Doug or Emmett had already been there," said Gaudio, now Prosser's top assistant at Wake Forest.

Wojcik finally took a job in 1999 with Matt Doherty at Notre Dame. He then went with Doherty to North Carolina and helped recruit the class that included Sean May, Raymond Felton, and Rashad McCants, only to watch everything fall apart during Doherty's last two seasons. When Doherty was fired, Wojcik was hired almost immediately by Tom Izzo at Michigan State. During his first year there, he was offered the chance to return to Navy and succeed the retiring DeVoe as head coach.

"For a long time I always thought that would be where I'd end up again when the right time came," he said. "I still love the place and I always will. But when I met with [Navy Athletic Director] Chet Gladchuk, I just didn't feel that comfortable with the conversation. I mean, he was talking to me about how great the weather is in Annapolis. I *lived* there for twelve years, I know all about the weather there. I wanted to know what he was thinking about doing to help a new coach improve Navy basketball. I talked to Tom [Izzo] about it and he said to be patient, maybe wait a year and see what happens."

Wojcik knew that Izzo assistants had landed good jobs in the past: Stan Heath is now at Arkansas, Brian Gregory is at Dayton, and Tom Crean has already taken Marquette to the Final Four. As tough as it was to say no to his alma mater, he decided to wait. The decision proved correct: soon after the regular season ended, Wojcik was named the coach at Tulsa, a school that has become a coaching cradle in recent years: Nolan Richardson, Tubby Smith, Bill Self, and Buzz Peterson have all coached there. As excited as he was about finally becoming a head coach eighteen years after playing his last game at Navy, Wojcik felt as if he had unfinished business at Michigan State.

"We felt this team had a lot of potential going into the season," he said. "If I'm leaving, I want to leave on an up note."

When the draw came out with Michigan State as the fifth seed in the so-called Austin regional, most people thought Wojcik would be starting work at Tulsa after the first weekend of the tournament. Old Dominion was a tough first-round opponent, and then would come a game with Syracuse, one of the hotter teams around.

Old Dominion proved to be difficult; the Spartans trailed midway through the second half before rallying to win. Syracuse did not — the Orange were upset by Vermont. Even though the Catamounts showed up wanting very much to beat Michigan State, their dreams had all come true in the Syracuse game two nights earlier. They hung around for most of the game, but Michigan State was in control down the stretch and won, 72–61.

That put the Spartans into the round of sixteen against Duke. For all his coaching accomplishments, Izzo had never beaten Mike Krzyzewski, losing to him in the 1999 Final Four and four times in the regular season. Wojcik had his own Duke memories: the Dawkins dunk in '86 and a 2–7 record against the Blue Devils during his three years in Chapel Hill. Still, he believed Michigan State had the quickness at guard and the strength up front to give this Duke team trouble. He was right. The Spartans won, again with relative ease, 78–68. Then they beat Kentucky in the double-overtime classic. All of a sudden, nineteen years after the "abandon ship" game, Doug Wojcik found himself in the Final Four.

"I can finally say I'm getting to do something David [Robinson] never did," he said with a laugh. "I now have exactly one thing on my basketball résumé he doesn't have. This will be an emotional weekend for me, regardless of what happens, because I know now that my last game here is coming soon. Win or lose, it will be tough to say good-bye to these players and to Tom. I always say that Skip [Prosser] is my coaching father. Tom's my coaching older brother. It will be tough leaving. But it's time."

Most people expect that someday Johnny Dawkins will succeed Krzyzewski as Duke's coach. If and when he does, he and Wojcik may very well meet again. "My guess," Wojcik said, "is that he can probably still dunk on me."

10

The Committee

IF THERE IS ONE GROUP OF PEOPLE at the Final Four that tries to stay under the radar as much as the referees, it would probably be the nine men and one woman who are in charge of the event. Technically, they are called the NCAA Men's Basketball Committee. To everyone involved in the sport, they are simply "the committee."

Being appointed to the committee is not quite as big a deal as becoming a Supreme Court justice, but the perks are just about as good. And although one is actually on the committee for only five years, those perks tend to last a lifetime. Very few former committee members pass up the chance to attend the Final Four — they all receive two tickets for life — and they are all quickly handed passes upon their arrival that allow them access to anything and everything Final Four–related.

"The one thing you have to give up," said George Washington athletic director Jack Kvancz, "is the police escort to the games. That's a killer, getting back on those shuttle buses with the regular people."

The reverence paid committee members sometimes borders on the ludicrous. The committee chairman (Iowa athletic director

Bob Bowlsby in 2004 and 2005) is frequently referred to by those interviewing him as "Mr. Chairman," as if he were a member of Congress, not simply someone leading a group charged with picking teams for a basketball tournament. The committee members are wined and dined throughout Final Four week. During the games, several committee members sit at the scorer's table wearing headsets to monitor the CBS broadcast. When the committee and the network meet during the summer, CBS often is handed a list of things that the committee wasn't happy with during the previous season's broadcasts. The complaints can range from too many mentions of the NBA (seriously) to referring to the "N-C-A-A" as the "N-C-double A." That is most definitely a no-no.

"That was a Walter Byers thing," Tom Jernstedt said, laughing, one morning in St. Louis. "He always insisted that people say both a's, and I guess we've stuck to it."

More than anyone else, Jernstedt is charged with keeping the committee members happy and moving forward with the job of putting on the tournament. Jernstedt has worked for the N-C-A-A since 1973. He grew up in the tiny town of Carlton, Oregon (pop. 1,054), and played football and basketball in high school. After graduating from Oregon, he went to work for an investment firm in San Francisco and was bored out of his mind. When he was offered the chance to come back to Oregon as the facilities manager in 1970, he jumped at it. "I was making fourteen thousand dollars a year and being provided with a car in San Francisco," he said. "At Oregon they offered me six thousand and no car. I took it in a heartbeat."

He met a number of people with NCAA connections when the school hosted the NCAA Track and Field Championships in 1972, and a year later was offered a job working as an administrator at NCAA headquarters. He wasn't sure if that was the right move, since his goal was to be an athletic director, but a number of people — including UCLA athletic director J. D. Morgan — told him this was a way to "spread his wings." He began working for Walter Byers in 1973, and thirty-two years later he is probably the second-most powerful man in the NCAA, behind only President Myles Brand. He has worked with the basketball committee ever since he arrived and has seen huge changes in the committee and the tournament it runs.

"When I first got there, it was a six-man committee," he said. "We didn't even bring people to headquarters [then outside of Kansas City] to select the field, we did it by conference call. I can remember some loud arguments even then, especially between J. D. Morgan and [then North Carolina State athletic director] Willis Casey. You were talking about some strong-willed people there."

Jernstedt was there when the decision was made to expand from twenty-five to thirty-two teams for the 1975 tournament and watched as the tournament kept growing until it got to sixty-four teams in 1985. "There was always debate on the committee about whether we were expanding too fast," he said. "Everyone wanted to be careful not to overtax the field. The guy who really pushed to go to sixty-four was [former Duke coach and Sun Belt Conference commissioner] Vic Bubas. Wayne Duke was the chairman at the time, and in the end he was the one who brought everyone along to get it done."

Duke was the Big Ten commissioner when he was on the committee — having once been Walter Byers's assistant, and only employee, at the NCAA — and was one of the people who played a major role not only in expanding the tournament but in agreeing to put the Final Four into domes. "That was something else Vic Bubas pushed for," Duke said. "We were all a little wary about it because the first time we tried it in the Astrodome [1971], it didn't work very well. Too many bad seats. Even the good seats were bad seats. But Vic kept saying if we were better prepared, if we let the people know that the seats upstairs were going to be less than perfect and far away, that it would work because it would allow so many more people to be part of the event. In the end, we decided to try it and he was right."

The second dome Final Four was in 1982 in New Orleans. That year marked the beginning of many new things. It was the first year of the CBS contract, the beginning of the dome era, and the first year when there was no consolation game for the Saturday losers.

"Thank goodness we finally convinced them to eliminate that game," said Dean Smith, echoing the sentiment of most coaches.

The last consolation game in the history of the tournament was played under the eeriest of circumstances. It was March 30, 1981, the day that John Hinckley shot Ronald Reagan outside a hotel in Washington, D.C. The national championship game between North Carolina and Indiana was scheduled to be played that night, with Virginia and LSU playing in the consolation game beforehand. Word reached Philadelphia before noon that the president had been shot.

"What I remember is that we were told initially that the president had not been hurt that badly," Duke said. "At first we thought we would hear back pretty quickly saying he was okay and there was no reason not to go ahead and play the games. But as the afternoon went on, it started to become apparent that it wasn't quite that simple, because he was still in surgery. That's when I got the committee together and said, 'We have to start considering alternative plans.' We decided to get together at the arena with the school presidents and the athletic directors, too."

Dave Gavitt was also on the committee at the time. He was then the commissioner of the Big East, but prior to that he had been a coach at both Dartmouth and Providence and had coached in the Final Four in 1973. "The sense I had was that Dave, as an ex-coach who knew something about the pressures of the Final Four, should be our liaison with the coaches," Duke said. "Of course, nothing Dave had been through could prepare them for a situation like this."

The only significant group that Duke decided not to consult was NBC. "This could not be about TV," he said. "Obviously, if something serious was going on with the president, they had to cover that anyway. But if there was doubt, one way or the other, I wanted the decision to be about what was right for the country and the event, not what was right for TV."

Two other important people were not consulted that day: Virginia coach Terry Holland and LSU coach Dale Brown. "I remember seeing Dale at some point during the day and saying to him, 'Why are we playing this game?'" Holland said. "He felt the same way. But they told us to show up and play, so we showed up and played. I know we won, but that's about all I know. I'm not sure there were a thousand people actually watching the game. None of us wanted to be there."

That is true of all consolation games, which is why all postseason tournaments have now eliminated them. Once, the NCAA made teams that lost in the regional semifinals play a consolation game. Those games were mercifully ended after the 1975 tournament. "We lost to Syracuse in the round of sixteen that year," Dean Smith said. "Then we had to come back and play the consolation game at ten o'clock on Saturday morning. Boy, was that depressing."

Virginia-LSU was even worse than that. The Philadelphia Spectrum was not only all but empty except for a small cadre of fans from LSU and Virginia, but it was almost silent. There were no cheers, because the game was meaningless and those few people watching were aware of what was going on down in Washington. "What was strangest about it," Holland said, "is that we were out there playing while the committee was behind closed doors deciding whether to play the championship game."

Several alternative plans were discussed: postpone the game for twenty-four hours, postpone it for a week, or even declare co-champions and send everyone home. "I remember thinking neither Bob [Knight] nor I would want to do that," said Smith, who at that point had not yet won a national championship. "In the end, we all wanted to play but we had to wait for a signal from Washington."

The signal finally came about two hours before tip-off, with Virginia and LSU still playing: the president was out of surgery and appeared to be doing okay. "We were in touch with the White House at that stage," Jernstedt remembered. "If they had told us to shut it down, obviously we would have. But the message to us was that they wanted us to play. So we did."

Indiana won the game, and Smith would later joke that maybe the co-championship would not have been such a bad idea after all.

The work done by the committee and how it does that work have changed radically since the days of a six-man committee and a Sunday conference call to pick the field. These days the committee consists of ten people, a mix of athletic directors and conference commissioners. There are always ex-coaches involved, although some coaches say not enough. One of the ex-coaches who became an athletic director and sat on the committee is Holland. He disagrees with the notion that more coaches are needed. "Some of the best guys I worked with and who have been on the committee were guys who didn't coach basketball," he said. "Maybe they worked harder because of that, I'm not sure. But I don't think we have a problem there."

The committee now meets several times a year: once in July to review the previous year's tournament and make any rule changes for the coming year; once in December to plan for the upcoming tournament; once in February to stage a "mock" selection of the field; and then in March to pick the field. The July and December meetings usually take place in good weather near good golf courses — certainly a coincidence. The February and March meetings are held in Indianapolis, which is where NCAA headquarters are now. Throughout the basketball season, the committee chairman holds a monthly conference call with basketball writers, which usually centers on how much weight the committee is going to give to the RPI; how many teams from certain conferences may be selected; how much emphasis will be placed on strength of schedule, on road wins, and on and on. No matter what the chairman says, everything usually changes by Selection Sunday.

To say that the committee's March meeting is taken seriously is a little bit like saying summits involving the future of world peace are taken seriously. The ten members fly in on Wednesday evening and check into the Westin Hotel in downtown Indianapolis. They are then taken to the top floor of the hotel, which is, for all intents and purposes, sealed off for the rest of the week.

No one can get onto the floor without credentials. Security patrols the hallways, and committee members are told not to leave the building unless they are in absolute need of a walk to clear their mind.

"One thing that isn't a problem is food," said Jack Kvancz, who was on the committee from 1998 to 2003. "They will bring you anything you want."

Especially ice cream. As Jernstedt remembers it, Arnie Ferrin, the former Utah athletic director, and Cedric Dempsey, then at Arizona but later president of the NCAA, were the ones who started the tradition of ending each evening with endless supplies of ice cream. "It started kind of innocently," Jernstedt said. "But then it became a tradition. It was as if no one could go to bed until they'd had their ice cream."

Nowadays most committee members go to Indianapolis fully prepared to gain five pounds while they are there. "There's a workout room you can use," Holland said. "But it doesn't do much good."

Each day becomes a bit more tense. On Thursday morning the group gathers formally for the first time. The members sit around a long table in a conference room along with Jernstedt and several key staff members, including Jernstedt's lieutenant, Greg Shaheen, and Bill Hancock, who handled all NCAA media through the 2005 tournament. For years Hancock was the "board master." Whenever a team had to be moved from one of the three large boards set up in the room, it was Hancock's job to do it. No one else was allowed to touch the board.

"My first year, we were talking about some kind of bracketing problem," Kvancz remembered. "I got very animated about something and I got up, went to the board, and I was about to say, 'Move this team here and that team there' — and I touched the Velcro strips with their names on them up on the board to make my point. Everyone started screaming, 'Don't touch the board, only Hancock touches the board!'"

Sadly, that tradition went away in 2005, when everything was put on computer so that someone can now press a button and move a team from one screen to another. But the principles remain the same: there are three screens (formerly boards). On one are the teams already in the field. On another are those not yet in but under discussion. On the third are those considered out. The middle board, the one with teams under discussion, is called the "cross-country board," in honor of Willis Casey. It was Casey who came up with the three-board concept. Since he was a former cross-country coach, the board where teams are, in effect, moving from one place to another (out to in, or in to out) is called the cross-country board.

The first thing the committee members do is make a list of the thirty-four teams they believe belong in the tournament. It should be remembered that even though there are sixty-five teams in the field, the committee's number to select is thirty-four since thirty-one of the bids go automatically to conference champions. Any team that appears on nine of the ten lists (which are actually submitted prior to the members' arrival in Indianapolis) is in the field and is placed on the "in" board. All the other teams that are named but don't get nine votes go on Willis Casey's cross-country board. Then the discussion begins. According to most who have served on the committee, things get a little more heated each day.

"The funny thing is, in the end, if you put thirty-four teams on your list, you're probably going to have thirty-two of the teams that get in eventually," Kvancz said. "Or maybe thirty-one or thirty-three or all thirty-four. But you have to go through the process. There are usually anywhere from eighteen to twenty-five teams that go in right away on the first ballot. There may be as many as six to eight more that get in fairly easily. Then you really get down to it for the last two or three spots."

As the weekend goes on, some teams eliminate themselves. In 2005 Maryland was on the cross-country board on Thursday morning. When it lost that afternoon to Clemson in the first round of the ACC Tournament, it was moved to the "out" board. Other teams move to the out board as spots dry up. For example, if a regular-season champion that is worthy of an at-large bid loses in a conference tournament, that takes up an at-large spot. In 2005 both Notre Dame and Miami of Ohio were on the cross-country board with at-large spots still open until Utah and Pacific lost conference championship games on Saturday night, meaning those two schools needed at-large bids to get into the field. Their losses eliminated Notre Dame and Miami.

By Saturday, heated arguments begin to break out. Charles Harris, then the commissioner of the Mid-Eastern Athletic Conference, got into the habit of jumping from his seat and doing push-ups at especially tense moments. Sometimes members would simply get up and leave the room in order to cool off. In 1984 Gene Corrigan, then the Notre Dame athletic director and one of the calmer men ever to sit on the committee, was so incensed that Dayton was being left out of the field that he got up in mid-argument on Saturday night and said, "I just don't want to speak to any of you anymore. This is just plain wrong."

The next morning, when everyone had calmed down, Dayton was placed in the bracket. The good news for Corrigan was that the Flyers made him look good by making it to the final eight. The bad news is that one of the last teams left out of the field that year was Notre Dame. "Me and my big mouth," he joked later.

Four years earlier, in 1980, UCLA was the topic of a heated discussion. The Bruins, under Coach Larry Brown, had started the season very poorly but had rallied late to put themselves onto the cross-country board. The sentiment in the room was that they belonged in the field based on their strong finish. Russ Potts, then the athletic director at Southern Methodist (and now a state senator in Virginia) kept insisting that the pro-UCLA members were basing too much of their feeling on UCLA's history. "This isn't the sixties or seventies, fellas," he kept saying. "Wooden isn't the coach. They just aren't that good."

Potts finally went for a walk. While he was gone, Wayne Duke, the chairman, decided it was time to end the UCLA conversation and vote. When Potts walked back into the room, UCLA was in the bracket, scheduled to play a first-round game against Texas A&M. Potts blew up.

"Russ, calm down," Duke said. "We put you down as a no vote, and UCLA still got in."

"I understand that," Potts said. "But you've got them playing Texas A&M." (A&M was a heated SMU rival and fellow member of the Southwest Conference.)

"So?"

"So, all those damn Aggies are going to kill me for letting you guys pair them against UCLA. They don't want to play *them!*"

"But you said they weren't even good enough to be in the tournament."

"I know I said that. But that was *before* they were in the tournament."

Eventually, after some bracket shuffling, UCLA played Old Dominion. The Bruins won that game and then upset number one seed DePaul in the west regional and ended up in the national championship game. Of course, its second-place finish was eventually "vacated" for NCAA rules violations, meaning it does not appear in any of the official records for the tournament that year. So, in a sense, Potts got his way.

Twenty years later a similar argument took place involving one of the sport's glamour teams: North Carolina. Like UCLA in 1980, the Tar Heels had struggled during the season. They had lost in the first round of the ACC Tournament to Wake Forest and had an 18–13 record. Their credentials were almost identical to another ACC team, Virginia. The conversation went back and forth. Carolina had been in the tournament for twenty-five consecutive seasons. The question many committee members was asking was whether they would even be under serious consideration if they weren't North Carolina.

Finally, Jack Kvancz turned to Les Robinson, the athletic director at Citadel, but formerly the coach at North Carolina State and a graduate there. Each committee member is assigned three conferences to follow during the season. He is expected to watch as many games involving teams from that conference as possible so he will know and understand the teams in great detail when questions are asked about them. One of Robinson's conferences that year was the ACC.

"When it comes right down to it, Les," Kvancz said, asking what is often the ultimate tiebreaker question, "who has a better team, Carolina or Virginia?"

Robinson paused for a moment and smiled. "You guys know it kills me to say this," he said. "But I think Carolina's better."

That was enough for Kvancz. "I said right then and there, 'Carolina must be better,' because there's no way Les is going to vote for them unless he has to."

Carolina was voted in as an eighth seed and almost matched what UCLA had done in 1980, upsetting number one seed

Stanford in the second round en route to the Final Four. The Tar Heels lost in the semifinals to Florida. Their finish, however, was not vacated.

Almost every year the longest and most heated discussions take place on Saturday night, when the field is almost always complete or virtually complete. Often committee members will ask for a "nitty-gritty" on a team. That means the members are shown every detail available: RPI, road wins, record in the last ten games, quality of cheerleaders — okay, there is nothing on the cheerleaders, but that's the *only* detail left out. Sunday is used to finalize seeding and to put the teams in brackets and then, finally, to spend the last hour briefing the chairman on what questions he should expect when he is interviewed on TV and radio and by the print media after the field has been unveiled. By Saturday evening in 2005, there were six unfilled spots in the field, with the committee understanding that the number could be sliced if heavily favored Utah and Pacific were to lose their conference championship games that night.

The teams still on the cross-country board who were under discussion were Northern Iowa, Iowa, UCLA, UAB, Miami (Ohio), Notre Dame, St. Joseph's, and George Washington. Earlier in the day Georgetown, Memphis, and New Mexico had been moved to the "out" board as the number of at-large spots available began to shrink because of the results in conference tournaments. Georgia Tech, which had been a "bubble" team (bubble being one of the most overused sports terms of the twenty-first century, along with "red zone" in football) going into the week, had played its way into an at-large bid with two wins in the ACC Tournament. So had North Carolina State. West Virginia had done the same thing in the Big East Tournament.

Exit Georgetown, exit New Mexico, exit Memphis. The latter

two could still get in by winning their conference tournaments. Memphis almost pulled it off, losing to Louisville in the final seconds of the Conference USA championship game. That was good news for the bubble teams. A Memphis victory would have taken away another spot.

As the day progressed, Iowa, UCLA, and UAB made their way — after lengthy discussion — from the cross-country board into the bracket. Northern Iowa, Miami, and Notre Dame were considered the leading contenders for the three spots still left at that moment, with St. Joe's on hold pending the outcome of its championship game in the Atlantic 10 with George Washington. If the Hawks won, GW would go onto the cross-country board as a possible at-large team, perhaps bumping one of the three teams under discussion.

On Saturday night everything changed as the evening wore on. George Washington won the A-10 final with relative ease. St. Joseph's went off the board. Northern Iowa was voted in, leaving Miami and Notre Dame needing wins from Utah and Pacific. When both lost — to New Mexico and Utah State, respectively — Miami and Notre Dame were finished. They would go where all teams blown off the bubble go: the NIT, or National Invitation Tournament, now known among major teams as the Not Invited Tournament. In fact, at major conference tournaments like the ACC, Big East, and Big 12, fans who suspect that an opponent is headed for the NIT will chant those letters tauntingly in the final seconds of a lost game.

Once the thirty-four at-large teams are chosen and the sixty-five-team field is decided, the teams must be placed into four brackets and seeded. In its own way, this is as much of a task as picking the field. There is always controversy about who receives the four number one seeds, and that was certainly the case in

2005, when the committee plucked Washington from a group of several candidates to be the fourth top seed, along with Illinois, North Carolina, and Duke. The problem, several committee members admitted later, was that they were all caught off guard when Kentucky — which had been slotted in the third of the four number one spots — was upset in the SEC Tournament final by Florida on Sunday afternoon. By midafternoon on Sunday, everyone on the committee except for the chairman, who stays behind, is thinking about getting to the airport for a flight home. They have all been locked up in the hotel since Wednesday and they all know they are facing three more weeks during which they will be on the road most of the time.

There is also the ongoing issue of those conferences that play their tournament finals on Sunday, such as the ACC, the Big Ten, the Big 12, and the SEC — all major conferences in which the outcome of the final frequently affects seeding and can knock an at-large team out of the tournament if a low-ranked team plays its way to the conference championship. The reason these finals are played on Sunday is simple: ESPN and CBS pay the conferences a lot of money to play on Sunday. In 2004, when everyone sprinted for the door, the Big 12 final was still going on. Oklahoma State beat Texas Tech and, in the minds of many, played its way into a number one seed. When the field was unveiled, Oklahoma State was the number two seed in the east regional, behind St. Joseph's. An argument could be made for either team being the top seed. But when Bowlsby said in the post-unveiling interview that one of the reasons Oklahoma State did not move up to number one after its victory was that the Big 12 title game was played too late to make a switch, many people were — justifiably — incredulous. Bowlsby then went on to criticize the conference for playing late on Sunday, a rather re-

markable statement since he is the athletic director at Iowa, a Big Ten member that readily gobbles up the money CBS pays the league to play on that same Sunday.

With all the money the NCAA spends on the committee — the hotels the members stay in during meetings are not exactly $39-a-night motels, and none of them would recognize a coach-class seat if it hit him in the head — the notion that they would simply break off their talks to get to the airport at the most crucial moments of their decision-making process stunned people.

Of course, Bowlsby's faux pas was nothing compared with what had happened to Jim Livengood in 2003. Livengood is the athletic director at Arizona, one of the truly decent men in college athletics, the rare athletic director who doesn't break into spin-speak whenever he is asked a question on a subject other than the weather. He was the committee chairman that year. For whatever reason, the committee had a very bad year in 2003. For one thing, it placed Brigham Young in a bracket where it would have to play a second-round game on Sunday. BYU is a Mormon school and has always made it clear that it will not play on a Sunday. The committee members simply forgot, causing an embarrassing scramble on Monday in which they were forced to switch BYU with another team to another bracket at another site.

The other problem was Kentucky and Arizona. There are years when separating the top two seeds from the others is difficult. In 2005, for example, Illinois was a clear-cut number one seed in the field, with only one loss — a buzzer-beater at Ohio State — all season. North Carolina was almost as clearly the number two seed in spite of a loss in the ACC Tournament. The next six to eight teams were all pretty even (although no one making mock brackets had Washington as a number one seed

and no one had Louisville as a number four; most people had the Cardinals as a one or two).

In 2003 Kentucky and Arizona had clearly distanced themselves from everyone else during the regular season. At that time the committee did not seed the number one seeds. It simply produced four number one seeds, placed them in brackets, and never told anyone who was considered number one in the field, who was number two, and so on down the line. When the brackets went up that night, everyone gasped: Arizona and Kentucky had been bracketed to meet in the national semifinals. How was that possible? How could the committee look in such detail at what every team had accomplished and not seed these two teams to meet in the championship game?

CBS always gets first crack at the chairman once it has revealed the bracket to the country, another perk it receives in return for the $6 billion it is paying over eleven years, a contract that extends now through the 2011 tournament. Jim Nantz and Billy Packer, on-site at one of those Sunday championships Bowlsby so dislikes, question the chairman along with the studio crew led by Greg Gumbel. When it was Packer's turn, he looked ready to jump through the screen to ask Livengood how in the world Kentucky and Arizona could be placed in the same half of the overall bracket.

One could not help feeling sorry for Livengood. In the hour-long briefing with his fellow committee members to prep him for his TV appearances, no one had brought up the Arizona-Kentucky question. There was a reason for that: no one had noticed.

"We just blew it," Kvancz said later. "We sat there and looked at the four brackets and somehow, because the four brackets were up there side by side, not one half together and the other half together, we all missed it. Everyone was responsible and

then poor Jim was the one who got stuck trying to explain something that was unexplainable."

Caught off guard, Livengood tried to get out of the question by talking about how well qualified all four number one seeds were (although a lot of people also took issue with Texas being a top seed over Kansas) and how hard the committee had worked. Packer wasn't buying. He again demanded to know how this could have happened. Finally, Livengood blurted out, "You know, it isn't our job to project matchups."

It is difficult to come up with an analogy to explain what Livengood said at that moment. It was a little bit like a pilot saying it wasn't his job to fly the plane or a hockey goalie saying it wasn't his job to stop pucks. Perhaps it was like a comedian saying it wasn't his job to be funny.

When all the talk and bluster and hoo-ha about RPIs and schedules and good wins and bad wins is over, the basketball committee has two basic jobs:

1. Select the field.
2. Seed the field.

What is the purpose of seeding? To project matchups.

If you don't want to project matchups, why seed the field? Just throw all sixty-five teams into a hat and begin drawing out names. If the top two teams come out to play in the first round, let them play — you aren't projecting matchups. But if you are seeding a field, lining up the number one seed in a bracket to play the number sixteen seed and working your way toward a matchup of the number one and number two seeds in the regional final if both teams keep winning, then you are — say it all together — projecting matchups.

It is difficult to be too harsh on Livengood, because he is a good man and because, as Kvancz pointed out, the entire committee was responsible for the screwup. The committee was taken off the hook a tiny bit when Kentucky and Arizona were upset by Marquette and Kansas in their regional finals. But that didn't change what had happened, and everyone knew it. That summer the committee voted to seed the four number ones so it would be impossible for the top two seeds to meet before the championship game. Thus, in 2005 there was no way that Illinois and North Carolina could meet before Monday night, April 4, in St. Louis.

That was a good thing.

However, in its infinite wisdom, the committee — partly, no doubt, to hide its embarrassment over the Arizona-Kentucky fiasco — announced that from now on, each regional would be named for the city it was being played in rather than by the simple geographic names — east, south, midwest, west — that had been traditional. So, instead of going to the east regional in 2005, North Carolina was sent to the "Syracuse regional." Illinois didn't go to the midwest; it went to the "Chicago regional."

This is confusing and silly and completely unnecessary.

Of course, it makes perfect sense to the committee. That makes ten people in the world who feel that way.

Making honest mistakes, especially under the pressures that are part of selection weekend, is both understandable and forgivable. It happens. We all make mistakes. Having said that, what the committee did five years ago when it created the "opening round" game — to use the committee's euphemism — was neither a mistake nor forgivable. It was done in the name of greed by men who clearly cared only about their own interests.

The problem began with the breakup of the Western Athletic Conference. The WAC had grown out of control, with sixteen schools spread out from Texas to Hawaii, and it was finally decided that eight of the schools should break off and form their own league, the Mountain West Conference. Since the MWC met the various criteria for an automatic tournament bid, beginning in 2001 there would be thirty-one conferences eligible for automatic bids instead of thirty. Which meant, logically, that the number of at-large bids would drop from thirty-four to thirty-three.

Anyone who knows anything about the history of the NCAA Tournament understands that the true magic of the event lies in the upsets that occur during the first week, whether it is Vitale standing on his head because Austin Peay beats Illinois or Bryce Drew beating the buzzer on the swinging-gate play so that Valparaiso can beat Mississippi, or Vermont beating Syracuse and Bucknell beating Kansas in 2005. Those games have produced indelible memories because they involved little-schools-that-could shocking power schools from power conferences. To fans of Vermont, beating Syracuse was every bit as big a moment as winning the national title was for North Carolina fans. Perhaps bigger, because it may never happen again.

All the schools that produce those moments are from the so-called one-bid conferences, the leagues where everyone knows that each year only the conference champion, the winner of the automatic bid, is going to the tournament. Regardless of what its RPI number was in 2005, Vermont was not going to get an at-large bid if it had lost in the America East Conference Tournament. "We were in the twenties in the RPI rankings all season," Coach Tom Brennan said. "That means, worst case, based on the numbers, we should be an eighth seed — maybe a nine or ten because we're not in a big conference. What were we? A thirteen! What's that tell you? It tells you we don't get in if we don't have the automatic bid."

Brennan's right. As a number thirteen seed, Vermont was ranked by the committee behind every at-large team in the field. The lowest-seeded at-large teams were eleventh seeds.

There are some coaches in power conferences who chafe at the automatic bids, saying the tournament should just be the sixty-four best teams in the country. They're wrong. If the tournament was the best sixty-four teams in the country, then sixty of the teams would come from the ACC, the Big East, the Big Ten, the Big 12, the Southeast Conference, the Pacific-10, and the Atlantic 10. Conference USA might get a bid or two, the Missouri Valley might get an occasional bid, and the Mountain West might sneak in a team every now and then. The America East? No way. The Patriot League — Bucknell's conference — no chance. Ivy League, SWAC, Mid-Continent (Valparaiso), and the Big Sky? Long gone. A major first-round upset would consist of the seventh-place team in the ACC upsetting the second-place team from the Big 12. So what? One school with unlimited resources beating another school with unlimited resources.

The committee is smart enough to understand that the one-bid leagues are a crucial part of the tournament. That doesn't mean they treat them fairly or well. Vermont should have been much higher than a thirteenth seed in 2005, just as Holy Cross should have been higher than a fourteenth seed in 2003. Even though committee members are assigned to follow the smaller conferences during the season, there isn't as much access to their games on TV and most committee members just don't care enough about how they seed those teams. At one point, a subcommittee on bracketing the teams on the thirteenth to sixteenth lines was formed, but it didn't help much, either. The little guys are allowed into the room, but they are expected to keep quiet, know their place, and pull an occasional upset so the committee can take bows and tell people how well the system works. The system does work, but it is more an accident of luck and fate than anything else.

When the committee was faced with the possibility of losing an at-large bid for the 2001 tournament, panic set in. Bids equal money. Each team that receives a bid to the tournament is paid one "unit" of the tournament's profits, which in 2005 was worth $300,000. Each time a team advances through a round, it receives another unit. That means an at-large bid is worth at least $300,000 and can be worth a good deal more should the team win a game or two — which can happen and has happened with teams that get in at the last minute. Witness Dayton in 1984, Virginia that same year (all the way to the Final Four), or, more recently, North Carolina in 2000.

The committee was being pushed hard by the big-money conference commissioners not to lose an at-large bid. Two of the men pushing hard were Roy Kramer, then of the Southeast Conference, and Jim Delany of the Big Ten — both former chairmen of the committee. Both also pushed to make sure that the committee chairman would always be from a big-money conference. In 2003 Kvancz, athletic director from George Washington, was supposed to be in line to become chairman in his last year on the committee. At the last minute, because of some backroom maneuvering, Jim Livengood from Arizona ended up as chairman. Which probably worked out for Kvancz, because it was Livengood instead of him left to answer all the questions about the mistakes the committee made that year in bracketing.

Pushed by Delany and Kramer, the committee decided to keep thirty-four at-large bids, as if that were some kind of magic number. It couldn't simply declare a league that met the criteria for an automatic bid no longer eligible for one, so it increased the number of teams in the tournament to sixty-five — thirty-one automatic bids, thirty-four at-large. How, then, do you get from sixty-five to sixty-four? Easy: send two automatic-bid teams from smaller conferences to, in effect, play off for the last spot in the sixty-four-team field. The committee smartly selected Dayton, a true college basketball hotbed, as the site of the play-in game and christened it the "opening round" game.

In other words, it created a second tier of teams, consisting of two schools among sixty-five. It made these two into second-class citizens, forcing them to play on Tuesday, then fly to another site, and play a number one seed on Friday. The losing team in Dayton never gets to go to a true tournament site. It doesn't get to take part in the day-before practices or the press conferences that are part of the Dance. They are in the Dance, but they end up dancing alone in an empty room with no one to talk to about their experience. To add financial insult to injury, the winning team in the play-in game isn't even credited with a financial unit for the victory. It's a win, but the NCAA doesn't really count it as a win. It is as if you've gotten into the Dance by winning your conference tournament and then you're told you have to go win another game to *really* be in the Dance.

It is insulting and it is demeaning and, in many cases, it denies kids whose greatest dream is to step on court in a packed building to take on a big-name team in the NCAA Tournament that chance. In 2005 the play-in game matched Oakland University (from Detroit) playing in its first-ever NCAA Tournament against Alabama A&M. There are two predominantly black

conferences that have automatic NCAA Tournament bids: the Southwestern Athletic and the Mid-Eastern Athletic. In five years of play-in games, there has always been one school from a predominantly black conference involved — never two, because the committee knows it would get killed politically if it sent both schools to the play-in game even if they were the two weakest teams in the field.

A year earlier, in 2004, the play-in game matched Lehigh from the Patriot League against Florida A&M from the MEAC. Lehigh was a great story. In 2002 it had won five games. Under Billy Taylor, a bright young coach, the school had turned its basketball fortunes around and in 2004 had gone from worst (in 2002) to first in the Patriot League and had won the conference tournament. Because of television, the Patriot League final that year was played on Sunday afternoon: bid day. A few hours after they had hugged one another on the floor of Stabler Arena and cut down the nets, the Lehigh players learned they weren't actually going to the Dance; they were going to Dayton. The next day they flew to Dayton, practiced, tried to learn about Florida A&M, and, forty-eight hours after the most emotional game of their lives, had to try to play Florida A&M in front of seven thousand neutral fans (a good crowd but a quiet one). They lost. Forty-eight hours after thinking they had made the big time, they went home having never seen the big time.

"It was a letdown," Taylor said later. "We had this great moment, winning the championship game, feeling that accomplishment, and then we sat there that night and saw we were going to Dayton. It really took away any chance to savor what we had done."

Lehigh was a senior-dominated team, meaning the seniors had no chance to come back and try to make it to the round of

sixty-four, and the underclassmen were unlikely to get another chance, either. They still had their conference title and an NCAA banner to hang in their arena, but not the memories that come with going to a true tournament site.

The committee members say they will not take away the thirty-fourth at-large bid. Okay, fine. What should be done then is that the thirty-third and thirty-fourth at-large teams should be sent to the play-in game. Sending two teams from major conferences means sending schools that will almost certainly be back in the tournament again soon; sending to Dayton players and coaches for whom playing at a true tournament site isn't nearly as big a deal as it is for Lehigh or Alabama A&M or Florida A&M or Oakland. For example, in 2005 the committee could easily have matched Iowa and UCLA — two of the last teams into the field. That would have been Big Ten vs. Pac-10. It would have been a far more glamorous TV matchup; it would have sold more tickets in Dayton, and the likelihood is that the players from the losing team would make the tournament again next year or the year after. Instead of putting the winner of the game into a number sixteen seed and feeding it to a number one, you put the winner into an eleventh or twelfth seed and match it up accordingly with a number six or a number five in the first round.

"It does make sense to do it that way," said Kvancz, who was part of the committee that created the play-in game. "I can see the argument. I don't think you will get a majority of the committee to see it that way."

Translation: the committee is always dominated and controlled by the major conferences. Perhaps if the entire committee — instead of one or two representatives — made the trip to Dayton and then went into the losing locker room after the game, they might feel differently.

11

Friday

FOR THOSE WHO ARE PART of the Final Four, Friday is when it begins to *feel* like a Final Four. The town is full; fans are everywhere; there isn't a restaurant reservation to be had. And for the first time, everyone gets a look inside the place where the games will be played.

Like most modern arenas and stadiums, the Edward Jones Dome is named after a corporation that pays a lot of money to stick its name all over the building. Once, it was named after an airline that went bankrupt (TWA) and is now named after an investment firm. The building is only ten years old, which means it was *built* with the idea of being used for basketball. So the seats sold for a basketball game — 47,754 for the Final Four — are not all as far away as in some of the older domes.

"In the Astrodome everyone was about five miles away," former committee chairman Wayne Duke remembered about 1971. "Going there probably set us back ten years in terms of domes. Everyone was wary for a while after that."

There are many people who will tell you that the best day of the Final Four is Friday. For one thing, people without the connections or the money to buy tickets for the actual games can walk in for free and watch the four practices. This has become a tradition to the point where most coaches allow their players to stage dunking contests during the last five minutes of their fifty-minute workouts for the specific purpose of entertaining the crowd.

"Not something you normally write into your practice plan," said Roy Williams, who *did* write it into his.

The unofficial attendance for the Friday practices in St. Louis for the 2005 Final Four was 31,000 — higher than the total season attendance for some Division 1 teams. It appeared to most people on the floor that at least 80 percent of those fans were from Illinois. They covered the building in blue and orange and went completely crazy when the Illini took the floor. "It felt like we were going out there to play a home game," said Luther Head, one of the trio of star guards who had formed the heart and soul of Illinois' remarkable season. "I mean, you don't usually run out there for practice and get a standing ovation."

The presence of so many Illinois fans may have been even more surprising to the players from the other three teams. "It was actually kind of overwhelming to run out of the tunnel and see how many people were there *and* how many of them were Illinois fans," said North Carolina walk-on guard Wes Miller. "We're so used to seeing Carolina fans everywhere we travel that to go to a place and see that many people from another school was kind of shocking."

When Carolina had gone through its open practice in Charlotte on the day before its first-round game against Oakland — the survivor of the dreaded play-in game — the Charlotte Coliseum had probably close to 10,000 Carolina fans watching. Even though Duke has become one of the strongest national programs under Mike Krzyzewski, the number of fans in the state who pull for "Carolina" — no one ever adds the "North" — dwarfs the number of Duke fans. Which makes sense: UNC is the public school in the state, it has a long and storied basketball tradition, and most of the people who go to school there come from the state and remain there after graduation. Duke, which has about 30 percent as many undergraduates, draws its student body from around the country and only a sliver of them stay after graduation. Most of the great players who have come from North Carolina — Michael Jordan, James Worthy, Jerry Stackhouse, Antawn Jamison, Brad Daugherty, Bobby Jones, Phil Ford, Walter Davis — have gone to North Carolina. The most notable exceptions are the great David Thompson and Tommy Burleson, who led North Carolina State to the national championship in 1974. The best in-state players to play at Duke? Probably Stuart Yarbrough, who played for Vic Bubas in the 1960s, and Kenny Dennard, who was on Bill Foster's Final Four team in 1978. The only highly touted player from the state Krzyzewski had successfully recruited was Shavlik Randolph, who was notable as a Duke player in that he was an oft-injured bust who left after his junior season in 2005 even though he had no chance of being drafted.

Wes Miller was one of those Final Four stories that should make people smile regardless of where they are from or which team they follow. Miller was the ultimate gym rat, a kid judged too small to be a Division 1 basketball player when he was in high school. Listed at five foot eleven and 185 pounds but looking smaller, Miller almost willed himself into a college scholarship. He left his home in Charlotte and played for three seasons at New Hampton Prep School in New Hampshire, where he roomed with Rashad McCants, who was as touted as Miller was unnoticed. But during his fifth year of high school (a lot of athletes spend an extra year in high school these days), he did attract some D-1 coaches because of his shooting ability and his willingness to do anything on the court to help his team win. He ended up going to James Madison and played solid backup minutes as a freshman, averaging 17 minutes per night and 4.1 points a game.

But the JMU program was in disarray. Sherman Dillard, the coach who had recruited Miller, was barely hanging on to his job (he was fired in 2004), and Miller's old friend McCants was urging him to transfer to North Carolina and try out as a walk-on. Most big-time teams have walk-ons these days, but Carolina has a genuine walk-on tradition. Dean Smith always encouraged good students to try out for his team, and frequently walk-ons would work their way into playing real minutes and receiving scholarships before they graduated. Having grown up in the state as a Carolina fan, Miller was aware of this. Even though it meant giving up his scholarship, he decided to transfer. He sat out the '03–'04 season, then became eligible to play the following year.

Miller had no illusions about where he would fit in as a Tar Heel. "My most important job is to run the blue [backup] team in practice," he said. "I try every day to make [starting point guard] Raymond [Felton] work as hard as I can. The minutes I get in the games are just a bonus." Miller's statistics for the season were a reflection of that. Coming into the Final Four, he had played in twenty-three of the team's thirty-five games, a total of 91 minutes, scoring 26 points and being credited with 12 assists and 4 rebounds. Almost all of that had come late in games, with Carolina in control of the outcome. But he was an important member of the team, in part because of what he contributed in practice but also because he got along well with everyone — including the sometimes moody McCants and the far less moody Sean May, the team's best player, who was his road roommate and a close friend.

On Thursday night Miller had talked to Mike Roberts, a high school teammate who had been on the Indiana team that reached the national championship game in 2002. Roberts had told Miller to make sure to look around all week and realize that he was going through a once-in-a-lifetime experience. He had told him to make sure to enjoy Friday because that was the fun day, the chance to play in front of a lot of people, with no pressure.

The focus at the Final Four is — naturally — on the coaches and the star players. But the backup players, the ones on the end of the bench, are just as thrilled to be there and find being a part of it just as memorable. "When we got out on the court and started doing our stretching, I was literally tingling with excitement," Miller said. "My whole life I dreamed of being on a Final Four team, but that was all it really was — a dream. Most of the time I heard I wasn't a D-1 player; and if I was, it would be low D-1 — not a team that would get to the Final Four. When I was at James Madison, the dream for us was to win our conference tournament and play in the first round of the tournament. Now I was on a team that had won four games but knew it still had work to do."

Roy Williams had reminded his players of that in the locker room before they practiced. They had accomplished a lot during the season already, but they had two more games to win. "Have fun, enjoy being here, but go out there prepared to work," he said. "I want forty-five hard minutes and then you guys can do whatever you want the last five. But give me forty-five first."

Carolina had arrived at the arena on the same bus it had taken on every road trip within the ACC all season. Williams, who is as superstitious as any coach, had the bus driven to St. Louis from Chapel Hill so his team could ride on it throughout the Final Four. He had been to four Final Fours at Kansas without a championship. He wasn't taking any chances.

During the forty-five minutes of real practice, it occurred to Miller that this was the time when he was most likely to make a real contribution if Carolina was to win. He was running Michigan State's offense for the blue team and he wanted to be sure that he helped the first team prepare for what they were going to see the next night. He was fully aware that once the game began, his major role would be as a cheerleader. Miller remembered hearing cheers during the Charlotte practice when he had drilled a couple of three-point shots. The next day he had gotten into the Oakland game with Carolina in control and made a three — his fifth of the season — in the late going. "That was a big thrill," he said. "Actually scoring in an NCAA Tournament game."

Now Miller could only hope that his team might get enough of a lead late to allow him to make it into a Final Four game. The good news was, unlike Dean Smith in 1952, he would not be left out of the box score if he got into the game. He hit a couple of threes during practice, which didn't seem to impress the St. Louis crowd as much as it had impressed the folks in Charlotte. That was okay with him. He was on the court practicing at the Final Four in front of more than 30,000 people. "In all," he said, "it was pretty cool."

When the Tar Heels began their dunking contest, Miller grabbed May's video camera and became the cameraman/play-by-play announcer. "I'm vertically challenged," he said. "This is the best role for me."

A good role player always knows his role — in practice or in a game.

*   *   *

Wes Miller was not, by any stretch of the imagination, the first player or coach to find going through the Friday practice at the Final Four emotional. Billy Hahn, who played at Maryland for four years under Lefty Driesell and then coached there later in his career for twelve seasons as Gary Williams's top assistant, remembers the chill that ran through him walking down the steps to the court in Minneapolis when Maryland went out to practice before the 2001 Final Four.

"It just hit me all of a sudden as we went down the steps," he said. "I've been in basketball all my life. I've watched the Final Four on television; I've come to it for years and seen all the games. Now I'm *in* the Final Four. Those kids walking onto the court are kids I recruited, I coached. It was just an unbelievable feeling. I got very emotional."

Williams wasn't as emotional at that moment, but he was aware of the road he had traveled to get there. "If you coach in college, I don't care what level you are at or whether you are an assistant or a head coach, the Final Four is the Holy Grail. Right or wrong, it is. We all talk about how we shouldn't judge our careers on making the Final Four or on winning it, but every single one of us wants to be there. To finally get there, to walk out on that court to run practice, was a big deal."

He smiled. "I had friends tell me to savor the moment on Friday because I didn't have to coach a game. I tried. I couldn't do it. I was too uptight."

One thing that has changed about Friday is getting into the building. Before 9/11, since there was no charge to get into practice and no tickets, people just walked in and found seats. Now, with post-9/11 security in place, everyone has to go through metal detectors or get wanded or both; there are limits on what can be brought into the arena; and anyone who doesn't have proper ID — including players and coaches — isn't going to get in.

That's a lot different from New Orleans in 1982, which was Roy Williams's first Final Four as a North Carolina assistant coach. "I had gotten into the habit during the season of eating a candy bar before every game," he said. "It started with the Wake Forest game. I had a candy bar before the game and we won. Superstitious as I am, I kept making sure I ate one before every game. Sometimes a manager would get me one, or I'd just go get one at a concession stand.

"Now we're in the national championship game against Georgetown and I get into the Superdome and I realize I forgot to stop and get a candy bar someplace. None of the managers have one. I go up to the concession stands, and they're not selling candy bars. Well, I've *got* to have a candy bar. If I don't have one and we lose, I'll never forgive myself. In those days we really didn't have any kind of credentials. We'd just all kind of come into the building off the bus, the guards would nod at us and wish us luck, and that was it.

"So, I go to one of the dome exits and I explain who I am, that I have to go out for a few minutes and will he be sure to remember me and let me back in. He says he will. I go out and it takes me a while, but I find a candy bar finally. I go racing back, it's maybe an hour or so before the game now, and I go to the same entrance. The guy's not there. He's been moved or something, and the guy in his place is looking at me like 'Yeah, sure, you're a coach and you went out for a candy bar.' I'm panicked. I'm thinking, 'Oh God, we're playing the national championship game in an hour and I can't get back in the building.' There were no cell phones. Finally, while I'm trying to talk this guard into letting me in, please, before Coach Smith kills me, another guard comes by and recognizes me. He tells the other guy it's okay, that I really am a coach, and I get back in."

In 2005 Williams would not have gotten back in. "That's true," he said. "Because I wouldn't have had my cell phone with me since you aren't allowed to bring them in these days."

One person who could relate to what Wes Miller was feeling as he went through practice on Friday was District Court Judge T. Bruce Bell of Lexington, Kentucky. Or as he was known during his days as a walk-on player at Duke, "Juice."

Bruce Bell is, almost without question, the only son of a Final Four referee ever to play on a Final Four team. Bell's father, Tommy Bell, who practiced law in Lexington throughout his adult life, was a top college basketball referee and one of the best-known referees in the history of the National Football League. In fact, it can be argued that Tommy Bell refereed the most important game in the history of pro football: Super Bowl III, the game in which the upstart New York Jets — 17-point underdogs — stunned the Baltimore Colts, 16–7. That was the last game played before the American Football League became a part of the NFL, and Jets quarterback Joe Namath had expressed pregame concern about having an NFL referee working the game. Late in the game Namath made a point of telling Bell that he had done an excellent job. "How can you say that, Joe?" Bell replied. "*My* team is losing."

Tommy Bell was a Kentucky basketball season-ticket holder, and his son grew up a fanatic UK supporter. He was a good high school basketball player, but not good enough to be recruited by

Kentucky or any of the other power basketball schools. At his father's urging, thinking he would follow him into law, he chose Duke, hoping he might be able to at least walk on to the team there, given that the Blue Devils had been struggling for several years. He was right. He made the team as a walk-on and became a starter during his junior season when starting point guard Tate Armstrong (a member of the '76 Olympic team who later played in the NBA) broke a wrist and his backup, Steve Gray, struggled. In Duke's last home game that season, Bell was matched against North Carolina's Phil Ford, who would later be the second pick in the NBA draft and the rookie of the year.

"Little bit of a mismatch," Bell said, laughing. "I remember I thought I'd stolen the ball from him once and then I heard the whistle. The guys all said later, 'What were the chances anyone was going to believe you stole the ball from Phil Ford without fouling?' I'm telling you, dang it, I stole it clean."

Bell really does say *dang it*. His teammates always delighted in mimicking his high-pitched voice and still mimic it every chance they get, regardless of how many people now refer to him as Your Honor. Naturally, they refer to him now as "Judge Juice."

Bell didn't play very much as a senior. Two transfers, John Harrell and Bob Bender, became eligible and took most of the minutes. That was the season when Duke exploded onto the national consciousness again, going from last place in the ACC to the national championship game, where, as luck would have it, they played Kentucky. Even though Kentucky, led by Jack Givens's 41 points, won the game, Bell doesn't remember the loss as much as he remembers the ride.

"To go from where we had been to be in the Final Four was just beyond amazing," he said. "We had high hopes when we started the season because we knew we were better with [Gene]

Banks and [Kenny] Dennard plus Harrell and Bender. But it wasn't until February really that we started to understand just how good we were."

Bell was the only senior on that team. On senior night he stood alone at center court while his teammates and schoolmates stood and cheered for him for three solid minutes. He still has a picture of that moment in his house. Duke went on to win the ACC Tournament for the first time in twelve years to get back to the NCAA Tournament for the first time in just as long. "Imagine that," Bell said. "Nowadays it's unthinkable for Duke not to be in the tournament. Back then, just getting back in set off wild celebrating on campus. When we beat Villanova to get to the Final Four, none of us could really believe it."

The Final Four was in St. Louis for the second time in five years, although it would not return again until 2005. Duke beat Notre Dame in the semifinals to set up the meeting with Kentucky. "I just couldn't believe my college career was going to end against Kentucky," Bell said. "And it was for the national championship. Of course, Givens just killed us. He did the same thing in my last high school game, too. I still have nightmares about him."

That night was probably the highlight of Givens's life. He had a relatively brief NBA career and landed a job as a color commentator for the Orlando Magic. But in 2004 he was arrested and charged with sexual battery and lewd molestation in a case involving a fourteen-year-old girl. Givens denied the charges, and the court case was still pending (he was acquitted in the fall) when college basketball returned to the scene of his finest hour in 2005. By then, Bell was a judge, a season-ticket holder for both Kentucky and Duke basketball games, and had two sons who had gone to Duke. And yet it can be argued that in a different way, St. Louis was as much a highlight for him — even though he never played a second in the national championship game — as it was for Givens.

"I still get chills whenever I think about that weekend," he said. "The connection I still feel to all those guys is amazing. It's been twenty-seven years, but we're *still* teammates. We have an e-mail circle that will get started sometimes on a topic and just go on for days. I remember after we lost the Kentucky game, we came back in the locker room and I asked Coach [Bill] Foster if I could say the postgame prayer because it was my last game. During the prayer I said, 'I love everyone in this room.' I know men aren't supposed to say things like that, but that's the way I felt at that moment. I still feel that way about all of them today — whether they like it or not."

Bell finally did get to see his school win the national championship in 1991. He and Rob Hardy, also a walk-on for the '78 Duke team, rented a limo and made the trip to Indianapolis when Duke played Kansas in the championship game. "I'd been in Dallas when they lost to Louisville and that was disappointing, but I just had a feeling this was going to be their time," Bell said. "When they won, it was a great feeling because I felt I was part of it. That's one thing Mike [Krzyzewski] has done well. He's tried to make everyone feel they're a part of the program, even those of us who didn't play for him. I know he's not the only coach who does that, but it still feels great to go back to a game at Duke and feel as if I'm a part, even a very small part, of all that's gone on."

These days there are people around Lexington who have no idea that the Honorable Judge Bell once played for Duke, now the team Kentucky fans love to hate most. "I play it kind of low-key," Bell said. "But if it comes up, I say, 'Yes, I played for Duke — on the team that lost to Kentucky in '78.' That seems to calm things down." He smiled. "Of course, every now and then I can't resist bringing up '92."

That was the year Christian Laettner hit the shot at the buzzer to beat Kentucky in the east regional final, a game Kentucky fans still rant about even though the Wildcats evened the score in '98 in the south regional final, rallying from 17 points down to beat Duke. In each case, the winner went on to win the national championship.

As thrilling as it has been to see his alma mater win three national titles, Bell's fondest memories are still of '78. "I'm not sure a Final Four team ever had more fun than we did," he said. "Maybe the pressure got to us a little bit in the Kentucky game when we walked out on the floor and realized we were in the national championship game. But until then, it was nothing but a joyride."

He smiled. "To tell you the truth, it still is."

While the four teams went through their paces in the dome, rumors continued to swirl around the coaches' hotel. By Friday afternoon it is just about impossible to walk from one end of the lobby to the other without being accosted by someone who has a rumor to spread, tickets to sell, or a story to tell. Someone spotted Buzz Peterson, the recently fired coach at Tennessee, strolling down a sidewalk with Coastal Carolina athletic director Moose Koegel. Within minutes word passed through the lobby: Peterson is going to Coastal Carolina. That one turned out to be true. He was named the following week.

The Virginia job was still the one creating the most stir. Terry Holland walked into the coaches' lobby and was set upon like bugs at a light because of his Virginia connections. Holland swore he knew nothing and fled for an elevator — then spent ten minutes waiting because the elevators simply couldn't keep up with the traffic trying to go up and down.

There were two theories flying around the lobby: One was that Craig Littlepage wanted to hire DePaul's Dave Leitao, that he had wanted a minority coach all along and that all the big names that had swirled about earlier — Rick Barnes of Texas, Mike Montgomery of the Golden State Warriors, Mike Brey of Notre Dame — were nothing but smoke screens. Perhaps that was true, but Barnes had been approached by ACC Associate Commissioner Fred Barakat the week before. The "Digger Phelps to DePaul" rumor still had life, too.

Theory number two was entirely different: it had Littlepage meeting with South Carolina coach Dave Odom. The two men were old friends. In fact, they had been assistant coaches together under Holland at Virginia. South Carolina athletic director Mike McGee was retiring, and there was talk that Odom, whose team had just won the NIT, might be a little nervous at the age of sixty-two about a new boss. He certainly had ties to Virginia and to the ACC, having gone from Holland's staff to Wake Forest, where he had been the head coach for twelve years.

Odom made the mistake of showing up in the lobby late that afternoon. "It just isn't true," he insisted. "I'm not going to Virginia."

Of course, that comment convinced everyone that a press conference was imminent.

While Odom was issuing denials, Mike Krzyzewski was arriving at the hotel. No one tries to be more low-key at the Final Four than Krzyzewski — except when he brings his team with him, which he had done for ten of the past twenty seasons.

Krzyzewski is now the most visible coach in the sport. His mentor, Bob Knight, once held that role and has also won three national titles, but because he is now coaching in Lubbock, Texas, and hasn't had a team in the Final Four since 1992 (when it lost to Duke), Knight isn't as visible as he once was. The only other active coach with more than one title is Connecticut's Jim Calhoun — who beat Krzyzewski en route to both his championships — but he has been to eight fewer Final Fours.

Krzyzewski is also a lightning rod, within his profession and among basketball fans. There are people who see Duke as the model for what a big-time college program should be: a good academic school that recruits kids who actually go to class and graduate and who can also play well enough to make the team a consistent national contender. Duke has had academic All-Americans under Krzyzewski as well as basketball All-Americans. Duke plays in one of the game's great settings, Cameron Indoor Stadium; it is part of one of the sport's great rivalries, Duke–North Carolina; and it is a member of one of the great basketball conferences, the ACC. It has a beautiful campus and a coach many national corporations have sought as a spokesman.

The perfect college basketball program.

All of which makes many people nauseous. For every college basketball fan who loves Duke, there are probably at least five who can't stand the place, the idea of the place, or the sainted coach. Where once North Carolina was the target throughout the ACC, Duke now is. Dean Smith makes the point that Duke faces far more vitriol than his team did when it was dominant in the 1970s and 1980s because back then there was no sports talk radio, no Internet rife with crazy rumors, no *USA Today,* no ESPN, and nothing approaching the obsession with sports that exists today.

Duke has now won six of the last seven ACC Tournaments and would have won all seven if not for a stunning collapse in the 2004 final against Maryland. It is a sign of Duke's dominance that Maryland fans were more excited about that game than they were about Maryland's victory in the 2002 national championship game. "I think for a lot of people, it *was* bigger," Gary Williams said. "Indiana [the team Maryland beat in the title game] isn't Duke. To beat them in the ACC final was very definitely a big deal for us. I'd be lying if I said it wasn't."

Williams's relationship with Krzyzewski in many ways symbolizes the way basketball people feel about him. Williams can rant about Krzyzewski and Duke at length: Duke gets all the calls from the officials; the officials were the reason Duke came from 22 points down in the 2001 Final Four to beat Maryland; the ACC schedule is set up to help Duke; the school isn't as hard academically, especially for basketball players, as people say it is; the media are all intimidated by Krzyzewski's aura. In the next sentence, he will tell you that no one is a better coach than Krzyzewski, that winning one ACC Tournament made him understand how amazing it is to have won five in a row, that one of the most touching moments in his career came in 2002 when Krzyzewski sent him a fax prior to the Final Four wishing him luck and telling him he thought Maryland had the best team. "Showed a lot of class," Williams said. "Especially given some of the battles we've had."

Williams and many of his fellow coaches were ready to do battle — though not to his face — with him again by the time Krzyzewski parked his car in the basement of the Millennium and sent his fund-raiser and right-hand-man Mike Cragg to check in for him at the front desk so he could avoid the lobby.

"Mike can't walk through that lobby," NABC executive director Jim Haney said. "I've been with him. If he tried to walk from the front desk to the elevator, it could easily take him three hours."

Which is why Krzyzewski would have breakfast in his room all weekend and slip out through the basement to go to the events he was scheduled to attend. The latest Krzyzewski-related battleground was an American Express commercial that had been airing during the tournament. It was one of the "My Life"–themed commercials that the credit card company had started with Robert De Niro walking around New York City. In this one, Krzyzewski talks about coaching and his relationships with players and coaches. The line that had some coaches losing their minds is: "I don't consider myself a coach, I consider myself a leader of men."

Hyperbole? Of course. That's what commercials are. But in the hypercompetitive world of college basketball coaching — and recruiting — seeing over and over on national television a competitor being portrayed as some kind of saint or icon was more than some coaches could bear. Krzyzewski had done a lot of national commercials before this one. In fact, he had been part of a very funny one for Allstate in which a group of men playing hoops in a driveway re-create the famous Laettner shot against Kentucky. As the shot drops through, Krzyzewski charges out of the bushes and begins hugging everyone, then disappears as quickly as he appeared, leaving the players staring at one another.

No one objected to that one, or others. But this one put people over the edge. "Unfair recruiting advantage!" they screamed, though not on the record. The most honest response came from Jim Calhoun: "As someone who recruits against Mike, I hate it," he said. "And if I had been offered the exact same thing, I'd have taken it in an instant."

Krzyzewski knew what was being said. He knew a lot of it was jealousy and almost all of it was out of his control. "When I hear the things people say about me and about our program, I know there's really only one way to stop all of it," he said. "Stop winning. I certainly don't want to do that. I worry sometimes because I don't think it's fair what the players have to hear sometimes and I do think sometimes the officiating goes the other way because guys are trying to prove that we *don't* get all the calls. But if that's what comes with winning, I'll deal with it. It's better than losing and having everyone talk about what a bunch of great guys we are."

Krzyzewski's entire weekend was planned. He had NABC meetings to go to. He would attend the Past Presidents Brunch on Sunday. On Saturday night he would gather a group of his ex-players and ex-coaches for dinner. The only thing he did all weekend that wasn't carefully planned was get up on Sunday morning to go to church. Pope John Paul II had died on Saturday and Krzyzewski, being both Catholic and Polish, felt it was important to attend a service that morning. He walked by himself to an early-morning Mass at a church near the hotel. One of the things many who deify him and many who crucify him miss about Krzyzewski is that he is intensely emotional and sentimental. The pope's death, even though it had been expected for weeks, was a very sad moment for him. As he was walking out of church, he bumped into Cliff Ellis, the former coach at Auburn and Clemson. He was surprised to see Ellis because he knew he wasn't Catholic.

"Cliff," he said as they shook hands. "A Catholic Mass?"

"I thought the pope was a great man," Ellis said. "I wanted to pay tribute to him."

Krzyzewski's eyes welled with tears, and he and Ellis hugged briefly. Then it was time to go back to being Coach K. He had a luncheon to get to.

12

The Senator and the Icon

IT MIGHT WELL HAVE BEEN that the most nervous man in St. Louis on Friday night was someone who would not be coaching, playing, or officiating when the games began on Saturday. He would simply be watching.

Dean Smith was always in his element when he was coaching. He readily admitted that since his retirement, watching North Carolina play had been very difficult for him. "I try to watch at home," he said. "But I get so nervous that sometimes I just turn it off. Sitting in the arena will be very hard — especially if things aren't going well."

Standing outside a St. Louis restaurant on Friday night, Smith, who had turned seventy-four on February 28, appeared relaxed after a good dinner. He wasn't. "I just wish," he said, "that everyone would stop saying we have the most talent."

There was a reason people were saying that North Carolina had the most talent: it did. It wasn't as if the other teams didn't have talent, too, but none of them had four players who would be among the first fourteen chosen in the NBA draft in June, including one — freshman Marvin Williams — who didn't even start but would be the second player selected. "Illinois is very good," Smith said. "Louisville can really shoot. Michigan State plays great defense."

All true. But Smith was doing what he had always done during his remarkable thirty-six-year career as the head coach at North Carolina: lowering expectations for his team. And there was no mistaking that the Tar Heels were very much his team. He still had an office in the building named in his honor in 1986 when it opened — the Dean E. Smith Center — and he had played a central role in all the machinations that had gone on involving the coaching job since his surprise retirement in October of 1997. It had taken until April 2003 to bring Roy Williams back home to North Carolina. Smith had very much wanted his longtime number one assistant, Bill Guthridge, to succeed him and to succeed as his successor. He had done both, taking Carolina to the Final Four in two of the three years he had been the coach. That wasn't good enough for Carolina fans, who frequently pointed out that the 1998 team had been built around Vince Carter and Antawn Jamison — both Smith recruits — and the 2000 team had struggled during the regular season before finding itself in time to make the Final Four after squeezing into the tournament as an eighth seed. What no doubt bothered the Carolina faithful as much as anything was his team's 2–6 record against Duke.

Of course, that record did lead to a great Guthridge line at the annual postseason banquet in 2000: "Duke beat us three times this year," Guthridge said. "They beat us in Chapel Hill, they beat us in Durham, and they beat us home from the NCAA Tournament."

Touché. The Blue Devils had lost to Florida in the round of sixteen.

Guthridge's decision to retire that June had set off dancing in the streets of Chapel Hill. Now, everyone said, Roy Williams would return from the plains of Kansas, march into town on his white horse, and lead the Tar Heels back to glory. Except that Williams wasn't quite ready to climb into that saddle. To the shock of everyone — including Smith — he turned the job down to stay at Kansas, feeling as if there was still more to be done there. Turning down the job wasn't a mistake: in fact, in many ways, Williams should have been applauded for his loyalty to the people he had spent twelve years with. "The hardest thing I've ever done in my life," Williams said later, "was say no to Coach Smith."

Williams made one critical error during the entire affair: when he called his press conference to announce that he was staying at Kansas, he declared that the next press conference he held like this would be to announce his retirement. He had violated the first rule of coaching: never say never.

While they celebrated in Kansas, people in North Carolina were hurt and angry. When negotiations with another Carolina prodigal son, Larry Brown, fell apart, and when Eddie Fogler also said he wasn't interested in the job, Smith and athletic director Dick Baddour finally turned to Matt Doherty. At another time, in another place, Doherty might have been the perfect choice. He had been a very good player on very good Carolina teams, a starter on the 1982 national championship team when he was a sophomore. He had worked on Wall Street for a while after graduation before deciding that his true passion was still basketball. Williams had hired him at Kansas, and in the spring of 1999 he got his first head-coaching job, taking over a long-dormant Notre Dame program.

Doherty did excellent work his first season. The Irish just missed making the NCAA Tournament — they hadn't been since 1990 — and reached the NIT final. Perhaps if Williams had taken the Carolina job, Doherty, who was still only thirty-eight, could have spent the next ten seasons coaching the Irish, waiting his turn to coach his alma mater. Now, quite suddenly, one year into his career as a head coach, it was Doherty's turn at Carolina. He almost had to take the job — the next person on the list was Randy Weil, the coach at North Carolina–Asheville.

He accepted Baddour's offer, but on one condition: he had to be allowed to bring his assistant coaches with him from Notre Dame. They had all left other jobs a year earlier to work for him, and he didn't want to leave them behind, where their future would depend on the whims of a new coach. It was exactly the kind of loyalty Doherty had been taught by Smith and Williams — but in this case it backfired. Smith had announced during Guthridge's retirement press conference that all three of his assistants — Phil Ford, Dave Hanners, and Pat Sullivan, each (of course) a North Carolina graduate — would be on the staff of the new coach. Now Smith had to scramble to find the three ex-coaches jobs within the athletic department. He also insisted that all three still appear in the next season's media guide.

Doherty made other changes: office personnel were moved around, longtime secretaries were reassigned. There is one thing you simply cannot do at North Carolina: anger Dean Smith. Doherty had done that. Smith and Guthridge moved to an office in the basement of the Dean E. Smith Center, and all was not well on the good ship *Carolina*. Dave Odom, who was still at Wake Forest at the time, got a sense of how difficult things were when Kansas came to play at Wake Forest early that season. Odom called Bill Guthridge to tell him that if he and Coach Smith wanted to come to the game to see their old pal Roy, he would make arrangements to get them in through a back door and stash them in a box where they wouldn't have to deal with the public. Then they could be whisked down to the locker room after the game. Guthridge thanked Odom for the offer and said he would get back to him. The day before the game he called back.

"We can't make it," he said. "Dean has some other commitments."

Odom was shocked. No one would have expected such a schism in the Carolina family. When he saw Williams at the shootaround on game day, he told him that he had invited Smith and Guthridge to the game. Williams just shook his head and said, "This has been really, really hard."

It got worse before it got better. Doherty's first season started well. The Tar Heels won at Duke in January and were ranked number one in the country in early February. But they faded in March, losing the ACC Tournament final by an embarrassing 26 points to Duke and then getting bounced in the second round of the NCAA Tournament by Penn State. This was basketball, not football. Star guard Joe Forte jumped to the NBA in the spring, and Doherty had a bare cupboard the next season. Carolina went an astonishing 8–20; astonishing because this was a school that had reached the NCAA Tournament a mind-boggling twenty-seven years in a row. The season began with losses at home to Hampton and Davidson, and things only got worse after that. There was a 112–79 loss at Maryland; an 86–54 loss at Connecticut; and, worst of all, an 87–58 loss at home to Duke.

The glimmer of hope was in Doherty's recruiting class: Raymond Felton, a jetlike point guard; Rashad McCants, a wonderful shooting wing guard; and Sean May, the son of former Indiana star Scott May, a six-foot-nine widebody with soft hands who came to Carolina largely because an embittered Bob

Knight told May's father he would never speak to him again if he allowed his son to go to Indiana.

Led by the three freshmen, Carolina became competitive again the next season, going 19–16 and reaching the NIT quarterfinals. There were encouraging moments: a win at home over Duke, an upset of defending national champion Maryland in the first round of the ACC Tournament. But there was also insurrection inside the team. The young players thought Doherty was too harsh, too quick to jump them in practice. Rumor had it that Felton had left school one night and driven home, only to be talked into coming back by Phil Ford.

True or untrue, there was certainly dissension. Shortly after the season ended, even though Carolina had won eleven more games in 2003 than 2002, Doherty was fired. It was a bitter moment for Smith, because firing one of his own went against everything he had ever preached or stood for. And even though it was Baddour who technically pulled the trigger, everyone knew it couldn't have happened without Smith's approval. Once again the question became: Will Roy come home?

At the time, Williams was busy taking Kansas to the national championship game. Those who liked to read the Roy tea leaves were sure he was going to take the job. He kept saying he was only focused on this Kansas team and not thinking beyond that. If he wasn't going, wouldn't he just say he wasn't going? In Kansas they were convinced Roy wasn't going anywhere; after all, he had promised in 2000 that he would never leave.

Kansas lost the national championship game to Syracuse. Williams, who curses more than Smith (who never curses) but less than 99 percent of his coaching colleagues, used a profanity on the air when CBS's Bonnie Bernstein asked him about the North Carolina job a few minutes after the loss. "Right now, I don't give a shit about the University of North Carolina," Williams said. "I only care about the brokenhearted kids sitting in my locker room."

He meant every word. A week later he was the new coach at North Carolina. Now he became Lord Voldemort in Kansas — which was unfair, given what he had done there in fifteen seasons — but at least partly because of what he had said three years earlier. Williams is a sensitive soul. The things being said about him in Kansas in 2003 were as crushing as the things said about him in North Carolina in 2000. The irony was this: if he hadn't been such a good coach, people wouldn't have cared so much.

Dean Smith breathed a sigh of relief on that April day in 2003 when Roy came home. Doherty had left very good players behind, and Smith knew Williams could recruit and could coach. Carolina's record against Duke since his retirement was 4–13. That was unacceptable. Smith is almost obsessive about Duke. That is understandable to some extent, because the schools are archrivals, but a little surprising since Smith had great success against Duke, winning 59 times to 35 losses.

Smith never liked the way the Duke students behaved. He thought their antics went too far at times, and there was nothing he enjoyed more than winning in Cameron Indoor Stadium. Vic Bubas was his first great rival in coaching and Mike Krzyzewski his last. Everything about Duke brought out the competitor in Smith, once described by columnist Mark Whicker (a North Carolina graduate) as "the only man I've ever met who would compete with you in an interview."

It was true. Smith has always tried to deflect personal questions. His father was a teacher and a coach who coached what is believed to have been the first integrated high school team in the state of Kansas. Dean was a good athlete as a kid — he played football, basketball, and baseball — and went to Kansas to play for Phog Allen, expecting to major in math and go on to teach and coach high school just like his father. He was never a starter for Allen, but by his junior year he was helping the coaches teach the younger guys the plays. It was apparent to everyone that he had a knack for teaching and coaching.

Kansas made it to the Final Four in Smith's junior year, 1952. The Final Four that year was in Seattle at the Hec Edmundson Pavilion on the University of Washington's campus, which seated 10,000 people. "I was the eleventh man on the team," Smith remembered, laughing. "My job was to take our tickets — we each had two — and see if I could sell them. It wasn't easy. I think the face value was about five or six dollars each. I'm not sure I got that much for them. It wasn't a very big event out there."

Kansas won the national championship, beating St. John's in the final game. With a comfortable lead, Phog Allen got Smith into the game. "Thirty-seven seconds," Smith said. "And then they left me out of the box score."

It wasn't until years later that the box score was amended to include Smith. The following year Kansas again made the Final Four and played Indiana for the title. "Because it was in Kansas City, we were scrambling for tickets," Smith said. "We all had friends and family who wanted to come. We thought we'd win; playing there was like having a home-court advantage. But Indiana was better than we were."

Smith did a stint in the air force after college — meeting Red Auerbach and Adolph Rupp in Germany when the two legends conducted a clinic at the base where he was stationed — and was then hired by Bob Spear as the first assistant basketball coach at the newly opened Air Force Academy. It was during the 1957 Final Four that he met Frank McGuire, who was then the coach at North Carolina. In those days, even the participating coaches hung out with one another, and Spear introduced his protégé to McGuire, who was impressed enough to offer him a job as his top assistant. "I felt guilty because I was rooting for Kansas to beat them in the championship game and I knew Frank was going to offer me a job," he said. "I guess that was the last time I ever rooted against North Carolina in anything."

He was McGuire's assistant for four years and always accompanied his boss on recruiting trips to New York and trips to the Final Four. "Traveling with Frank was a great experience," Smith said. "He knew everyone, he knew what restaurants to go to. He was just a lot of fun to be around."

The most important thing Smith did as an assistant coach had nothing to do with basketball. Not long after he arrived in Chapel Hill, he began attending the Binkley Baptist Church and became friendly with the pastor there, Dr. Robert Seymour. It was Seymour who pointed out to him that Chapel Hill's restaurants were segregated and that it might take someone who had the clout of the North Carolina basketball program to put an end to that tradition. Soon after, Smith walked into a well-known local restaurant with a member of the church who happened to be black. The two men sat down at a table, daring the restaurant's management to say something. No one said anything. Everyone knew that Smith was Frank McGuire's assistant coach. That was the beginning of the end of segregation in Chapel Hill restaurants.

Twenty-three years later, Seymour told that story to a reporter whom Smith had reluctantly agreed to cooperate with on a newspaper profile. "I wish you'd write about the players and not me," he had said when first approached. He finally agreed because the reporter told him he had been assigned to write the story with or without Smith's cooperation. When the reporter asked Smith about the restaurant story, Smith was clearly perturbed. "Who told you that story?" he asked.

When he heard that it was Seymour, he shook his head. "I wish he hadn't done that."

"Why?" he was asked. "Aren't you proud of what you did?"

"I did what I thought was the right thing," Smith said. "I don't think you should take bows in life for doing the right thing. You should just do it."

No story says more about Dean Smith.

A lot of Frank McGuire's success was built around recruiting in New York City, his hometown. According to Auerbach, McGuire's genius lay in whom he brought to the house with him on recruiting visits: "The priest of the local parish and the local police captain," Auerbach said. "Especially when he was recruiting an Irish Catholic kid. He knew just how to get to the parents."

McGuire left for the NBA after the 1961 season, and Smith was named his successor at the age of thirty. As has been frequently chronicled, he struggled his first few seasons. Saddled with an NCAA probation left over from McGuire and the fact that Duke and Wake Forest were both national powers, Smith was 66–47 his first five seasons, certainly respectable but not what was wanted or expected at North Carolina. He was famously hanged in effigy by students after a loss in 1965 to Wake Forest — an effigy that a furious Billy Cunningham tore down as the team got off the bus and saw what the students had done.

"I don't remember much about that," Smith has said. "But I do remember Billy tearing it down."

Several days later Smith got his first victory over Duke and Vic Bubas. In 1967 he won his first ACC Tournament title and went to his first Final Four. He did it again the next year and in 1969 — three in a row for both the ACC Tournament and the Final Four. This was in the midst of the UCLA run, and the one time Carolina reached the title game it was overwhelmed by UCLA and Lew Alcindor. After the three straight Final Fours, Smith's legend grew and Carolina became the dominant program in the ACC. Even so, it wasn't until 1982, when Michael Jordan hit his famous shot against Georgetown, that Smith finally won a national title — on his seventh trip.

"I really noticed a big change in the event between the time we went to Los Angeles in 1972 and the next time we went when it was in Atlanta in 1977," he said. "In '72 I don't remember that we even had press conferences. We just stood outside the locker room and talked. I really felt as if it had doubled in size by the time we went back in '77."

They were still playing a consolation game in 1967. After North Carolina lost in the semifinals to Dayton, it had to play Louisville in the consolation game. "I just told the players to be on time for the game," Smith said. "We didn't practice, do a scouting report, or anything. The game just didn't matter once we had lost to Dayton." As it turned out, Smith, an absolute stickler for being on time, almost missed the start of the game. "I never took consolation games seriously because I didn't think they should be played," he said. "When we got into town that week, I ran into Al McGuire. He had forgotten to make a hotel reservation. I told him he could stay in my room for the week. On the day of the consolation game I went to lunch with Al and [his ex-boss] Bob Spear and Don Donoher [whose Dayton team was playing in the final that night]. We got to talking and I lost track of the time. I finally looked at my watch and said, 'Oh God, I have to get to the game.'"

That is the difference between McGuire and Smith. McGuire would have let the game start without him. Smith made it to the arena before tip-off.

In 1982 the NCAA finally got rid of the consolation games Smith hated so much. Carolina avoided playing in the consolation game in 1977 by beating UNLV in the semifinals to get to the championship game against Marquette. It can be argued that getting to that game was one of the great achievements of Smith's career, because no fewer than three starters — Tom La-Garde, Walter Davis, and the great Phil Ford — were injured during Carolina's run, which included a huge comeback in the round of sixteen against Notre Dame. "On St. Patrick's Day," Smith liked to point out when the subject of the Irish's lack of luck late in that game came up.

Marquette was also a surprise finalist. It had just squeezed into the tournament at the last possible moment, and some wondered if the Warriors would have been invited if Al McGuire hadn't announced that he was retiring at season's end. As had been the pattern throughout the tournament, Carolina fell behind, then rallied, tying the game with a little more than eight minutes to go. When the Tar Heels got the ball back with the score tied, Smith immediately went to his famed four corners. Even with an injured hand, no one ran the offense the way Ford did, and Smith saw this as Carolina's chance to pull Marquette out of its zone and to wear down the Warriors by chasing Ford. As soon as Carolina got the ball back, Smith sent star freshman Mike O'Koren to the scorer's table to check back into the game.

O'Koren had scored 31 points in the semifinals and was being given a brief rest. In his place was Bruce Buckley. With Ford running the four corners, assistant coach Eddie Fogler leaned over and asked Smith if he wanted to call time to get O'Koren, who was quicker than Buckley, back into the game. Smith said no — at least in part because he would never do that to a senior. It can be argued that Smith's greatest strength as a person — his loyalty — might have been his only failing as a coach.

Buckley made a move toward the basket and Steve Krafcisin passed him the ball for what looked like an open layup. But Bo Ellis, Marquette's brilliant center, came flying in from out of nowhere to block the shot. "At the time I thought it was goaltending," Smith said years later. "But when I saw the tape, I realized Ellis just made a great play."

The block led to a layup at the other end. Carolina never got even again. Marquette won the game, 67–59.

"I've never regretted it," Smith said. "First, it would have been wrong to do that to Bruce. Second, it took a great play to stop us from scoring."

Smith insists he still has fond memories of that Final Four. "I was president of the coaches association that year," he said. "But because we were playing, I didn't have to go to all the meetings."

Carolina continued to be hugely successful after winning the national title in 1982 but wasn't quite as dominant as it had been. The Tar Heels, who had been to seven Final Fours in sixteen seasons from 1967 to 1982, didn't go back until 1991. By then, Mike Krzyzewski — whose early years at Duke had been even shakier than Smith's start at Carolina — was there for the fifth time in six years. That was the year Duke finally won, and then it won again the next year. When North Carolina came to Cameron Indoor Stadium the next season, the Duke students all arrived wearing T-shirts that had a picture of Smith with the caption "I Want to Be Like Mike." This was soon after a Michael Jordan commercial had come out with the slogan "I Want to Be Like Mike."

The students were referencing a different Mike than the one in the commercial. Smith graciously accepted one of the shirts when it was offered to him and then went on to win the national championship that year, evening the score with Mike at 2–2. He reached the Final Four twice more — in 1995 and 1997 — but by then some of the joy of coaching was gone. In the aftermath of the '93 championship he had brought in a great freshman class: Rasheed Wallace, Jerry Stackhouse, and Jeff McInnis, the first two arguably the best high school players in the country that season.

But as often happens in sports, more can be less. The championship team lost only one starter, but he was crucial: George Lynch, the unquestioned leader of the team even if he wasn't the best or most talented player. Wallace and Stackhouse were instantly resentful of Smith's loyalty to more experienced players, and the team was rife with dissension and underperformed the entire year, losing in the second round of the NCAAs to Boston College. A year later, led by Wallace and Stackhouse, they reached the Final Four, at which point both sophomores bolted for the NBA. McInnis stuck around for one more season, and Carolina was again — by its standards — mediocre, again going out in the second round of the tournament.

During the 1997 season, Smith admitted that retiring had crossed his mind the previous season. He would never say it, because it would have sounded like a put-down to his players, but coaching Wallace, Stackhouse, McInnis, and many of the "modern players" wasn't as much fun as coaching Charlie Scott or

Bobby Jones or James Worthy or Michael Jordan, among others. Carolina rallied from a poor start in '97 to win the ACC Tournament and reach the Final Four. In the second round of the tournament, Smith broke Adolph Rupp's all-time record of 876 victories when the Tar Heels beat Colorado. Even so, Smith was exhausted by season's end. "I *am* tired right now," he admitted a few weeks after the season. "I'm sixty-six. I don't bounce back as fast as I did. But I think by October I'll be fresh again and want to coach. If I'm not, like I've always said, that's when I'll retire."

October came. The freshness didn't. A few days before the start of practice, Smith stunned the basketball world by retiring, handing the reins to Guthridge. What happened over the next seven seasons — even with Guthridge's two Final Four trips — was very tough for Smith to take. There was open bickering inside his cherished "Carolina family." Even with Williams back, all didn't go well right away. Carolina did make it back to the NCAA Tournament and did beat Smith's first employer, the Air Force Academy, in the first round. But then Texas took the Tar Heels out in the second round. The only good news about the early exit was that none of the three star sophomores — May, Felton, and McCants — had done enough to make themselves guaranteed lottery picks in the NBA draft. If Felton or McCants had been locks, they almost certainly would have left. Instead, all three returned, as did Jawad Williams, who would be a senior. Roy Williams added a superb freshman, Marvin Williams, and Carolina came into '04–'05 looking loaded. The team had lived up to the hype, winning the ACC regular-season title and earning a number one seed, even after being upset in the ACC Tournament by Georgia Tech, an event Roy Williams used to work McCants back into the playing rotation after he had missed three weeks with an "intestinal disorder."

Now the Tar Heels were back in the Final Four. But with most people convinced that at least two of the juniors *and* Marvin Williams were bound for the NBA draft, there was a now-or-not-for-a-while feeling around the team. Williams had been to four Final Fours at Kansas. Always protective, Smith had called North Carolina SID Steve Kirschner to tell him he needed to mention in his game notes that Williams's percentage after sixteen years as a coach was the best in history. Kirschner *had* mentioned it. Smith wanted it in the notes for *every* game.

Smith had first attended a Final Four forty-eight years earlier. He hadn't missed many since. The argument could be made that this would be the most difficult one he had ever attended.

Bill Bradley had been to a lot fewer Final Fours than Dean Smith — to be precise, he had been four times: once in 1961, when he and several of his high school buddies made the trip from Crystal City, Missouri, to Kansas City to see Ohio State play Cincinnati in the national championship game; once in 1965, when he and his Princeton teammates made the trip from New Jersey to Portland, Oregon, as the east regional champions; once in 1966, as an Oxford Rhodes scholar on a break from his studies; and once in 1998, when he was about to run for president of the United States and made the trip to San Antonio as a visiting professor at Stanford to watch Stanford play Kentucky in the semifinals.

"I've only been four times," Bradley said. "But I can honestly say I had four very different experiences."

Bill Bradley served three terms in the U.S. Senate and ran for president in 2000, losing the Democratic nomination to Al Gore. He also scored 58 points against Wichita State in the consolation game of the 1965 Final Four — still the Final Four record for points in a game, a record surpassed in the history of the *tournament* just once, by Notre Dame's Austin Carr, who scored 61 in a first-round game in 1970.

"What I remember about that [consolation] game was the beginning," Bradley said. "Every time I passed the ball to a teammate who I thought had a good shot, the ball would come back to me. I'm thinking, 'What's going on here, why are they passing up open shots?' Finally Coach [Butch] van Breda Kolff calls time and says to me in the huddle, 'Bill, this is your last game, will you please shoot the damn ball!' So I did what I was told."

It wasn't until years later, when he was retired from the Senate and politics and was spending most of his time speaking and writing, that Bradley got a sense of just how good he had been that night. "Some guy came in [to his New York City office] with a bunch of memorabilia that he wanted me to sign. One of the things he had was the box score from that game. I'd never really looked at it, but when I did, I think my line was twenty-two of twenty-nine from the field and fourteen of fifteen from the line. I looked at it and thought, 'Hey, I guess I was pretty good that night.'"

Bill Bradley was good on a lot of nights, from high school through Princeton through his ten-year career with the New York Knicks. His first basketball hero was Wilt Chamberlain, who arrived at the University of Kansas just when Bradley was beginning to emerge as a standout player. "During his sophomore year, I was in the eighth grade," Bradley said. "I kept a scrapbook on him. Everything he did, I put it in the scrapbook. I still remember them losing the final in triple overtime to North Carolina and how disappointing that was to me."

Bradley became a star in high school and was recruited by all the basketball power schools. In those days, high school players didn't make final decisions on college until the end of their senior seasons. Bradley's senior year at Crystal City High School ended with a huge disappointment when the school lost the state championship game by one point. "We were down one in the final seconds and I managed to steal the ball," Bradley said. "One of my teammates broke ahead of everyone and I passed him the ball. He had an open layup at the buzzer — and missed."

The teammate was Tom Haley. "He became Rabbit Angstrom," Bradley said, a reference to the famous Updike character who never got over his days as a high school star. "He just couldn't get past it. He dropped out of college, went into the military, and then came back to Crystal City. To this day — forty-four years later — I think people still bring it up to him all the time." Haley did have one moment of stardom, though, when Bradley ran for president. Looking for a boyhood friend, many members of the media found Haley to ask him about his old teammate. "I was happy that my running did something positive for him," Bradley said, laughing. "I think he enjoyed it."

Perhaps because of his team's near miss in the championship game, Bradley decided to go to Duke, where Vic Bubas was building a power. He'd had a chance to witness the national championship game shortly after his high school career ended. "The finals were in Kansas City again that year, and some of my friends and I drove up there and went to the final. I don't even know how we got the tickets but I don't remember that it was a big problem. I *do* remember that we somehow got down to the hallway where the Ohio State players were walking from their locker room to the court. I remember standing there watching them and seeing Jerry Lucas, who would later be a teammate on our '73 championship team, and John Havlicek, who would be the toughest guy I ever played against, going out onto the court. Of course, I had no idea I'd be connected to them later. I just remember being surprised when Cincinnati beat them. Ohio State had won the year before and I think we all thought they'd win again.

"I knew I wanted to go to school someplace where I could play for the national championship. Duke had Art Heyman and Jack Marin and seemed to be building a team that could win a championship. That's what I wanted to do. The fact that it was a good school helped, but I was driven by the idea of a national championship."

Basketball history changed when two things happened: First, Bradley broke a foot and "got a look at life without basketball." Second, he went on a summer trip — "thirteen girls and me" — to England and visited Oxford. "Fell in love with the place," he said. "Fell in love with the whole idea of the place. That was when I first heard of the Rhodes scholarship. I read someplace that Princeton had produced more Rhodes scholars than any other school. So, at the last possible second, I changed my mind and decided to go to Princeton."

This was long before the NCAA had come up with the one-sided idea of the "letter of intent," which basketball players are now allowed to sign almost a year before they are scheduled to enroll in school. If a player changes his mind because he hears about the Rhodes scholarship or, more likely, because the coach who recruited him leaves to take another job, he can't simply decide to go elsewhere. If he doesn't go to the school with whom he "signed" (imagine a "student" signing a contract with a college), he must sit out one year before he can play. Coaches who change jobs aren't required to sit out a year before they coach again; athletes are.

In 1961 Bradley could change his mind. H
League wasn't as powerful as the ACC and th
league champion lost in the first round of the l
ment. But he remembered seeing Yale's Johnny Le
of *Sports Illustrated* when he was a high school fresh
figured the quality of ball couldn't be all that bad.

"A lot of the basketball cognoscenti said I had give
winning the national championship when I decided to
Princeton," he said. "I didn't see it that way. I still wanted to
it. I became a recruiter. I talked to kids when they came to ca
pus; I went and *visited* kids [which was still legal then] to te
them to come to Princeton. We got some very good players: Ed
Hummer and Gary Walters were the best. Then we added Don
Rodenbach and became a very solid team. Our center my senior
year was a six-nine walk-on named Robby Brown. He had some
qualms about the morality of winning, but he was a pretty good
player anyway."

Princeton improved each year Bradley was there and went
into the '64–'65 season thinking it had a chance to do something
special. Bradley, Michigan's Cazzie Russell, and UCLA's Gail
Goodrich were considered the three best players in the country,
and Princeton had already attracted a good deal of attention because it was winning with smart kids and because its best player
had already said he would pass up his rookie year in the NBA if
he got a Rhodes scholarship. In December the Tigers faced
Michigan and Russell in the semifinals of the Holiday Festival in
New York. In those days there was no bigger in-season tournament. It was an eight-team tournament, and almost without fail,
several of the teams were nationally ranked. Princeton-Michigan
in the semifinals was a complete sellout: 18,499 packed into the
old Madison Square Garden.

"I remember what the building seated," Bradley said. "I know was sold out. But since that game I've had at least twenty-two housand people come up to me and say they were there that night."

Those who were there saw Bradley and his teammates dominate Michigan, which was ranked number one in the country, for thirty-six minutes. The Tigers led by twelve when Bradley fouled out. Once he was gone, the game changed completely, and Russell hit a shot in the final seconds to give Michigan a one-point win.

"It was disappointing, very disappointing," Bradley said. "But I think our attitude was 'We had the number one team in the country on the ropes for thirty-six minutes, we're good enough to play with anyone.' Our goal was to play them again because we knew if we did, it would be in the Final Four."

It wasn't called the Final Four back then, but the goal was the same: Princeton wanted to win the east regional championship and get to Portland. In those days, only twenty-three teams made the tournament and they never traveled outside their own geographic region. Princeton had to play a first-round game — fourteen teams played in the first round while nine teams had byes. The Tigers beat Penn State to get to the regional in College Park, Maryland, and then beat ACC champion North Carolina State in the round of sixteen. Providence won the second game, 81–73, over St. Joseph's. The Princeton players had stayed to watch the second game. They were stunned when the Providence players cut the net down after their win.

"It was as if they thought they were already in the Final Four," Bradley said. "We took note of that."

To put it mildly. The next night — in those days the regionals and the final four (no caps back then) were played on Friday and

Saturday — Princeton put on one of the most stunning basketball clinics ever seen. "I think there was one stretch where we hit eighteen of twenty shots," Bradley said. "It was the way you dream about playing basketball. I can still see most of the plays in that game in my mind's eye very clearly. I can remember Don Roth, who later became the treasurer of the World Bank, throwing a perfect pass to Ed Hummer for a dunk. The feeling of satisfaction was just incredible." Princeton won the game by the remarkable final score of 109–69, a score Bradley can still pull out of the air on command.

"I remember we cut down the nets and really celebrated," he said. "All the games and all the teams I played on, that was, without question, one of the two or three best performances I was ever part of. It was a great high.

"And then, on Monday, we all went to class."

Bradley's memories of the Final Four are vivid, but not quite as satisfying as the regionals. "We flew out on Thursday to play on Friday," he said. "I don't think we even went to the arena to practice. Princeton was very tight. We stayed in some motel that didn't have any beds in the rooms — just pullout couches. It was the classic fleabag motel. Really awful. Here we are, getting ready to try to win a national championship and we're sleeping on pullout couches. We couldn't believe it."

Nowadays, the NCAA is so flush with its network billions that it pays the expenses for all sixty-five teams to travel to game sites as well as their hotel bills. It has been a long time since any team playing in the opening round, much less the Final Four, has stayed in a motel with only pullout couches for beds. Back then, the schools received a per diem of $25 a day for each player — probably enough for a decent hotel room but apparently not enough to get Bradley and his teammates a real bed to sleep on.

"When we got to the arena, I think it hit us for the first time that this was a big deal," Bradley said. "We're playing Michigan again and UCLA is playing Wichita State in the second game. Michigan had been ranked number one all year, and UCLA was the defending champion. We started out very nervous. They got ahead and stayed ahead. We made a run in the second half, but then I got the fouling disease again and fouled out. I think we were down three or four when I fouled out." Michigan ended up winning the game, 93–76. It might well have been losing that made Bradley realize how important the game was to him.

"It was crushing," he said. "I think we all believed we were going to win the national championship. To sit in that locker room and realize we weren't was about as difficult as anything I can remember. People tell me now how great the next night was [when he scored the 58], and I explain to them that it wasn't. Yes, I played well; we played well but we didn't meet our goal. Our goal was to win, not finish third.

"After the game, Henry Iba came into the locker room to see me. I had played for him on the '64 Olympic team. He said I'd had a great game and a great career. It was really nice of him, but it all felt pretty empty right then. I don't think we even stayed for the championship game. In some ways, it almost felt as if we weren't there, it was all over so quickly. We flew home the next day and went back to school. That was it."

Bradley has never seen a film or tape of that game — because there is none. The game wasn't on TV, and in those days teams didn't routinely tape — or film — games the way they do now. "A couple of grainy highlights," he said. "That's it. Fortunately, most of it is still inside my head."

The Princeton players missed a second remarkable performance in the Michigan-UCLA game, Gail Goodrich's 42 points, which led UCLA to its second straight title. John Wooden still calls that the greatest individual performance he witnessed in the Final Four. Between the two of them, Bradley and Goodrich scored exactly 100 points that night. Their paths would cross again in the NBA finals a few years later when Goodrich played for the Lakers and Bradley for the Knicks and the teams played each other for the championship three times in four seasons.

Bradley returned to the Final Four a year later on a break from Oxford and was in the building in College Park on the night Texas Western beat Kentucky in what has become the most famous and arguably the most important Final Four game ever played. For Bradley, the return to Maryland's Cole Field House was bittersweet. The night when he and his teammates had cut down the nets in that same building felt more like a lifetime ago than just a year.

Bradley graduated from Oxford and joined the New York Knicks the following season. In a twist of fate, it was an injury to Cazzie Russell that elevated him to the starting lineup and turned the Knicks into a championship team. With Russell coming off the bench to lift the team offensively at key moments, the Knicks won their first title in 1970 and won again three years later. They haven't won an NBA title since. "I don't go to see them play very often even though I work right here [in Manhattan] now," Bradley said. "I really have trouble watching the NBA game. So much of the time the offense consists of two guys running the pick-and-roll or a big guy pitching and catching with someone shooting a three-point shot. I really think the three-point shot has damaged the game a great deal. You have four guys playing and six guys watching most of the time.

"I was taught that you play the game with your feet. Now the game is played with the chest; it's all about strength. It looks more like sumo wrestling than basketball to me, and I find it more or less unwatchable. I try to watch the finals or pick one team I like every year just to keep up with it, but it's very, very hard. It's just a boring game to watch. Every year I'll try to go to one game, put my toe in the water to see if it's warmed up at all. It's still freezing."

Bradley didn't return to the Final Four for thirty-two years after 1966. For ten years he was playing in the NBA and soon after that he launched his political career. In 1998 he was teaching at Stanford and got involved with Mike Montgomery's team. Most of the players knew he had been a U.S. senator and had played in the NBA. But they had little clue that he had been one of college basketball's great players. "One of the kids, Mark Madsen, had read *A Sense of Where You Are* [Princeton professor John McPhee's legendary book on Bradley and the '65 Princeton team], so he knew. But that was about it. Still, they were smart kids, real students, and I enjoyed the way they played. I started going to practices, got to know Mike very well, and for the first time in years I became a real fan."

Stanford made the Final Four that year, for the first time since 1942, and Bradley, who was doing some commentary for CBS News, got to go as part of his role for the network. "But I was there as a fan," he said. "I was devastated when they lost to Kentucky because I liked the kids so much. Still, it was fun to feel passionate about the game that way again. I enjoyed it."

He hasn't been back since, but does sit down to watch the games on television. He enjoys the college game more than the NBA because he sees passion in it. "It just has more human drama," he said. "I follow the first round, looking for those upsets that happen. I still remember the Princeton-Georgetown game in '89 and how beautifully Princeton played all night and thinking [Princeton center] Kit Mueller got fouled on that last play. You see mental blunders, you see how much it means to the kids. I find myself flashing back to '65 and remembering how much it meant to all of us.

"I really don't follow Princeton closely, to be honest. I might sit down and watch a big game in which I think we have a chance, but that's about it. I loved [Pete] Carril and I like it when they play well, but I guess life moves on."

Bradley did go back to Princeton in the winter of 2005 for a fortieth reunion of the 1965 team. Every member of the team and van Breda Kolff, now eighty-five, made it back. "It was very emotional to see everyone all together again," he said. "It's amazing how clear my memories are of that season."

Bradley's devotion to the game he played so well is still apparent when he talks about it. He sounds almost angry when discussing what he sees as the fall of the NBA, the commercialization of the college game, the lack of passion he sees so often. And, he says, he still thinks basketball is an excellent window into someone's soul.

"I think I can learn more about a person's character by playing basketball with them than by sitting down and interviewing them for an hour," he said. "Not that I play very often these days. A few years ago I was looking to hire a state director in New Jersey. I was interviewing a guy named Kevin Rigby and we were down at the Jersey Shore. We were walking on the beach, talking, and we came on some people playing half-court. We stopped and got into a three-on-three game. Kevin was a perfect teammate: passed the ball, played hard, knew how to box out. When the game was over, I said, 'Kevin, you're hired.' He was one of the best people I ever had work for me."

Nowadays, Bradley stays busy speaking and writing and traveling. He says he has no plans to run for public office again, even though there are many Democrats who would like to see him run for president in 2008. He still believes, even with all the changes in the game since his playing days, that character and heart are as important as talent. "You have to have some degree of physical skill," Bradley said. "We had that in '65. I've heard people say that we won because we were smarter than other teams. I really don't believe that. I believe we won because we had more heart than other teams, that we cared about what we were doing. I still believe once you reach a certain talent level, the difference between teams is in their character. [John] Wooden's teams had great talent, but they had character, too. They were so well prepared that he didn't even coach very much during the games. They knew how to play and they went out and played. Seeing basketball played the right way is still something I find beautiful. That's why Stanford was so much fun in '98.

"It may be why I think back to our team so often. I can still see so much of it so clearly. And all these years later, it still looks great to me."

13

Saturday

THE WAITING BEGINS on Saturday — for everyone. Thursday and Friday are all about getting into town, finding your way around, and, for the teams, going through practices and tape sessions and (sometimes) a little sightseeing.

Saturday, though, everyone waits. The first game doesn't start until 6:07 eastern time — an hour earlier in St. Louis because of the different time zone — and no one, especially the teams, wants to do very much. Each goes through a brief shootaround in the morning and then returns to its hotel, all with orders from the coaches to "stay off your feet."

All of the teams have been through this during the regular season, especially nowadays when so many college basketball games don't start until nine o'clock — for television, of course, which is the ultimate dictator of all starting times in college basketball, as in most sports. When the Final Four was last played in St. Louis, in 1978, the first semifinal began at 12:30 local time and the second one was over by just after five o'clock — almost the exact same time that the games would now begin.

"It was a lot harder waiting at the Final Four than any other time during the season," Wes Miller said. "It wasn't anything new, but that was part of the problem. Sean [May] and I had been roommates the whole tournament, and by the time we got to St. Louis, we had ordered every movie there was to order from every hotel we'd been in. On Saturday we spent a lot of time arguing about whether it was worth ordering a movie for the third time or not. We finally ended up not ordering anything. Instead, Sean tried to sleep — which wasn't working — and I walked around the room in circles, playing with a deck of cards or flipping TV channels. It was a long four hours between our morning meal and our pregame meal."

Most teams eat a pregame meal four hours before tip-off. Once, everyone ate the same thing for the pregame meal: steak. The last thing you wanted to do was eat anything that was heavy, like pasta or pancakes. Then, about twenty years ago, someone discovered the concept of carbo-loading and now most pregame meals consist of pasta and pancakes. Many coaches serve pasta at 8:00 A.M. pregame meals when their teams play at noon.

"It's all probably ridiculous," said Texas coach Rick Barnes, whose team made the Final Four in 2003. "During the summer all the guys eat is McDonald's and Burger King, and that's probably when they play their best basketball."

Barnes was in the lobby Saturday morning, killing time like everyone else. He had just finished his eighteenth season as a head coach — one year at George Mason, six at Providence, four at Clemson, and seven at Texas. He had won twenty games in his one season at George Mason and built programs that consistently made the tournament at his next three stops. But he had never been past the Sweet Sixteen until his Texas team made its run in 2003.

"Sometimes it's still hard for me to believe that I actually got to the point in my career where I coached a team in this event,"

Barnes said. "It seems like it was about fifteen minutes ago that I was a twenty-two-year-old assistant coach at Davidson making twenty-five hundred dollars a year, and now I've been a head coach for almost twenty years. I remember early in my career I looked at the guys coaching in the Final Four and they were like gods to me. Dean Smith, are you kidding me? I grew up in North Carolina. Jim Valvano? Coach Wooden? I can't even call him John Wooden, he's just Coach Wooden to me."

Given Barnes's roots, it is ironic that he and Smith came close to a fight during the 1995 ACC Tournament. Barnes was an ACC rookie coach trying to rebuild a sputtering Clemson program. The overmatched Tigers played North Carolina in the first round of the ACC Tournament, and as expected, the game was a blowout. But a couple of chippy plays late in the game angered Smith, who began yelling at one of Barnes's players, Iker Iturbe. Barnes told Smith that if he had a problem with one of his players to yell at *him* — which he did. The two men ended up having to be held apart by referee Rick Hartzell while Smith yelled at Barnes, twenty-two years his junior, "Go ahead and hit me."

The incident made Barnes a pariah in most of North Carolina but seemed to establish what he wanted to: that Clemson wasn't simply going to be rolled by the ACC's powers anymore. In 1997, after a loss at Duke, Barnes showed up the next morning in Greensboro at the office of Fred Barakat, the ACC's officiating supervisor, insisting he had tapes that proved Clemson got the short end when it played Duke and Carolina. His team made it to the Sweet Sixteen that year, losing in double overtime to Minnesota, which went on to the Final Four. A year later Barnes took the Texas job, in large part because he believed no matter what he did at Clemson, jumping over the league's two superpowers would be virtually impossible.

He quickly built Texas into a perennial contender in the Big 12, where Kansas and Roy Williams were just about as big an obstacle as Duke and North Carolina. When Texas beat Connecticut and Michigan State to win the south regional in 2003, Barnes found himself in a place he had never really dreamed of reaching. "I remember all the phone calls and notes," he said. "It was great. But the amazing thing is the phone call that really got to me was from Amp Davis."

Amp Davis had played on Barnes's George Mason team, his first real problem as a head coach. The two clashed almost from the day Barnes took over the program: over conditioning, over class attendance, over just about everything. "He spent more time in my office being lectured than any player I've ever coached," Barnes said. "The fact that either one of us made it through that season was a miracle."

Davis played well in the second half of the season, made it to class, and became one of the team's leaders. On the night Texas beat Michigan State, Barnes got home and found a message from Amp Davis. "When I called him, he was crying," Barnes said. "He said he felt as if he were a part of it in a small way, that he knew he'd never play in a Final Four, but now he felt like he was part of a Final Four. By the time I hung up, I was crying, too."

Having been once, Barnes yearns to go back. He had thought his 2005 team had a chance to make an impact in the tournament until P. J. Tucker, his best player, was declared academically ineligible for the second semester. "It's very hard to go the first time and not feel totally fulfilled, whether you're a player or a coach," Barnes said. "Part of it is there's so much to do during the week, you just feel like you don't get time to prepare for a basketball game. It didn't really hit me that we had a game to play until

I walked on the practice floor on Friday and I heard my assistants talking about what we were going to do to try to stop [Syracuse's] Carmelo Anthony. Even then, I caught myself looking around the [New Orleans Super] dome thinking, 'This is a long way from Davidson.'"

The manner in which Barnes got his first two coaching jobs is legendary among his colleagues. In 1977, having just graduated from Lenoir-Rhyne College in the western corner of North Carolina, he got a friend to set up an interview with Davidson coach Eddie Biedenbach for a part-time coaching position. The appointment was for nine o'clock in the morning. Not wanting to be late, Barnes was there at eight. Eleven hours later he was still sitting in the unair-conditioned gym. The assistants had told him they expected Biedenbach back at any moment throughout the day. They had left at six. An hour later Barnes decided that eleven hours was enough and was getting up to leave when Biedenbach walked into the gym. When he saw Barnes, a look of horror crossed his face. "You're Rick Barnes, aren't you?" he said. Barnes was so tired by then that he wasn't 100 percent certain who he was, but he nodded his head. "Oh God, I completely forgot," Biedenbach said. "Come on in."

Thirty minutes later Barnes had the job. Two years later, when Joe Harrington was hired at George Mason and was looking for an assistant coach — he could hire only one full-time assistant — Biedenbach's assistants, Tom Abatemarco and John Kochan, told him he was crazy not to hire Barnes. "They told me he was the hardest-working young coach they'd ever seen," Harrington said. "They said he was in the office every morning at five o'clock. I decided to call their bluff. I set my alarm one morning and called the Davidson basketball office. Someone picked up the phone and I said, 'Is this Rick Barnes?' He said, 'Yes, it is.' I said, 'Rick, this is Joe Harrington at George Mason. You're hired.'"

Eight years later, when Harrington left George Mason to take the job at Long Beach State, George Mason athletic director Jack Kvancz hired Barnes. By then he had worked at Alabama for Wimp Sanderson and at Ohio State for Gary Williams. "I learned a lot from both of them," Barnes said. "Of course, my wife has never completely forgiven Gary because he taught me how to curse."

Barnes has cursed more than a few times but has now won 363 games as a head coach and been to the Final Four. "Once you've been, you want to go back and you want to win," he said. "Most coaches don't win the first time they go. I guess Jim Calhoun's the exception, but he had a great team that was on a mission — and he's a Hall of Fame coach. I'm fifty now. I know I'm on the back nine of my coaching career. I want to win the thing once so I can retire someday with a smile on my face."

Coaches who have won once would tell Barnes it isn't that simple. Two of them were in the lobby Saturday afternoon taking bows and telling stories. Word had started to circulate that morning that when the Hall of Fame announced its class of 2005, Jim Calhoun and Jim Boeheim would be two of the people going in. Calhoun had been a finalist a year earlier and had somehow not been selected. His second national championship — which he won on the night the Hall announced he had *not* been chosen — made it impossible for him not to get in. Boeheim had been winning more than twenty games a year at Syracuse for close to thirty years. He had been to three Final Fours and three national championship games, and in 2003 his team had beaten Barnes's Texas team and Roy Williams's Kansas team to win the national title.

Boeheim had coached in the Big East from the day the league began play in 1979. Calhoun had coached at Northeastern and had taken over a moribund Connecticut program in 1986. They had competed against each other for nineteen years. They had both survived prostate cancer and returned to coach. Boeheim had been ridiculed early in his career as someone who recruited great talent but couldn't harness it. Syracuse had spent a year on probation in the early 1990s and had bounced back to reach the championship game in 1996. Calhoun had been hailed as a savior at UConn and then been questioned when he couldn't get to the Final Four. Some of his key players had had brushes with the law, including star point guard Khalid El-Amin, arrested on drug charges soon after the 1999 national championship, but he had come through it all standing.

Now Calhoun and Boeheim would go into the Hall of Fame together. Both spent a good deal of time accepting congratulations.

"It's still almost an adjustment for me to realize that this is where my career is now," Calhoun said. "I still remember when I first came here, being openmouthed walking through the lobby, seeing people like John Wooden and Dean Smith and Louie Carnesecca. It sort of hits you at moments like this that now you're one of the guys people are looking at. It's a nice feeling." He smiled. "It's also an old feeling."

Boeheim may be the most ridiculed great coach in history. He played at Syracuse — as a walk-on — on very good teams alongside Dave Bing in the 1960s and succeeded Roy Danforth when Danforth left to take the Tulane job after getting Syracuse to the Final Four in 1975. "Even though we'd been to a Final Four, I really didn't think we had a national program back then," he said. "We were pretty good but we weren't at the level where I thought of us in the same sentence as the true national powers. The Big East changed all that. When we became part of the league, it gave us a chance to be a national power."

Many people (including this author) have made fun of Boeheim through the years because he always appeared to be in pain on the bench during his early years as a coach. He has a nasal voice that makes him sound as if he's whining when he's not. As he acknowledged, he had some very good teams in the '80s that suffered some frustrating losses and some embarrassing ones — not the least of which was a second-round loss to Navy in the Carrier Dome in 1986. "They *did* have David Robinson," Boeheim pointed out.

Nevertheless, to be a national power playing on your home court and lose to a team filled with future naval officers was embarrassing. A year later Syracuse and Boeheim bounced back, upsetting North Carolina in the east regional final to make the Final Four. "The feeling of relief was unbelievable after the years of not getting there," Boeheim said. "It just felt great."

Even so, there was a moment in the postgame press conference when Boeheim was talking about Carolina's late rally and the mistakes his team had made that almost cost them the lead. Finally, center Rony Seikaly, sitting on the podium next to Boeheim, said, "Hey, Coach, cool it, man — we won!"

Boeheim laughed.

A week later Syracuse easily beat Providence, coached by former Boeheim assistant Rick Pitino, in the semifinals but then lost to Indiana in the final on Keith Smart's off-balance jump shot from the corner with five seconds left. Boeheim never forgot what Bob Knight said to him when they shook hands that night: "You'll be back."

He was — nine years later — only to lose to Pitino, who by then had become the King of Kentucky. The third time was the charm. "The road from zero national championships to one is miles and miles and miles long," Boeheim said. "From one to two is a few yards. I always knew my life would change if we ever won, but I never dreamed how much. It isn't as if I can do no wrong now, but it certainly makes up for a lot of things. We lose the way we did to Vermont this year with a senior team, I'm getting killed right now. As it is, people are disappointed, but they can still talk about '03. And we'll have other chances. We'll be pretty good again down the road."

Boeheim has strong opinions about the way the tournament is run. He believed that the best team had not made it to St. Louis. "I think Arizona was the best team," he said. "They had Illinois by fifteen *in Chicago*. That was a home court for Illinois. There's no way Arizona loses that game if it is played any place that's even a little bit neutral. I'm not knocking Illinois, it was a great comeback, but it just isn't fair that way. They don't have to keep teams at home to sell tickets. We would have played in Austin this year, and there were thirty thousand people in Syracuse to see North Carolina, Wisconsin, North Carolina State, and Villanova. The tournament has gotten that big. They say they keep high seeds home so teams don't have to travel as much. If you look at it, teams are traveling just as much — it's just different teams traveling.

"The advantage of being a number one seed should be that you play the number sixteen seed first and then the eight-nine winner and so on. It should *not* be that you get some kind of home-court advantage. This should be a neutral-court tournament — for everybody. And I say that as someone who has benefited from home court or near home courts in the past. It's just not right."

Boeheim is one of the few big-time coaches who never leaves the Final Four until after the championship game. "I still love the whole thing," he said. "I love going to the games, I love being here. The lobby's not the same. I miss staying up late at night and just listening to coaches talk basketball and hearing guys like Jimmy V. tell stories. But I still love coming here and being a part of it. I love all of it."

A radio guy walked up to Boeheim, wanting to know if he had "just a couple minutes."

Boeheim smiled his wry smile. "Okay," he said. "Maybe I don't love *all* of it."

The only coach among the four still working who had not previously been in a Final Four was Bruce Weber. He had been a late bloomer as a head coach, not getting his first job until he was forty-two, when Southern Illinois hired him in 1998. Weber might have lacked experience compared with the other three Final Four coaches, but he didn't lack smarts. On the Monday of Final Four week, he had called Jim Calhoun — the last coach to win the championship in his first trip to the Final Four. Winning the Final Four in your first trip isn't impossible — after all, you have to win only two games — but it doesn't happen often. Since Don Haskins did it in the *Brown v. Board of Education* game in 1966, it has happened eight times — Norm Sloan in '74, Jud Heathcote in '79, Jim Valvano in '83, Rollie Massimino in '85, Steve Fisher in '89, Jim Harrick in '95, Tubby Smith in '98, and Calhoun in '99. Interestingly, only Fisher ('92 and '93) and Calhoun returned, and only Calhoun won a second time.

Calhoun's advice to Weber was simple and direct: "You divide the week into two parts," he told him. "The first part is to celebrate the achievement of getting there. Let the kids get out and see the town, let them enjoy themselves and realize that being in the Final Four is a big deal. But then, at some point late Thursday or early Friday, you have to let them know that it's time to work. They've had their playtime, now there is a job to do: there are still two more games to be won and then you can celebrate for as long as you want. But playtime is over. The key is making sure when you walk on the court Saturday night, your team is as well prepared mentally and physically as it has ever been to play a game."

That doesn't always happen. Many coaches admit that, especially the first time, the hoopla and demands of Final Four week can overwhelm them. "The first time we went [Dallas '86] I honestly think I spent more time on ticket requests than on preparing my team," Mike Krzyzewski said. "It happens whenever you go, but especially the first time, people come out of the woodwork and want to be there. On the one hand, you understand it and appreciate it. On the other hand, you have to find a way to get away from it, or you'll show up unprepared."

Calhoun agrees with that but thinks there can be an advantage to being a first-timer. "You're almost an innocent," he said. "Yes, the demands can overwhelm you. I felt that a little bit in '99. But in a way there's less pressure because by getting there, you've already answered that one big question — 'Can he coach a Final Four team?' — and until you get there and don't win, no one is asking the other question — 'Can you win the Final Four?' — because you haven't lost one yet. In a sense, that first time you're playing with house money. When you go back a few times and haven't won it yet, then you start to feel the pressure."

Jim Boeheim agreed. "If you have a program where you can get there more than once, after a while you feel like you *should* win at least once," he said. "I know I felt that. I'm sure Roy feels it. We all say the same thing when we haven't won it yet — Dean [Smith] said it, Mike [Krzyzewski] said it, I said it, and now Roy is saying it: 'It isn't that big a deal, I won't be a better coach if I win it, I'm not losing sleep over it.' You know what? We're all wrong. It *is* a big deal and you just can't know how big a deal it is until it happens." He smiled. "It's a little bit like parenting. People can describe it to you all you want, but you can't understand it until you experience it."

In a sense, it was good for Roy Williams to be coaching a different team and school in this Final Four than in the past. His players were certainly aware of his last-weekend failures at Kansas, but they hadn't lived them with him, hadn't been there to feel the acute disappointment. They had dealt with their own set of crises: the three seniors on the team had been freshmen during the 8–20 year, and the seniors and the juniors had lived through the Doherty-to-Williams coaching change. In fact, the media rarely brought up to the players the question of Williams's winning a Final Four. That would not have been the case had he still been at Kansas.

In an experienced Final Four group of coaches, Williams was making his fifth appearance, as was Rick Pitino, and Tom Izzo his fourth. But Pitino and Izzo each had a title. Williams was also the most superstitious coach in the group. Since his team had bused from Chapel Hill to Charlotte for the first weekend of the tournament and been successful, Williams had had the same bus driven up to Syracuse. Now it was in St. Louis. Carolina had an off-season trip scheduled for the Bahamas. One had to wonder how Williams would get the bus *there* if they won in St. Louis.

"One thing I think has really changed in the last ten years is that there's no clear-cut favorite or clear-cut underdog any-more," Boeheim said on Saturday afternoon as he prepared to leave for the arena. "You go back ten or fifteen years ago, there was almost always one team people were saying should win and there was almost always one team most people didn't think could win. Look at these four teams. Sure, you have to give an edge to Carolina and to Illinois, but will anyone be shocked if Louisville and Michigan State win tonight? I don't think so. You get here, you're playing well. Everyone going out there tonight thinks they're going to win."

A lot of coaches were walking over to the arena, a ten- or fifteen-minute jaunt from the hotel. Others were taking buses that would drop them at the front door. One ex-coach waiting for a bus was George Raveling, who had coached successfully at Washington State, Iowa, and Southern California before leaving coaching in 1994 after health problems. He did some radio and TV work and then became the honcho of Nike basketball, tak-ing over after Sonny Vaccaro, who had first come up with the idea of paying coaches a lot of money to put themselves and their teams in Nike gear, jumped to Adidas. (Vaccaro has since jumped again, to Reebok.) Raveling once worked at Maryland for Lefty Driesell and was an assistant coach to Bob Knight at the '84 Olympics and to John Thompson at the '88 Olympics. So he has plenty of stories to tell about people in basketball.

But his most interesting story has nothing to do with basket-ball or basketball coaches.

That's because sitting in George Raveling's house are the original notes from which Martin Luther King Jr. read his "I Have a Dream" speech in Washington, D.C., on August 28,

1963. Raveling was a young assistant coach at the time, having grown up in Washington, from where he had gone on to play at Villanova. He was home in Washington on the day of the rally and was planning to attend. He was walking around the Mall early in the morning with a friend when someone walked up and asked him if he might be available to serve as one of Dr. King's bodyguards that afternoon. Raveling is six foot five and in those days was a lean twenty-four-year-old still in basketball-playing shape. "I guess they didn't have anything formal the way they do nowadays and they just wanted some big guys to be around Dr. King," he said. "I said yes, sure I'd do it, and the guy told me to report someplace at a specific time. We walked onto the podium with Dr. King, and I just stood behind him with several other guys while he was speaking.

"It wasn't hard to tell that something extraordinary was going on. I listened in awe while he spoke. When it was over, he just started to walk away and I noticed he had left his speech notes sitting there on the lectern. I picked them up and I said, 'Dr. King, do you want these?' He said, 'No, you can go ahead and keep them. Maybe they'll be worth something someday.'"

Raveling laughed at the memory. "I read through them later, they're pretty readable, and nowhere did I find the words 'I Have a Dream.' That must have just come to him while he was speaking, I guess. A few years ago someone offered me six million dollars for them and I said no. I'm hanging on to them. Someday I'll give them to my son. If he wants to sell them, he can. But I won't do it."

Raveling was one of the first African American coaches to have consistent success, taking all three schools he coached to the NCAA Tournament. He never got past the Sweet Sixteen and didn't achieve the fame or notoriety of John Thompson or, later, Nolan Richardson, African American coaches who went to multiple Final Fours and won the national championship. But he is one of basketball's most respected and best-liked figures, someone who knows everyone and is known by everyone. When he was still coaching, he was consistently one of the captains of the "all-lobby" team, the unofficial group put together every year by observers consisting of those who spent the most time hanging out in the lobby.

"It was how you learned," Raveling said. "John [Thompson] and I used to argue every year about who the all-lobby captain was, because it was almost always one of us. Now I have to spend a lot of time up in the [Nike] suite. It isn't the same. Times change."

They certainly do. Having been where he was on that August afternoon in 1963, Raveling can certainly attest to that.

What may be the most amazing thing about major sporting events post-9/11 is that everyone does eventually get into the building. People are allowed to arrive earlier nowadays because security checks make getting in a much more complicated process. Even the players go through security checks, though not nearly as thorough as those performed on everyone else. If you have a lapel pin that shows you are part of a team's official party — players, coaches, managers, trainers, doctors — you are usually waved through pretty quickly.

"It was a lot easier getting in last year than this year," Georgia Tech coach Paul Hewitt said as he waited to go through a security check. In 2004 Hewitt's team played in the championship game. In St. Louis he was just a spectator. "It's a lot harder to go back to watching after you've been in it than it is to watch when you've never been in it," he said. "I can certainly understand why coaches who have been a few times don't want to come when their team isn't in. This isn't easy."

Mike Krzyzewski had skipped Final Fours in the past when Duke didn't make it. Like his mentor, Bob Knight, he found it tough to be there when he wasn't competing, for the same reasons Hewitt found it tough — only more so because of his visibility. "When you've been a few times, people sort of expect you to be there," he said. "So, when you're not, even in a year like this one, where it really wasn't reasonable for us to expect to make it, you know a lot of people are going to ask, 'What went wrong?' Some years that's a legitimate question when you don't make it. Other years it isn't."

Krzyzewski had just completed one of his most gratifying years in coaching. After his team's devastating loss to Connecticut in the 2004 semifinals, he had been rocked by freshman Luol Deng's decision to turn pro. He had expected Deng, who was a good student, to stay at Duke for at least two years or perhaps even three before turning pro. But Deng's family, after hearing that he would be a lottery pick, wanted him to take the money while it was there. Deng ended up being the seventh pick in the draft and had played well in Chicago as a rookie before getting injured.

Krzyzewski had expected to lose one starter, point guard Chris Duhon. When Deng decided not to return, he had lost two. Then, when high school star Sean Livingston, who had been slated to fill Duhon's spot at the point, decided not to go to college at all, Krzyzewski found himself without a point guard and two holes he hadn't counted on. This wasn't brand-new to him — since 1999, when three underclassmen left, Duke has lost more underclassmen to the draft than any other major program. Krzyzewski learned after 1999, when Elton Brand left (as expected) and William Avery and Corey Maggette left (unexpectedly), to try to prepare for early defections. "If they're lottery picks, it's hard for them to say no to that kind of money," Krzyzewski said. "I don't always think it is the best thing for them. But they aren't always going to listen to me."

To some degree, Krzyzewski is a victim of his own success: not only in recruiting top players but in sometimes making them look better than they actually are — at least in terms of pro potential. Mike Dunleavy was taken with the third pick in the draft, Avery (who is now out of the league) the fourteenth pick, and Jason Williams (who was badly hurt in a motorcycle accident and may never play again) second. About the only Duke player who has ever been *under*rated was Carlos Boozer, who didn't go until the second round because he was considered a center in a forward's body. He has become a very good (and wealthy) player.

Duke started the 2004–05 season not picked in the ACC's top three for the first time in years and not picked in the national top ten for the first time in just as long. But with J. J. Redick emerging as a much better all-around player, Shelden Williams becoming a force inside, and Krzyzewski squeezing minutes out of freshmen like DeMarcus Nelson and David McClure, Duke finished a strong third in the ACC and then won the ACC Tournament to finish 25–5 and earn a number one seed in the NCAAs. Some thought Krzyzewski had done his best coaching job even after Michigan State had "upset" the Blue Devils in the round of sixteen. Duke had now reached the sixteens for eight straight seasons. No one else had a string going of longer than three years.

After missing several Final Fours, Krzyzewski had decided

years earlier that he should show up with or without his team. There were meetings he felt he should attend and people he should see. He also decided to pick up on an old Knight tradition by getting all of "his guys" together for dinner one night. Before Knight stopped holding them, Knight's dinners had grown almost massive, because they included ex-players and assistant coaches, old friends, fishing buddies — anyone in town who knew Knight was invited. Krzyzewski's dinners were a little more exclusive: you had to have coached under him or played under him.

"You know, when I first came up with the idea, I didn't give it much thought, it just seemed like a fun thing to do — in part, to take my mind off not having a team to coach during the weekend," he said. "But now, having done them a few times, I realize that they mean a lot more to me than just an enjoyable evening. When I look around during these dinners, I see the people who have shaped my life — outside of my family — and brought me to where I am. These are the guys who had the faith to choose me as their coach — some of them when doing that was a big gamble — and were willing to come work for me, some of them after they played for me, some not. In a sense, it's a way of having my team with me at the Final Four even when that year's team isn't playing. I know that sounds corny, but it's true."

Krzyzewski's dinner was scheduled for 7:30 on Saturday night, just a few minutes before the scheduled tip-off of the North Carolina–Michigan State game. "It was the only time we could get a reservation," he said, smiling.

No doubt that was true. And who would want to eat dinner at, say, 5:30. "We'll drink a toast to Carolina," Krzyzewski said.

He didn't mention what he would say in that toast.

*   *   *

An hour before tip-off of the Louisville-Illinois game, it was quickly becoming apparent that this was going to be a Final Four in which, even playing in a dome, one school would have a home-court advantage. It appeared that almost all of the seats upstairs had been bought by people wearing Illinois blue and orange. Downstairs was divided the way it always is: four sections with the big-bucks fans who had bought their tickets through the school allotments, and then several sections filled with coaches and the NCAA and CBS's corporate guests. Or as they liked to call them at CBS and the NCAA, their "corporate champions."

These matchups may have been as eagerly anticipated as any in recent Final Four history, if only because the previous weekend's regional finals had been so remarkable. North Carolina's victory over Wisconsin had been decided in the final minute, and that had been the most one-sided of the four games. In fact, it was the only one that didn't go into overtime. Louisville had come from 22 points down in the first half to beat West Virginia — the most surprising final eight team in the field — in overtime in the opening game on Saturday. Most people thought that one would be the game of the weekend. Except later that evening, Illinois had pulled its impossible escape against Arizona, coming from 15 points down in the last four minutes and then winning in overtime. Clearly *that* game wouldn't be topped. Only Kentucky–Michigan State (following Carolina's "rout" of Wisconsin on Sunday) went double overtime, reaching overtime after the officials spent more than ten minutes watching replays of Kentucky's Patrick Sparks's shot at the buzzer that (a) hit the rim twice before going in, (b) came either just before or just after the buzzer, and (c) was released with his toe either just on or just off the three-point line.

Remarkably, the officials got the call exactly right after watching the play in super slow-motion from every conceivable angle: Sparks was an inch (maybe less) outside the three-point line and he had released the ball with just about one-tenth of a second left. It can be said, without exaggeration, that millions of people around the country sat transfixed at dinnertime, watching the replay over and over exactly as the officials were watching it.

When overtime began, it was almost impossible to believe that Michigan State could recover and still win the game. The Spartans fell behind, rallied, and then fell behind once more in the second overtime. Again they rallied, and this time they hung on to win what has to be considered one of the great games in tournament history.

That was the backdrop as the Jones Dome began to fill up. With the exception of some seats in the fat-cat Michigan State and North Carolina sections, it was full by the time Illinois and Louisville tipped off. Sitting in his front-row seat on press row, covering the Final Four for a thirty-third straight year, Dick Weiss of the *New York Daily News* was amazed by how he felt as the final seconds ticked off the clock before the player introductions began. "I still get chills," he said. "All these years, all these games, it is still the only event in sports that makes me tingle just before it starts."

A lot of people feel that way about Saturday. It has now become such a big deal for a team just to get there — winning four games is never easy — and the hype throughout the week makes that moment when the games finally begin and the hype ends special. The NCAA tries to choreograph everything. In the "game itinerary" that the teams are given, this line is included:

"After the coaches are introduced, they are to walk to the scorer's table and shake hands." As staged as it all is, the building is still electric, and everyone — even those in the upper reaches of the dome — feels that electricity. Almost everyone feels the exact same thing as the first game begins: *Boy, am I lucky to be here.* Or as Bill Bradley once said of the way he felt before playing in the seventh game of the NBA finals: "There is no place on earth I would rather be at this moment than right here, doing what I'm about to do."

That's the way the Final Four feels just before tip-off on Saturday night.

Sometimes, much like the Super Bowl, the games don't (or can't) live up to the hype. That turned out to be the case in 2005. The games were similar to each other. In the opener, Louisville stayed close to Illinois until almost midway through the second half, trailing by just 50–49 with 10:04 left. But the Illini, a veteran team built around three guards — Dee Brown, Luther Head, and Deron Williams — who kept firing three-point shots all night, finally wore the Cardinals down, outscoring them 22–8 in the game's final 10 minutes. The last five minutes were little more than Louisville shooting threes and fouling to try to slow the game down, to no avail. The final was 72–57. The best moments of the second half came during the (endless — almost three minutes apiece) TV time-outs during which the Illinois band began playing the Michigan State fight song to try to get the Michigan State fans to pull for them — one Big Ten group pulling for another. The tactic worked. The green-and-white-clad fans, who had been watching the game quietly, responded to the familiar music and chimed in with the Illinois fans — not that Illinois really needed more support.

During the second game, the Illinois fans returned the favor, pulling quite noisily for Michigan State. This was for two reasons: the support showed by the Michigan State fans for their team, and — more important — their understanding that their chances of winning the national championship on Monday night would be greatly enhanced if they were to play the Spartans instead of the Tar Heels. For twenty minutes it looked as if they might get their wish. A drive straight to the basket by MSU's Kelvin Torbert through a defense that appeared stuck in cement put Tom Izzo's team ahead, 27–25, with 5:44 left in the half. At halftime it was 38–33, Shannon Brown's layup in the final minute upping the margin to five.

The buzz of upset ran through the building.

It didn't last. Roy Williams decided on his way to the locker room that this was not the time to stay calm, to soothe frazzled nerves. This was the time to let his team have it, to tell his players they were being outplayed, outhustled, and — most of all — outfought in a Final Four game. "I really let them have it," he said later. "I was angry and I needed them to understand why I was angry. We'd worked so hard to get where we were, we couldn't just throw it away without putting it all on the line. If they put it all out there and got beat by a better team, fine. I'm disappointed, but I can live with it. This, I couldn't live with."

Wes Miller hadn't heard his coach this angry very often during the season. Then again, he thought, neither he nor his team had been in this position before. "It was the first time since we got to the point where it was 'lose and go home' where we had played poorly in the first half," he said. "Coach wanted to make sure we understood the consequences of playing another half like that one."

Clearly, they got the message. The Tar Heels scored the first six points of the second half to take the lead, 39–38. The game seesawed to 49–49 with 15:17 left. At that point Carolina exploded, scoring 12 straight points. No one knew it, since there were still twelve minutes to go, but the game was over. A Torbert three made it 61–52, but Sean May answered immediately with a rebound basket and Michigan State never got to within single digits again. Carolina just had too many weapons, especially with senior Jawad Williams, who had struggled for most of the tournament, shooting 9 for 13 and producing 20 points and 8 rebounds. It was tough enough stopping May (22 points), Rashad McCants (17), and Raymond Felton (16 points, 7 assists). Throw in a hot Williams and Michigan State had no chance.

As Carolina pulled away, word reached the Krzyzewski party at Kemoll's Restaurant that their archrivals were in control of the game. "I'd like to propose a toast," Krzyzewski said, holding up a glass of wine. "This is to all of you who have played for me. From here going forward you will always be known as 'Coach K's players BC.'"

Everyone held up their glasses and waited for the punch line. "BC," Krzyzewski repeated. "Before Commercial."

With Carolina comfortably ahead, Wes Miller got in for the game's final minute. This was his turn to tingle. "Coming out of the tunnel was an unbelievable feeling before the game," he said. "We'd played in big places before big crowds in big games during the season. But this just felt different. Then the first half was such a disappointment. But the way we turned it around and then to get into the game was just unbelievable. It's a memory I'll always treasure."

Miller didn't shoot — Williams didn't want his team trying to score at that point — but he made the box score in a Final Four game. At the very least he matched Dean Smith — and he wouldn't have to call the NCAA to tell them to make a correction. He was there when the final box was handed out, just below another walk-on, Charlie Everett, and just above Marvin Williams, who would be the second pick in the NBA draft in a couple of months.

When the game was over — final, 87–71 — Williams was direct with his team again in the locker room: "If you play on Monday night the way you played the first half tonight, we have no chance to win," he said. "If you play the way you did in the second half, there's no one in the country who can beat us. It's that simple."

It was also this simple: Illinois — ranked number one at the end of the regular season — vs. North Carolina — ranked number two at the end of the regular season — for the national championship. It was the first time since 1975 (UCLA vs. Kentucky) that the regular season's top two teams had made it to the championship game.

Louisville and Michigan State had both had memorable seasons. Clearly, though, the better teams had won on Saturday. There was no doubt that the two best teams in the country would play for the title.

There was only one question left now to be answered: which one was the best?

The answer wouldn't come until Monday night.

14

The Long Wait

UNTIL 1968 THE FINAL FOUR WAS, for all intents and purposes, a forty-eight-hour event. Teams would fly in on Thursday, and the semifinals would be played on Friday night. The finals were on Saturday night, and everyone would head home on Sunday morning. Bill Bradley's description of his final college game sums it up well: "We played, took a shower, ate a cheeseburger, and flew home to New Jersey the next morning."

It isn't anything like that anymore. In 1968, the first year that NBC televised the event on network TV (before that it had been syndicated to markets that had an interest), the championship game was moved to Saturday afternoon because it wasn't a big enough event to merit prime time on a network. That made it impossible to play the semifinals on Friday, since the teams would then have only about fourteen hours prior to the finals. So the semifinals were moved to Thursday. Five years later NBC decided to take a chance and move the final to Monday night in prime time. But it still wanted games to be played on Saturday afternoon. So the semifinals were moved into the Saturday afternoon slot occupied by the finals (there were still two games on the last day then, since the consolation game didn't go away until 1982).

Which created what everyone in college basketball now calls the Wait.

It isn't that teams aren't accustomed to having forty-eight hours between games. In fact, the two teams playing for the title have already been through two similar weekends, playing either Thursday/Saturday or Friday/Sunday in their regionals. But this is different. For one thing, as Wes Miller pointed out, there are only so many movies that can be ordered on hotel television systems. For another thing, this is the third straight weekend they have spent away from home, cooped up in a hotel, waiting to play. More than anything, though, is the pressure. Everyone knows what Monday night means. Playing in the championship game is something every player dreams about, every coach wishes for. When it becomes real and you have to wait . . . and wait . . . the forty-eight hours between games feels like an eternity.

"I remember waking up on Sunday morning after we beat UNLV and being ready to go out and play," said Bruce Buckley, recalling his experience with the Wait in 1977 while a North Carolina senior. "Every hour waiting, even if you were lying down, you could just feel the energy draining out of you. After a while you find yourself thinking, 'Are they *ever* going to play this darned game?'"

The players and coaches aren't the only ones who feel that way. A lot of people leave town on Sunday; others stay for the coaches' dinner on Sunday night and leave on Monday morning. If you peruse the coaches' section on Monday night, you aren't likely to see many of the game's stars. Jim Boeheim is always there, and coaches who have a friend in the game might stay. Most of the big shots get out of town on Sunday or early Monday. They have had enough.

"You come in on Wednesday or Thursday and you're usually

happy to see people," Maryland coach Gary Williams said. "You might spend time in the lobby; you talk to old friends. You go out Thursday and Friday and probably stay out too late. By Saturday, you're tired but you want to see the games — even though it's a lot tougher to sit there and watch when you've been in them before. Even so, that's okay. But by Sunday, it's time to go. You know you've got work to do at home. You watch on Saturday and think, 'I need to get our team better so I'm not here watching again next year.' It's fun to go most of the time, but you reach a point where you just feel like you're done."

Williams had taken Maryland to the Final Four in 2001 and 2002. After his team lost in the round of sixteen in 2003, the shock of not getting back to the Final Four didn't hit him until he checked in to his hotel in New Orleans. "For the first time in three years," he said, "I used my real name at check-in. It didn't matter if anyone called. I had no work to do."

The fans of the two losing teams on Saturday usually clear out of town on Sunday, too. The best time to buy tickets for Monday night is right after the games on Saturday, when fans of the two losers come streaming out of the dome looking to dump their Monday tickets. Most accept face value if you simply take the tickets off their hands so they can start planning their escape. Few fans want to stick around and watch the team they have just lost to play for the national title. One of the few exceptions was in 2001, when many Maryland fans stayed in Minneapolis to root heartily and often angrily *against* Duke in the final.

The city was considerably quieter on Sunday — especially in the morning, when most people were still sleeping in since the second game on Saturday didn't end until after eleven o'clock eastern time and clocks were set forward by an hour early Sunday morning for daylight saving time. If you see people on the streets early on Sunday morning at the Final Four, it is for one of three reasons: (1) they're on their way out of town, (2) they still haven't gotten back from Saturday night yet, or (3) they're morning people who can't sleep in no matter how late they've been up the night before.

Other than the players and coaches of the two teams in the final, there is one group that always stays in town until Tuesday morning: the media. Most are happy to do so, even though the weekend can get long for them, too. They arrive on Wednesday and Thursday, and because of the way the event has grown, they have much less to write about than they did years ago, when the event was smaller.

"My first one was in 1970, Cole Field House," said Dick Weiss of the *New York Daily News*. "I can remember after practice on Friday, Coach [John] Wooden came over and just sat in the stands and talked for about half an hour. There couldn't have been more than twenty-five of us there. If you wanted a player one-on-one, you just went and got him."

Like a lot of veteran writers, Weiss understands that times change and that all events in sports have grown to the point where intimacy is nothing more than a memory. Once upon a time, the White House press corps would pile into the Oval Office once a day to chat with the president. To some who have covered basketball for a long time, the growth of the Final Four is something they have mixed emotions about. On the one hand, they're pleased to see their sport appreciated and its popularity has been good for them professionally. On the other hand, they grimace when in the massive Friday press conferences a columnist who hasn't seen a basketball game all season asks Sean May what it means to follow in his father's footsteps as a basketball player, a question May has been answering since high school.

Dick Weiss is known to everyone in basketball — including his wife — as "Hoops" for the simple reason that basketball has been his greatest passion, dating back to his boyhood, when he grew up in Philadelphia following the Big Five. Weiss started going to Big Five games when he was ten, riding the el downtown from Sixty-ninth Street to Thirty-fourth Street with a group of friends from St. Bernadette's CYO, where he first learned the game. In those days Saturday doubleheaders were routine, with the Big Five teams playing not only one another but national teams who wanted to come in and play in the Palestra. Weiss loved the games and the atmosphere and to this day can recite the names of all the great Big Five players of the late '50s and early '60s. "I especially loved the '61 St. Joe's team that Jimmy Lynam was a sophomore on," he said. "I remember them getting to the Final Four and losing to Ohio State in the semifinals but then beating Utah in four overtimes in the consolation game to finish third in the country. That was a big deal.

"Then, a week later, we started hearing stories that the New York District Attorney's Office was investigating several of the players for point shaving. That was the beginning of what I call the Curse of Philadelphia. If you look at the NCAA official record book for 1961, it reads 'vacated' for third place — which is where St. Joe's is supposed to be. Then you go ten years further to 1971 and second place is vacated because of Villanova and Howard Porter."

Howard Porter was the star of the Villanova team that shocked an undefeated (28–0) Penn team in the regional final, beating the Quakers, 90–47, after having lost five straight games to their Big Five rival. Weiss was working at the *Trenton Times* by then, having graduated from Temple in 1969. It was there that he first acquired the "Hoops" nickname from friends because of his devotion to basketball at all levels. In the last game of his senior year, Temple beat Boston College in the NIT final (the NIT was still a big deal back then), ruining Bob Cousy's exit from Boston College as coach but turning Weiss's exit from Temple as a student into a celebration. Weiss was thrilled to be working in Trenton in '71 when the two Philadelphia teams hooked up with a trip to the Final Four at stake.

"It was just shocking the way Villanova dominated them, because Penn was vurry, vurry good." (Like most Philadelphians, Weiss always says *vurry* instead of *very*, and almost always says it twice when describing something.) "We thought they were the Final Four team from the city. The worst part for Penn was that both teams flew home on the same plane. In the meantime, the Villanova students marched on the Penn campus to celebrate. A week later, when they beat Western Kentucky [in double overtime] to get to the championship game, they marched on the Penn campus again."

The marching ended soon after that. UCLA beat Villanova to win its fifth straight title, and shortly thereafter it was revealed that Porter had signed a contract with the American Basketball Association (which at the time was competing with the NBA for players) and had forfeited his eligibility. "The Curse of Philadelphia, part two," Weiss said.

Weiss moved to the *Philadelphia Daily News* in 1974, first covering high schools and later covering both the Big Five and the Philadelphia 76ers. He enjoyed covering the NBA playoffs, but his true love was always college basketball. As a sideline, he ran one of the first basketball camps for girls, to the point where in the 1980s, when women's basketball began to catch on at the college level, it seemed as if every star player had once been one of Weiss's campers.

Not surprisingly, Weiss's favorite Final Four memory is 1985, when Villanova not only won the championship but managed to keep its name in the record books after it was over. "To cover a team that actually won it was a thrill," Weiss said. "I'd be lying if I told you I was unaffected by it. People say a lot of things now about Rollie [Massimino] and what happened afterwards — and a lot of them are true — but the fact is, the guy could really coach and he had built a wonderful program that peaked at just the right moment."

Villanova was no fluke. The Wildcats had reached the final eight in both 1982 and 1983, losing to powerhouses both years: North Carolina with Michael Jordan, James Worthy, and Sam Perkins in '82 and the Hakeem Olajuwon–led Houston team a year later. Their victory in 1985 was one of the great upsets in the history of the Final Four, and Weiss not only got to fly home with the team the next morning but was actually in the victory parade, riding on the same flatbed truck on the ride from the airport to City Hall as the players and coaches. "To see the people lining the streets that way was amazing," he said. "I looked at the players and had to pinch myself because this was a team that barely squeezed into the tournament [eighth seed] and then had to play Dayton at Dayton in the first round. I remember going out there thinking I'd fly someplace else for the weekend after Villanova lost on Friday."

Weiss left the *Philadelphia Daily News* in 1992, the same year that Massimino left Villanova — though the circumstances were different. Massimino fled to UNLV, hoping to start anew after Villanova was never able to climb to the heights of '85 again. Weiss was offered a job by the *New York Daily News* as its national college basketball writer (few papers have a full-time national writer) and agreed to take the job only if the paper allowed him to continue to live in Philadelphia — which he does to this day. It was right around then that Weiss began to feel as if the Final Four had grown out of control.

"I think it was '94 in Charlotte that it really hit me," he said. "The city just couldn't handle the event, it was too big. When President Clinton came, no one could get to the arena. I began to look around and notice a lot of what I call 'event' guys. Some of them came because they had to do TV or radio from the Final Four. Others came because it has become an event, like the Super Bowl or the World Series or the Masters. I knew it was bad when I heard guys complaining before the games started on Saturday that they were actually missing a few days of spring training to be at a basketball game. *Spring training?* Are you kidding me? The NCAA has all these rules about newspapers and TV and radio stations having to have covered a certain number of games during the season to get credentialed. They ought to have that same rule for columnists."

Or perhaps a test of some kind: if you can't name Mike Krzyzewski's three daughters (who have been on TV about as often as David Letterman the past twenty years), you can't cover the Final Four. Or perhaps you should be required to know why Roy Williams always claps for the other team's starters when they're introduced. (Because, as with most things Williams, Dean Smith always did it.) One person who would pass any or all tests is Bill Brill, a proud graduate of the Duke class of 1952, who has covered almost as many Final Fours (forty-eight) as Rich Clarkson. There's no doubting his allegiance to Duke — he retired to Durham in 1992 after a distinguished career as the sports editor and columnist of the *Roanoke Times and World News* — but to simply label Brill a "Duke guy," as many people do, is a great oversimplification. For one thing, his wife, Jane, graduated from North Carolina and Brill has always gotten along well with both Dean Smith and Roy Williams. More important, Brill probably has a better understanding of the basketball tournament historically and in terms of how it has evolved than anyone in the sport — including the members of the committee. In fact, it is a long-standing Saturday night tradition at the ACC Tournament that Brill unveils *his* tournament bracket about eighteen hours before the committee unveils its bracket. Brill is so precise in announcing his brackets, placing teams into specific regional and subregional sites, that in years past there have been occasions when young reporters who don't understand the process have actually believed that Brill's bracket was the real one and began making travel plans before gently being told that the Brill bracket wasn't quite as official as they thought.

Maybe it should be. Brill puts together his bracket based not so much on what he thinks is right as on what he thinks the committee will do — and *should* do, based on past history, all the various rules about who can play whom, RPI/quality wins/road wins, and how a team finishes. Brill sticks to these rules better than the committee does and knows all of them cold. He certainly knew in 2003 that Brigham Young couldn't go in a bracket to play a Sunday game and he also had Arizona and Kentucky opposite each other in the draw. In 2005 he had Kentucky as the fourth number one seed — before its loss on Sunday — and Louisville as a number two. Like everyone else, he was stunned when the committee opted to make Washington a number one and Louisville a number four — and was proved right when Louisville easily beat Washington in the round of sixteen.

Brill usually has almost the same field as the committee — "They get one wrong every now and then," he says, not kidding — and more often than not, his seedings and bracketing are very similar to the committee's. All kidding aside, his bracket often makes more sense than the committee's. Which calls into question all the time and money that is spent by the NCAA on the committee. The group meets four times a year: in the summer to review the previous year's tournament; in December to begin preparing for that season's tournament; in February to put together a "mock" bracket; and then for five days in early March to put the field together. There are ten committee members, innumerable NCAA staffers, reams and reams of computer printouts.

After all of that time and money and hours and hours of staff work, the end result is virtually the same as that produced by a retired sportswriter working by himself, fortified by several beers and cheered on by a few friends during Saturday night dinner at the ACC Tournament.

Perhaps just as silly is the absolute secrecy the committee insists upon during its deliberations. Although the information leaks out every year, committee members don't like to talk about how the teams left out ranked and how early (or late) they were removed from consideration. The committee members insist — quite angrily at times — that politics never enters into the equation. There are all sorts of rules about committee members having to leave the room if the school they work for or even a school from their conference is being discussed in earnest. Are we supposed to believe that the other nine members don't *know* what the missing member thinks? In 2005 the committee was chaired by Iowa athletic director Bob Bowlsby. As luck would have it, three teams from Iowa were on the bubble — Iowa, Iowa State, and Northern Iowa — and all three got into the field. When someone jokingly asked Bowlsby if he was planning to run for governor of Iowa, he didn't even crack a smile: "Obviously I had nothing to do with those three institutions [committee members insist on calling colleges *institutions,* just as they ludicrously insist on calling players *student-athletes*] getting into the field," he said.

Almost undoubtedly he didn't. And just as probably, they all deserved their slots. But by acting as if the future of the planet is at stake when they walk into their conference room, the committee members make people suspicious of their actions. In the past when it has been suggested to them that a pool reporter be allowed to sit in on the deliberations, most committee members have reacted as if someone had suggested they fly coach for the rest of their lives. "Not gonna happen" is the standard answer.

Why not? Congress's deliberations are public and frequently on TV. Murder trials are frequently televised these days. Ten people are selecting sixty-five teams for a basketball tournament. They insist there are no politics involved, that no one is ever given a break — good or bad — that they are America's ten most honorable people. Okay, fine. Let one reporter sit in for the weekend. Specifically, why not let Bill Brill, who probably knows the rules better than anyone on the committee, sit in. Heck, if he had been there in 2003, he might have been able to whisper in someone's ear and the Arizona/Kentucky and Brigham Young debacles would have been avoided. More important, when the committee members report that the presence of Bowlsby as chairman had nothing to do with the Iowa teams getting in or when they say that Charlotte got into the field as a number nine seed in 2002 (when it had been on the bubble) because it deserved that seeding, not because Charlotte athletic director Judy Rose was on the committee, there would be an outsider to vouch for those statements.

Of course, the committee members insist they don't care what people think or that the media frequently speculates on politics influencing their decisions. And then they get angry every March when people question them.

It is all part of the tradition.

If Bill Brill is the Bracket King among the media, then Jim O'Connell is the King of Games. Sunday at the Final Four is tough on O'Connell, who has been the AP's lead college basketball writer since 1987, because there's no game to cover. "It's brutal," said O'Connell — Occ to everyone he knows — "all you've got are those endless press conferences."

If there's one thing everyone — players, coaches, media — agree on, it is that the worst day of the Final Four is Sunday and the worst part of Sunday is the press conferences. Like the rest of the Final Four, it has simply gotten to be too big — and too long. "How is it that we're scheduled to spend more time talking to the media than we are practicing?" Roy Williams asked, noting that he and his players were supposed to be with the media for an hour and forty-five minutes and on the practice floor for ninety minutes.

Years ago, the Sunday press conferences were an hour — and that was plenty. The five starters and the coach would sit up on a podium for thirty minutes and answer the usual desultory questions. Then the players would spread out around the room and talk to writers in small groups — sometimes as few as two or three writers with one player, because a lot of people would stay with the coach, who remained on the podium — and most of the electronic media would have the sound bites they needed and would leave. Now everything is formalized. After the first thirty minutes, the players are taken into separate rooms, where they are put on podiums with microphones. This does four things: makes life easier for TV people, who can set their cameras on the risers in the back of the room rather than scrambling for position if the player is talking more informally; almost guarantees that the answers will be stilted and clichéd, since the player is very aware of the cameras and the microphones being used not only by him but by the questioners; allows the NCAA to put its logo on the backdrop of everyone being interviewed; and gives each moderator the chance to say the NCAA's two favorite words, *student-athlete,* several dozen more times.

In truth, the Sunday press conferences — like most NCAA press conferences — are something out of a *Saturday Night Live* parody. They make a presidential news conference look informal; at least there, the president calls on questioners himself and tends to know many, if not most, of the reporters by name.

The NCAA — surprise — has very strict rules. You may not ask a question until someone brings you one of the roving microphones so that questions can be picked up on the satellite feed sent out by the NCAA, which is second to none when it comes to feeding trite answers to the outside world. You must identify yourself before asking a question, even a follow-up question. This is how the asking and answering of two questions can sound:

MODERATOR: Questions for the student-athletes. Yes, left
    side, second mike.
REPORTER: Sean, when you first got to North Carolina —
MODERATOR: Identify yourself, please.
REPORTER: Oh, right. Barry Svrluga from the *Washington
    Post.* . . . Sean, when you first got to North Carolina, the team
    had just gone 8–20; did you think when you got there, you
    guys would reach this point either this quickly — or ever?

SEAN MAY: We thought we had a lot of talent, and that talent just had to come together. It took us a while, but we knew we had the potential to get to where we are now.

REPORTER: Just to follow up, was there a game —

MODERATOR: *Identify* yourself, please.

REPORTER: Again?

MODERATOR: Yes.

REPORTER: Barry Svrluga. Sean —

MODERATOR: Please identify your publication also.

REPORTER (sighing): Barry Svrluga, still from the *Washington Post.* To try to follow up, was there a game this season when it hit you that you had turned a corner to becoming a very good basketball team? And Roy [Williams], could you answer the same question after Sean, please?

MODERATOR (interrupting May as he begins his answer): We're only taking questions for the student-athletes now. You can ask Coach Williams the question later.

This isn't even an exaggeration or an aberration. It is, in fact, typical. At least after the games, when everyone is on deadline, the press conferences don't last very long. Even on the Friday practice day the time on the podium is limited to fifteen minutes for the "student-athletes" and fifteen minutes for the coach. Sunday is torture for everybody.

"What you have to do on Sunday is already know from Saturday what you're going to write or who you're going to write about," O'Connell said. "If you just walk in there hoping a story is going to appear magically, you're going to be in a lot of trouble. And you're going to sit through a lot of very boring answers."

Very occasionally a Sunday story will magically appear — though not in recent years. In 1975 John Wooden stunned everyone on Saturday when he announced that the championship game would be his farewell. On Sunday he sat and talked to reporters about his decision and his coaching career. "Maybe twenty guys sitting around at a hotel pool," Dick Weiss remembered. "It was amazing. No moderator, no cameras, no one identifying themselves, just him sitting there talking."

In 1981 Bob Knight had made news late on Saturday night when he got into an altercation with a drunken fan and ended up stuffing him into a trash can. Coming two years after his confrontation with a Puerto Rican policeman at the Pan American Games, Knight, who desperately wanted to be the Olympic coach in 1984, was concerned about the incident overshadowing his quest for a second national championship. Prior to the Sunday press conferences, Knight asked Dean Smith if he would defend him (not about the incident, which Smith obviously hadn't witnessed, but on more general terms) in his press conference. Smith launched into a lengthy diatribe about how Indiana and North Carolina stood for what was right about college basketball, about how he and Knight insisted that players go to class and graduate and play by all of the NCAA rules. (He did make the mistake of referring to his players as *players* rather than *student-athletes*. No doubt he was reprimanded.) One reporter stood up at the end of Smith's monologue and asked him if he was saying that the final matchup was a triumph for truth, justice, and the American way.

Smith smiled. "I didn't say that," he said. "But if you want to write it that way, it would be fine."

In 1986 a shouting match broke out among media members during the Duke press conference. A number of writers had laughed about the brevity of the answers given by the Louisville players and had joked about Milt Wagner, the Cardinals' star guard, commenting that all he and his teammates had known about (first-round opponent) Drexel was that "they're one of those academic-type schools." The Duke players, by contrast, were loquacious and funny. At one point each of the starters was asked if he aspired to play in the NBA: "I'd give my left arm to play in the NBA," Jay Bilas answered. "But I don't think there's much call for one-armed players in that league."

In the back of the room, Mike Lupica, the superb columnist for the *New York Daily News,* and Charlie Pierce, the equally superb feature writer who was then with the *Boston Herald,* began railing at several writers who were praising the wit and charm of the Duke players. Lupica, a close friend of Larry Brown's, was still upset about a couple of critical calls that had gone Duke's way late in its victory over Kansas on Saturday. Pierce was upset because that is just his way. They began telling people that the reaction to the two teams was racial — which didn't really make much sense: Louisville had four black starters, Duke three.

"They're the Cosby kids," Lupica insisted, referring to the then popular TV show in which Bill Cosby played a well-to-do doctor whose kids were good-looking, smart, and spoiled. It got loud, even while the Duke players were still answering questions. The next day those who read newspapers in New York could see a prime example of how the same event could produce radically different viewpoints: Dave Anderson, the Pulitzer Prize–winning *New York Times* columnist, wrote about how remarkable it was to hear a group of players good enough to be 37–2 and in the national championship game express themselves in complete sentences while clearly enjoying the chance to address the nation's media. Lupica wrote about his colleagues wanting to embrace the "white" team and not understanding the backgrounds from which the Louisville players came.

There was a transitory moment in the sport's history during the 1989 Sunday press conferences when Seton Hall's P. J. Carlesimo mentioned that one of the reasons he felt close to Michigan coach Steve Fisher was that "we're both Nike schools." It was a great moment for branding, if not for the sport.

There hasn't been much to write home about — or to write about, period — since the formalization of the press conferences. In 2003 Roy Williams and Jim Boeheim were bombarded with questions about what it would mean to each of them to finally win a national championship: Williams had been in four Final Fours and two title games, Boeheim three and three. The two of them spent so much time insisting it didn't matter that you wondered why either would even bother showing up for the game the next night. The most ludicrous moment of the day came when Tom Izzo, working as a commentator for CBS, said he would readily change his record — which included the 2000 national title — for either Boeheim's or Williams's record. That's a little bit like saying being vice president for two terms is better than being president for one.

"I love being at the Final Four," O'Connell said. "But I don't love the press conferences. I don't think anyone on either side does."

If Weiss sounds like pure Philadelphia when he talks, O'Connell is as New York as it gets. He has a round Irish face, thinning black hair, and a quick smile. Growing up in Queens, he was a St. John's fan, often going to games at nearby Alumni Hall and to the college doubleheaders at Madison Square Garden. "I remember in '71 when Digger [Phelps] had the great Fordham team and beat Notre Dame in the Garden," he said. "Then he went to Notre Dame, and when he came back the next year we all chanted, 'Digger is a mercenary.' Hero to goat, just like that."

He went to St. John's and worked in the sports information office as a student, becoming friends with the legendary Lou Carnesecca. By the time he was a junior, O'Connell knew he didn't want a "regular job." He went to talk to Carnesecca, who set him up to work as a stringer for the Associated Press. He can still remember Gordon White, the *New York Times*'s longtime college basketball writer, showing up for a St. John's game with the first computer anyone had ever seen at a basketball game. "Fans just stood around behind him while he was writing because they had never seen anything like it," he said.

O'Connell worked for two years after graduation as the SID at Fordham, which is where he met his wife, Annie — who to this day is the all-time leading rebounder in women's college basketball history. "She finished with one thousand nine hundred and ninety-nine," O'Connell said. "In her last game she needed thirteen to get to two thousand. They were counting it down on the P.A. With three minutes left she gets the thirteenth rebound, but one of the refs calls her for going over the back — and it's her fifth foul."

That official would have made a great NCAA press conference moderator.

O'Connell begins most answers during his frequent radio appearances by saying, "Deffanaly," as in, "He's deffanaly a great player." Like Weiss, he is an absolute basketball purist. Every November the AP flies him to the Maui Invitational. O'Connell watches all twelve games — four a day for three straight days — writes about all of them, never puts on a short-sleeved shirt, and has never once been on the beach that is about twenty-five yards from the front door of his hotel room. "It's not what I'm there for," he said. "I'm there for two things: to watch basketball and to write about it."

O'Connell has three children, which makes his travel schedule from mid-November to early April difficult. Fortunately, Annie remains as big a fan as her husband, and O'Connell frequently takes the kids to games in the New York area. He loves covering Duke-Carolina but gets just about as much of a buzz covering Wagner–Long Island University. "I just like being in gyms," he said. "When I'm on the road and I'm on my way to a game or at a game, I'm having a great time. I get back to the hotel room, I miss my family."

O'Connell laughed when talk of how big the Final Four has gotten came up. "My first one was '79, Magic vs. Larry in Salt Lake," he said. "I remember the older writers talking about how it had gotten too big *then*. It's deffanaly lost its homey edge, you can't argue that. I miss being in real basketball arenas [the last nondome Final Four was in New Jersey in 1996] and the fact that you can't do real reporting when you're at the event. It's become what I call ASAP journalism. People just wait for the quote sheets."

ASAP (as soon as possible) is a business that has sprung up in the past ten years. At most major events now, ASAP supplies dictationists who transcribe every word of every press conference. The transcripts are handed out within minutes of the end of a press conference. ASAP is a boon to deadline-pressed reporters, especially in this era when TV has pushed starting times deeper and deeper into the night. But it does give many people an easy excuse never to go into a locker room or even attempt anything resembling reporting.

O'Connell has made a career of writing incisive leads with little time to think about what he is going to write. When Kansas won the national championship in 1988 — with the team dubbed "Danny and the Miracles" because Danny Manning was so clearly the team's star — O'Connell's lead that night said: "The one-man team is number one." He is very good at pithy descriptions of some of the basketball people he has dealt with over the years:

JIM BOEHEIM: Cynical, sarcastic, and misunderstood. You spend time with him, you're gonna be surprised because you're gonna like him.

JOHN THOMPSON: Imposing and often right.

DEAN SMITH: Complicated, tough, always finding an angle.

JOHN WOODEN: The man who never lost.

JIM CALHOUN: Intense and funny — often at the same time.

MIKE KRZYZEWSKI: The guy I wish I could be as good as.

ROY WILLIAMS: Dean Jr.

DICK VITALE: I enjoy talking to him on the phone more than listening to him on TV. On the phone, he's just Dick; on TV he's Dickie V.

BILLY PACKER: Honest — never gives in. Does it his way.

HOOPS: My alter soul. If you cut us both open, there would be basketballs bouncing around in there.

BILL BRILL: The guy who knows everything going on and will tell everyone what he knows.

O'Connell would probably describe himself this way: he's the guy who gets home from the Final Four after seeing 150 games in a season and sits down in front of the TV set on Tuesday night and feels lost because there's no basketball game to watch. "I pick up the remote and don't know what to do," he said, laughing. "All there is to watch is baseball. It kills me. For one night every year, I hate baseball."

O'Connell became the AP's lead basketball writer in 1987, succeeding a man named Dick Joyce, who had been on the beat for years. Joyce, a sweet, friendly man, called O'Connell over to his desk after he had been told the job was his. "Kid, I want to show you the key to success in your new job," Joyce said. O'Connell nodded, waiting for a sage piece of advice about how to deal with deadlines or coaches or writing game stories. Joyce led O'Connell over to a desk where newspapers were stacked. He picked up *USA Today* and opened it to the national weather map. Jabbing a finger at a section of the map covered in blue to show cold, and probably snowy, weather, Joyce said: "Stay out of the blue."

O'Connell has heeded that advice. "Except when the Alaska Shootout has a really good field," he said. "Then I have to go — blue or no blue."

15

The Music Stops

IF SUNDAY IS THE DAY when almost nothing happens at the Final Four, Monday is the day when everything happens — late. Very late. It is college basketball's longest day.

Television dictates a 9:22 P.M. eastern time start; in St. Louis that meant 8:22, which is a little better, but not much. The two teams playing in the championship game have now been in the same town and the same hotel for five days. On the biggest day of the players' lives, they have to wait for hours and hours. They can't go out and be tourists; it is too late for that. They don't really want to hear the coaches' scouting reports again. The opponent is always someone they are familiar with. Unlike the old days, when players could meet in the championship game without ever having seen one another play, players see the other top teams on TV constantly. And tapes of virtually every game they have played are available to them. If Raymond Felton didn't know what Dee Brown's game was about, or vice versa, by the time they stepped on the court on Monday night, something was very wrong.

Sean May had managed to get his hands on a DVD of Indiana's victory in the 1976 title game over Michigan. His father had been voted to the All-Tournament team of that Final Four.

He started watching it soon after breakfast on Monday morning, and by the time it was over, most of his teammates had wandered in for a look. "It was cool seeing my dad play in the game I was about to play in," he said later. "It helped get me ready to play."

Beyond that, everyone waited. The teams had their final walk-throughs and shootarounds at the dome in the middle of the day, the building locked up tight until three hours before tip-off, when spectators would be allowed to enter. The town had been taken over, or so it seemed, by Illinois fans. There were occasional pockets of people in baby blue and white walking around, but everywhere one looked was orange and blue. At one point in the afternoon, four fans dressed in orange and blue with their faces painted orange got on an elevator in the official hotel with Jack Kvancz, the George Washington athletic director and former committee member.

"So," Kvancz said with a straight face, "who are you guys pulling for tonight?"

There were still a few meetings going on. The U.S. Basketball Writers Association held its annual awards brunch. Like most of the other events held at the Final Four, this can be a drawn-out affair since almost everyone in basketball with any kind of official title is invited to speak. Most understand that the best speech is a short one: "Thanks for having me — anytime I can help, give me a call." Of course, there is always someone who feels the need to speak for fifteen minutes. The USBWA inducts new members into its Hall of Fame during the brunch. One year, one of the inductees spoke for about fifteen minutes and just when everyone thought he was finishing up, he said: "And so, to begin at the beginning . . ."

There have been some memorable moments at the brunch, too. The USBWA gives an annual "Most Courageous" award, and some of the winners have had remarkable stories to tell. In 1981 the winner was Mark Alcorn, who had been a walk-on at LSU and then had been stricken with cancer. He had come back to be part of the team after beginning cancer treatments. LSU had lost to Indiana in the semifinals that year on Saturday and had to play in the consolation game on Monday afternoon. Even so, Dale Brown brought his entire team to the brunch to be there for Alcorn. Even cynical reporters were moved by the sight of all the Tigers leading the applause for their stricken teammate.

The USBWA also presents what is called the Katha Quinn Award, given to someone in basketball who has greatly aided those who cover the sport. It can be an SID, someone who works for the NCAA, even a reporter. In 2002 the *Washington Post's* Mark Asher, who continued to cover college basketball after kidney and pancreas transplants, was given the award. One NCAA basketball committee chairman, Tom Frericks — the former Dayton athletic director — received the award. As chairman of the committee, Frericks, over the objection of both the NCAA's then media director and most of the committee, took the unheard-of step of agreeing to have committee members actually meet directly with the media. Until then, any requests from the media on issues such as telephone lines, locker-room access, or press conference scheduling had to be funneled through Dave Cawood, who was then the media director. Most of the time the answer to requests was simple and direct: No. When Jim Delany, Frericks's predecessor as committee chairman, was approached by the USBWA with the notion of direct contact, he reacted as if he had been asked to donate both his kidneys to Mark Asher. Out of the question, was his response. "Dave Cawood does a fine job representing the interest of the media to the committee," he wrote.

That was a little bit like saying that Karl Rove did a fine job of representing the interests of the Democratic Party in the White House.

One of Frericks's first acts when he succeeded Delany was to schedule a meeting with the USBWA. The two groups — committee and writers — have met regularly since then and the world has somehow remained spinning on its axis.

Most of the award winners have been very proud to win the Katha. That's because almost all of them knew Katha Quinn. She was St. Johns's SID, and one of the first women to hold that post at a big-time college basketball school. Part of her genius was in persuading writers to see the lovable side of her coach, Lou Carnesecca, as opposed to the paranoid side. "People forget that in 1985 when Louie made the Final Four, he kept his team as far away from Lexington as [Georgetown coach] John Thompson kept his team away," Dick Weiss likes to point out. "Louie was just more charming about it than John. And John never had Katha working for him."

Katha Quinn was one of those SIDs who figured out a way to make the answer yes even when the easy answer was no. Writers loved her for that. They also loved her for her sense of humor — she did a wicked Dean Smith imitation — and because she could drink most of them under the table and be at work ready to go first thing the next morning. There was really nothing that could slow Katha Quinn down.

Except cancer. When she was first stricken in 1987, no one really believed it. Or wanted to. She never stopped working. She would go for chemo in the morning and be at the press table that night. She was thin, she was drawn, she often looked horribly sick, but she was always there. And she was still Katha. She joked about her chemo and talked about all the different wigs she was planning to buy when her hair fell out. "I'm not gonna die," she would snarl at writers. "Louie would never forgive me."

As luck would have it, the USBWA had decided the year before to create an award to give people who had gone out of their way to help writers through the years. When it came time to discuss who the first winner should be, there really wasn't any discussion: Katha.

And so, on that morning of the Kansas-Oklahoma national championship game in Kansas City, the writers gathered for their brunch and went through all their annual rituals. The first class of USBWA Hall of Famers was inducted that year, with six very deserving men being honored. Arizona's Steve Kerr, who had been unrecruited as a high school senior, who had dealt with his father's assassination in Beirut as a college freshman, and who had come back from what had appeared to be a career-ending knee injury, was the Most Courageous winner. Kerr's speech was witty and emotional and most years would have easily been the highlight of the morning.

But that day he was upstaged by a woman who hadn't been sure she would be able to walk to the podium, a woman who was afraid she wouldn't have the strength to get through her speech. He was upstaged by a woman who would not be alive the next time the Final Four was played.

Her speech was, as her good friend Malcolm Moran, then of the *New York Times*, now of *USA Today*, liked to say, "pure Katha."

She was funny — as always — making fun of herself, talking about how she'd always wanted to lose weight but not this way. She told stories about writers and coaches and about *her* coach, Carnesecca, who sat a few feet away with tears streaming down his face. She talked about all the friends she had brought to "her fight" and how very much she loved St. John's and the players she had worked with.

By the time she finished, the room was utterly silent except for the quiet sounds of her friends all crying. People who had never met her before that day were crying, too. The standing ovation — once people collected themselves — lasted several minutes. The applause still rings in the ears of everyone who was there.

Soon after that day, the award she had received was given a name: the Katha Quinn Award. She died on the Sunday before the Final Four in 1989. St. John's dedicated its victory that week to her. Every year when the Katha is presented, those who were in Kansas City in 1988 flash back to that morning. Without fail, they laugh — and cry — all over again.

On Monday afternoon the coaches' hotel feels like a ghost town. The meetings are over. Most of the coaches have gone home. The few that linger are snapped up by the now-desperate radio producers. Even some of the radio people have gone home, knowing that what was *the* sports place to be on Thursday, Friday, and Saturday is now being dismantled. There are even people in the hotel who have no idea that a championship game will be played in town that night. They are here on business that has nothing to do with basketball.

Coaches will tell you that the most trying time before any game is the last few hours before tip-off. "You keep thinking about what you haven't done, that there must be something else to do," said Maryland coach Gary Williams. "Deep down, though, you know there's nothing. You just have to hope the players are ready. If there's any one thing that will drive me out of coaching, it is the waiting around on game day."

Williams was lucky in 2002, the day his Maryland team played for the national championship. His daughter, Kristen, had brought his then eighteen-month-old grandson with her to Atlanta, and since Maryland was staying out near the airport, the little boy spent most of the afternoon pointing out airplanes to his grandfather. "It made the game feel very far away," Williams said. "At least for a little while."

Every coach who reaches the championship game understands that what Al McGuire used to say is true: coaching on Monday night is something to be savored — at least until game time. But that becomes more difficult when you have been there and not yet won. "You reach a point," Jim Boeheim said, "where you don't want to wait anymore. You don't want to answer the questions anymore."

Bruce Weber could savor the day. He could look around and think about how far he had come in eight years to reach this moment in his life. Roy Williams would insist he could savor it, too. But this would be his third Monday night. Like Boeheim, he was tired of waiting. "I never thought that winning the national championship would make me a better coach," he said. "There is no question, though, that it makes you a coach people look at differently."

The players understand that the night is special — sort of. "I think they understand that it's a big deal because it has become such a big-time event," Bill Bradley said. "But I'm not sure there's any way for them to understand the long-term impact it will have on them. The short-term impact they understand: feeling great because they won or awful because they lost. But it takes time to really get a grasp on how much it meant to you to play. I still regret not having gotten to the last game, just as I know there are guys who got there and didn't win who think about it all the time."

Wes Miller, who knew he would play at a critical juncture only if his team was beset by injuries or foul trouble, felt as if he understood the significance of what was to come. "When I was a kid, playing in the Final Four was a dream," he said. "Each step of the way I had to stop and pinch myself to believe I was going through this experience. I felt it on Friday and again on Saturday. There was no question in my mind that running onto the floor on Monday night was going to be unlike anything I'd ever experienced in my life. And I had to take the approach — I think we all had to take the approach — that this was a once-in-a-lifetime thing. It could happen again, but it's certainly not something you can count on, especially after you've seen how tough it is to do once."

Years ago, when the teams ran onto the court for the championship game, Frank Fallon, who was the Final Four's P.A. announcer for twenty-three years, would say the following: "Ladies and gentlemen. On October fifteenth, 326 teams began practicing, each of them pointing for this night. Now, two are left. They are . . ."

It was always a thrilling moment when the names of the two schools were announced, especially by Fallon, who had one of the great P.A. voices of all time. For some reason — no one is quite sure why — that tradition has been abandoned, which is a shame. Still, players and coaches will tell you that there is nothing quite like the feeling of running onto the court on Monday night, knowing you are playing in the last game of the season, knowing you are about to be part of history, one way or the other. "You kind of know you're going to end up on [ESPN] Classic down the road when you play in the final," Shane Battier had said on the eve of his last game at Duke, the 2001 final. "You want it to be a game you can feel proud about having people watch for years to come."

For many years it seemed as if every championship game was a classic or near classic. In fact, from 1982 through 1989, the only game decided before the last minute was the Georgetown-Houston game in 1984, and that was still a compelling matchup: Patrick Ewing and Hakeem Olajuwon squaring off at center. That string ended in 1990, when UNLV beat Duke, 103–73 — the largest margin ever in a final. Since then, finals have blown hot and cold: Duke-Kansas in 1991 was taut until the last thirty seconds; Duke-Michigan a year later was a 20-point blowout. Carolina-Michigan in '93 was memorable because of Chris Webber's time-out that wasn't a time-out because Michigan was out of them, and Scotty Thurman hit the late three for Arkansas in its win over Duke the following year. Then came relatively easy victories for UCLA and Kentucky, followed by Arizona's spellbinding overtime win over Kentucky in 1997.

Since then, there have not been too many games worth remembering. UConn over Duke in '99 was a superb game, Duke over Arizona in '01 was a good one, and Syracuse holding off Kansas in '03 was very good. The others are remembered only by the fans of the teams that won, including UConn's blowout of Georgia Tech in 2004.

No one (except the coach or the fans on the winning side) wants a blowout on Monday night. It is bad for TV ratings, especially on the East Coast, where people simply go to bed if the game isn't competitive. It is bad for the fans in the arena. It is bad for the media, except perhaps some of the print reporters, who can start writing their stories early. Deadlines on Monday night, with the game ending not long before midnight eastern time, are brutal.

"It's hard to be very good when you have to hit the send button the instant the final buzzer sounds," Tony Barnhardt of the *Atlanta Journal-Constitution* said.

Carolina-Illinois had all the makings of a final everyone could feel good about. The two teams had a combined record of 69–5 coming into the game. One of Carolina's four losses had come in its opener against Santa Clara when point guard Raymond Felton didn't play. The other losses had been at Wake Forest, at Duke, and to Georgia Tech in the ACC Tournament. Illinois' only loss had been in the regular-season finale at Ohio State. Carolina was in the championship game for the seventh time; Illinois had never been there before.

The dome filled early. People didn't want to take a chance on having trouble getting in because of security lines, and since no one has very much left to do on Monday afternoon, they tend to arrive early — almost as if getting in the building early will somehow get the game started sooner. It never works out that way.

Like most major sports organizations, the NCAA likes to harp on patriotic themes in the post-9/11 world. No one has commercialized patriotism more than the NFL, but the NCAA isn't all that far behind. The playing of the national anthem featured the unleashing of a bald eagle, which fluttered down to the court a few feet away from where Wes Miller was standing. "It gave me chills," Miller said. "Just to be on the court, to see that eagle land, to be part of it in a small way. I remember I looked over at Coach [Joe] Holladay and he smiled at me as if to say, 'Yeah, this is really cool, isn't it?'"

Moments before they went on the air, Jim Nantz spotted a

flaw in the way Billy Packer's tie was tied and put his microphone under his arm to tighten it for him. Standing a few feet away, John Thompson, who was doing color on the radio broadcast, laughed as he watched Packer and then the two coaches as they walked onto the court. "I'll tell you the biggest change in coaching since I started," he said. "The way coaches dress. How much do you think Roy's suit cost? I guarantee you it's more than all the clothes I owned when I started at Georgetown. I never wanted to wear anything too nice anyway, because I knew I was just going to sweat right through the damn thing before the game was over."

Exactly how much Bruce Weber's outfit cost was a different question. He was wearing a bright Illinois-orange jacket that looked as if it would glow in the dark. If nothing else, he had to feel very secure to wear a jacket of that color, knowing millions of people would be watching him.

There is nothing quite like the tip-off of the national championship game. After all the waiting, all the hype, and all the pregame pomp, the scripted introductions, and the scripted coaches' handshake, by the time the players finally walk to center court and shake hands all around one more time, the building feels as if it is about to burst. As soon as Ed Corbett threw the ball up, thousands of flashbulbs went off from cameras around the building. Fans are allowed to carry very few items into places where major sports events are being held these days, but cameras are still okay. It seemed as if about 47,000 of the 47,262 in the building wanted a picture of the opening tip.

Illinois won the tip and Deron Williams buried a jumper 30 seconds into the game, causing about three-quarters of the building to explode in orange-and-blue joy. There wasn't any more of that for the next two minutes as North Carolina raced to a 9–2 lead. Frequently the championship game begins with a lot of missed shots. But both teams came out looking comfortable and confident in spite of what was at stake. Illinois quickly tied the game, at 9–9, with 15:32 left.

The first critical moment came early. With 12:57 left, Deron Williams started a drive to the basket and Raymond Felton fouled him. It was his second foul. Carolina had played several games without Rashad McCants and had hardly missed a beat. Sean May was invaluable but didn't have to score in huge numbers for his team to win. Felton was the player the Tar Heels could least afford to lose for an extended period of time. That they had lost to Santa Clara when he didn't play was evidence of how key he was to his team's success.

The unwritten rules of college basketball say that when a player picks up his second foul in the first half, he comes out. Once, coaches would let players stay in until they picked up a third foul in the first half, but in the past twenty years that has changed. Rarely does a player stay in the game with two fouls or come back in before halftime unless his team falls way behind. In 1984 Michael Jordan had picked up his second foul early in a round-of-sixteen game against Indiana. Dean Smith took him out and kept him out for the rest of the half. Indiana built a big lead by halftime and Carolina never caught up. It was Jordan's last college game.

Roy Williams learned at Dean Smith's side. One of the reasons Smith believed in taking a player out with two fouls was that you had to show faith in your bench; you had to let the non-starters know that you believed they could step in and play if needed. What's more, Felton's backup was Melvin Scott, a senior, and you always had to have faith in your seniors.

As soon as the whistle blew, Felton knew the foul was on him.

He also knew that Williams's first instinct was going to be to take him out of the game. He made a dash toward the bench where Williams was standing, arms folded.

"Coach, it's okay, I'm all right," Felton said.

"I've heard that before," Williams answered.

Still, he made no move to send in a sub for Felton.

There are, in every coach's life, moments when he has to take a risk, one that involves stepping out of character. In 1982 Dean Smith, who always believed in putting the game — and each season — in the hands of upperclassmen, turned to a freshman as his team came out of the huddle in the final minute of the national championship game against Georgetown. Carolina trailed, 62–61, and Smith knew there was no way the Hoyas were going to allow the ball to get to James Worthy, his best player, anywhere near the basket. He might have instructed Jimmy Black, his senior point guard, to try to create space either for himself or Worthy or even sophomore Sam Perkins.

But deep down, Smith knew that Michael Jordan would be open. And he knew Jordan could make the shot. "Knock it in, Michael," he said to Jordan as his players returned to the court. A few seconds later Black reversed the ball to a wide-open Jordan, who followed his coach's instructions perfectly and drained the shot that won Smith's first national championship. Smith had to go against all his instincts to put the game and the season in the hands of a freshman, but his coaching gut told him that was the moment to do it.

Now Williams let his coaching gut take over. He went against the rules and tradition and left Felton in the game. Carolina led at that moment, 14–12. Williams missed both free throws, and on Carolina's next possession, Felton fed Sean May for a dunk. The game stayed close for the next eight minutes and Felton was careful not to commit his third foul. Then, with Carolina leading, 27–25, he drilled a three-pointer. Dee Brown missed at the other end, and Felton found Jawad Williams open for a three: swish. The lead was 33–25. A minute later Felton fed McCants for another layup and the margin was suddenly 10 and Illinois had to call a time-out. Williams got Felton out for the last minute of the half to make sure he didn't commit a tired foul. McCants hit one more three and at halftime Carolina led, 40–27.

No one had expected either team to build that kind of lead. A year earlier Connecticut's 41–26 halftime lead against Georgia Tech wasn't that big a surprise. This was.

Neither team thought the game was over. Illinois hadn't gotten to 37–1 on good fortune. Carolina had shot 6 of 11 from outside the three-point line, Illinois 5 of 19. The Illini simply had no semblance of an inside game, which had allowed Carolina, normally not a good defensive team against the three-point shot, to extend its defense and make it difficult for Illinois to find open shots. During the break, each coach said essentially the same thing to his players but for different reasons: the first five minutes would be crucial. Williams knew if his team could extend the lead, the game would be over. Weber knew his players needed a jolt of confidence, and closing the gap would do that.

It was Weber who got what he needed: after May opened the half with another basket inside, Illinois went on an 18–7 run, punctuated by Deron Williams's three-pointer with 15:11 to play. The momentum seesawed: every time Illinois crept close, Carolina would stretch the lead, mostly on the strength of May's play inside. He was simply too big and too strong for anyone from Illinois to guard him one-on-one. He was a smart, gifted passer, so when the Illini attempted to double-team him, he would find Felton, Jawad or Marvin Williams, or McCants on the perimeter.

Illinois' inability to handle May was never more evident than during a two-minute stretch after Carolina's lead dwindled to 52–50. First he posted up and powered to the basket for a layup and was fouled. He made the free throw and then hit a short jump shot to push the lead to 57–50. A few seconds later, after Deron Williams had answered with a three-pointer at the other end, he recognized a double-team and fed a wide-open Jawad Williams for a three that stretched the margin back to 60–53. May ended up scoring 10 points and assisting on the Williams three during a 13–5 Carolina run that pushed the margin back to 65–55 with under nine minutes to play.

But as often happens, Carolina forgot how it had kept control of the game. With Illinois putting more and more defenders in the lane to try to deny May the ball, the Tar Heels got jump-shot happy and began to make mistakes. Illinois, showing the resilience that had gotten it this far, rallied one more time. A three-point shot by Luther Head with 2:40 to go tied the game at 70, and amid the cheers of the Illinois fans you could hear the kind of rumble that goes through an arena when something special is about to happen. One way or the other, this was going to be a memorable championship game, one that was going to show up on Classic for years to come. It was either going to be the story of Illinois' remarkable comeback from a 15-point second-half deficit or the story of Carolina righting the ship at the last possible moment to finally win a title for Roy Williams.

After Head's shot, Williams again stepped out of the Dean Smith school of how to coach a game: he called time-out. In thirty-six years as a head coach, Dean Smith probably didn't call a dozen time-outs that weren't part of the absolute endgame, usually in the final minute. Williams had even joked on Friday that no one in history had taken fewer time-outs than he had. If there was anyone who had done so, it was his old boss and mentor, who now sat directly across from the UNC bench, his face creased with tension.

"I was far more nervous right then than I would have been if I'd been coaching," Smith said. "When you're coaching the game, you don't have time to be nervous. You aren't thinking about what might happen if you lose or if you win. You're focused completely on figuring out what to do right at that moment. When you're just watching, it's a helpless feeling because there's nothing you can do to help."

If he had been at home watching the game on TV, Smith might have turned off the set and paced around for a while, too nervous to watch. But now there was no place for him to go or hide. He had to sit, watch, and hope.

Just as Smith would have been, Williams was completely calm as his players jogged over to the bench for what is euphemistically called a 30-second time-out. (They tend to last almost a minute so that CBS can get in a commercial and reset the game once they return.) "We're fine," Williams told his players in a calm, steady voice. "We've been through this before. We've been in much worse situations than this. Take a deep breath and let's go finish the job."

Calm was just what the Carolina players needed at that moment. The place was in absolute bedlam, the Illinois fans convinced that their destiny was to win. After all, why else had they come from 15 down in four minutes against Arizona? Why else had they just come from 15 down to tie?

The teams traded misses by Williamses — Marvin Williams, whose jump shot never made it to St. Louis, missing for Carolina;

Deron Williams missing for Illinois, a three-point attempt that, had it gone in, might have been a dagger in the heart for the Tar Heels. Carolina came down again and worked the ball around the perimeter. Sean May was trying to post up, but half the population of Illinois appeared to be guarding him. With the shot clock winding down, McCants drove from the left side into a bevy of defenders. There really wasn't time for him to pass, so he forced up a horrible shot, the ball popping high into the air with absolutely no chance to get to the rim, much less the basket.

Luck and talent now came into play. With the ball spinning skyward, Marvin Williams came flying in from the top of the key. He didn't have a chance to think about the moment or be nervous or worry about what was going on around him. He was playing on pure adrenaline and he flew over everyone, grabbed the ball out of the air, and pushed it into the basket before anyone from Illinois could even think to move for it. In some ways it was reminiscent of another freshman, Louisville's Pervis Ellison, grabbing a Jeff Hall airball out of the sky and laying it in during the final minute of his team's victory over Duke in the '86 championship game. In a completely different way it brought back memories of another Carolina freshman, Michael Jordan, burying the jumper against Georgetown twenty-three years earlier.

The Carolina bench went wild. The score was 72–70, but there was still more than a minute left. Illinois pushed downcourt, and Head missed another three — Illinois would end up attempting a mind-boggling 40 three-pointers — and this time it was Jack Ingram of the Illini getting the rebound. Now Weber called time, wanting to be sure his team got a good shot. But his team was out of bullets, perhaps worn out by the comeback and by the fact that it had missed its best chance to take the lead a possession earlier. Deron Williams missed another three, Illinois rebounded again, and Weber called time again.

This time Weber demanded that the ball get inside somehow, someway. Deron Williams tried, but Felton stole his pass to Head, and Williams had to foul him. But Felton made only one of two free throws, and trailing, 73–70, the Illini had one last chance to tie. Now they *had* to shoot a three, and Carolina's entire defense grouped on the perimeter. Head finally forced up a shot from beyond the arc with 16 seconds to go. It hit the back rim and — naturally — May was there for the rebound. He slipped the ball to Felton, who was fouled again with 9 seconds to go.

Carolina was now one free throw from the national championship. Roy Williams almost couldn't look, even though if you glanced at him at that instant, you might have thought he was sitting in an easy chair, reading a book. "If I looked at all calm," he said, "it was because I didn't think Raymond was going to miss another free throw."

He didn't. Both shots went in. Head missed one last time — Illinois missed its last five field-goal attempts, all of them threes — and May grabbed his tenth rebound, the last of his collegiate career. He began looking for Roy Williams because he had told him he wanted the first hug when the game was over. May had played one of the great championship games of all time: 26 points on 10 of 11 shooting, 10 rebounds, 2 key assists, and a blocked shot on a rare Illinois foray inside. Twenty-nine years later, he had actually surpassed his father. He would be voted the Most Outstanding Player of the Final Four.

For Illinois, as is always the case for the loser on Monday night, the defeat was devastating. It never occurs to a team good enough to win five games in the NCAA Tournament that it might lose one step from being remembered forever. "It hurts a lot at the moment when it happens," Jay Bilas said. "But you're in shock a little bit. The real pain doesn't really set in for a while."

The Illini would be celebrated at their school as the first team to reach the championship game, as a team that won as many games as any team in college basketball history (tying Duke 1986, UNLV 1987, and Duke 1999, all teams that also failed to win the national title), and as a team that brought great joy to an entire state in the winter of 2005. Banners would go up in Assembly Hall: Big Ten Champions, Final Four, NCAA Finalist. But the banner they all wanted — and expected — would go to Chapel Hill.

That banner would hang with three others — 1957, 1982, and 1993 — amid the dozens of banners that hang in the Dean Dome. (Carolina hangs so many banners — ACC CHAMPIONS — REGULAR SEASON TIE rates one — that Jim Valvano once joked that he was going to put up banners in Reynolds Coliseum that read NATIONAL CHAMPIONS — ALMOST.)

There was no *almost* in this banner or in this championship. Roy Williams never got around to putting his arms in the air, but he did get to feel the joy that comes with winning your last game and spending an entire summer doing what Mike Krzyzewski calls "a victory lap."

It can be argued that no one has ever been more entitled.

Epilogue

CELEBRATIONS DON'T LAST LONG in college basketball. The best moments for the North Carolina players and coaches came after they had gone through the seemingly interminable on-court ceremonies: the cutting of the nets (which lost its romance years ago when the NCAA began providing platforms for people to walk onto), the presentation of the trophy, and then the playing of the unbearably sappy "One Shining Moment." The only thing that makes playing the song defensible is that the players and coaches actually enjoy it. At that moment there are very few things they wouldn't enjoy.

Once Roy Williams had chased down Bruce Weber, he asked Dick Baddour, his athletic director, if there was any way to get his wife and children down near the court so he could see them. "I knew there was no way Wanda was coming out on the court," he said. "But I wanted one moment with her and the kids before we accepted the trophy." When Wanda Williams came downstairs with Scott and Kimberly, they all enjoyed heartfelt hugs. Williams saw tears in his wife's eyes and felt a little bit choked up himself. But unlike in the past, when tears had come so easily, he didn't cry. "I did get a little bit teared up during 'One Shining

Moment,'" he said. "I always made a point to watch that every year when I was home because I wanted to see the looks on the faces of the winners. I would sit there and think, 'I wonder what it is like to feel *that* good.' It was something I wanted to feel — more a dream than a demand — but to stand there did get me pretty emotional."

Once the last notes of the song were played, the Tar Heels escaped to their locker room, where they found both Dean Smith and Michael Jordan waiting. Jordan had flown in for the game and had watched from a luxury box. They had both made their way to the locker room during the awards ceremony and were there when the players came in. Smith's presence was no surprise, as he was often at practice and was frequently seen around the building that bears his name. Williams still slipped on occasion and referred to "Coach Smith's office" while sitting in the chair Smith once occupied. Jordan was another story. None of the players had been born when he hit the shot that beat Georgetown, and even though he still showed up in Chapel Hill on occasion, he was almost a mythical figure to the players.

"Seeing the two of them when we walked in there, arguably the greatest coach and the greatest player of all time, made me realize all over again what we're all part of," Wes Miller said. "Seeing Coach Smith and Coach Williams hug one another made all of us get kind of emotional."

In a sense, those locker-room moments, away from the public eye, are the best for any team that has just won — or lost — a championship. Players who have lost on Monday night talk about how close they felt to their teammates in those few minutes a team is allowed in the locker room before the doors are opened and the TV lights go back on. "I'm not sure I remember a word anyone said," Bruce Buckley recounts. "But I vividly remember how intensely emotional it was. The hugs and the feeling are something I've carried with me since that night."

"Men aren't supposed to say, 'I love you,' to one another, especially jocks," said Bruce Bell, the only senior on Duke's 1978 team. "But I told everyone in the room that night that I loved them and they said the same thing back to me. It was the right thing to say."

The emotions winners feel are different. There is a glow to a winning Monday night locker room because every goal a team can set prior to a season has been reached. "There's a feeling that, as you go forward in life, no matter what else happens, no one can take this away from you," said Duke assistant coach Johnny Dawkins, who dealt with the emotions of defeat as a player in 1986 and as an assistant in 1999 before finally being part of a Monday night winner in 2001. "You almost can't feel totally satisfied when you've been so close but haven't gotten over that last hump."

There were no humps left for the Tar Heels. No more questions for Roy Williams and a feeling of complete satisfaction for all the assistants and players. Of course, the moment the locker-room door opened, the questions started again. The three juniors — Raymond Felton, Sean May, and Rashad McCants — were asked if they were going to turn pro. So was freshman Marvin Williams. Wes Miller probably should have been insulted that no one asked *him* if he was turning pro. May had turned twenty-one on Saturday and Miller had bought him a bottle of champagne. Now they could truly celebrate.

Everyone knew McCants was leaving; he and Williams had more or less thrashed that out in January. He had played well in the championship game — 14 points — but had been bailed out of long-lasting infamy by Marvin Williams's rebound of his wild shot with the score tied at 70. Most people expected Felton to leave, too. He was a lock top-ten pick and, especially after winning the national championship, was more than ready to make a move. Marvin Williams probably would have liked another year of college. He was only a freshman, and what exactly was there not to like about being a star freshman basketball player at the University of North Carolina? But the way basketball works today, if the NBA says you are a top-five pick, you almost have to go because there is no guarantee you will be as highly sought in another year. There are too many examples of players whose draft status has slipped after another year of college to risk not making the jump when the money is, for all intents and purposes, dumped at your feet.

The only real question mark among Carolina people was May. He had been saying emphatically, both publicly and privately, that he was coming back for his senior year. No one doubted that he meant it. In fact, Rick Brewer, who had worked at North Carolina in sports information and as an associate athletic director since the Civil War, was so certain May would return that he bet on it during the Final Four.

"Even if we win, he's coming back," Brewer said. "He likes college."

No doubt May liked college. But after his performance in the Final Four, a lot of pro scouts who had talked about his being a "tweener" — too small to play the low post in the NBA, not quick enough to play forward — were rethinking that position. May had great hands, great vision, and a great feel for the game. Because he was also the kind of person you wanted on your team, his stock soared. He went from a late-first- or second-round pick to a high- to mid-first-round pick. There was another issue: May had climbed the mountain. He had done it with Felton and

McCants, whom he had arrived with three years earlier. With Felton, McCants, and Marvin Williams gone, Carolina — with May and a great incoming freshman class — would still be very competitive in 2006. But they weren't likely to return to the Final Four. When you've celebrated your twenty-first birthday with national championship champagne, it is awfully hard to think about starting a season with the Sweet Sixteen as a reasonable goal.

May was the last of the four to announce that he was leaving. "That was the one that felt like a kick in the stomach," Roy Williams said. "Obviously, I knew Rashad was going and I suspected Raymond was. Marvin really had to go. But I had thought Sean would come back. I understood the decision completely, but I'd be lying if I didn't say it hurt."

The pain was lessened by the victory lap. Williams had almost come to dread being recognized in airports. "It isn't that people weren't nice," he said. "Most of the time they are. But you really get a little tired of hearing 'Is this the year, Coach?' or 'You think you're finally going to get it done?' It's nice just to have people walk up and say, 'Congratulations, I'm real happy for you.' I think people were happy for me because they knew it wasn't easy. I think a lot of them had felt sorry for me all those years. Now they didn't have to feel that way anymore."

Letters came in from colleagues: Mike Krzyzewski, Gary Williams, and Clemson coach Oliver Purnell wrote letters that were there almost as soon as Williams got home. Jim Boeheim and Jim Calhoun both wrote, too. So did some of his ex-Kansas players. The new president of Duke, Robert Brodhead, also wrote. The letter Williams may have enjoyed the most came not from a friend or a coach or a fan or a relative. It came from Lenny Wirtz, the longtime ACC referee who might have had more on-court duels with Dean Smith than anyone who ever officiated. Wirtz was now retired but he wrote to Williams to tell him how pleased he was for him. Williams was touched by the letter from someone he and his mentor had battled with through the years.

He knew that next season would be different. Four underclassmen gone to the NBA — plus three seniors graduating — would make for a very young team. Four talented freshmen would arrive, but they would be freshmen. There would also be an entirely different feeling at Carolina. Much like Duke in '05, the season would start with lower expectations than normal. "It will be easier to go to practice every day and look up and see that banner," Williams said. "It will help when I get frustrated during the season. But it isn't going to make me want to win any less. I don't see that changing."

That wouldn't change. The great coaches are always hungry for the Next Thing — whatever it may be. Krzyzewski, whose Duke team would enter the '05–'06 season as one of the favorites to win the whole thing much the way Carolina had entered '04–'05 — wants a fourth title as much as he wanted his first. Jim Calhoun — another preseason favorite, at UConn — wants a third. Jim Boeheim and Roy Williams want a second. Gary Williams may want a second more than he wanted a first.

"I always thought if I ever won the national championship, I'd feel less pressure," he said. "I think, if I'm being honest, I feel more pressure now. I feel as if more people are watching what our team does and when we lose, it's a bigger deal than it used to be — because it *is* a bigger deal than it used to be. We miss the NCAA Tournament, and our fans are very unhappy. I understand. I'm unhappy, too. But now, in the back of my mind, I catch myself thinking, 'If I could just win one more, that would be enough.'" He smiled. "Of course, that's not true. It wouldn't be enough."

It is never enough. Because when one Final Four ends, when one city clears out and another — Indianapolis in 2006 — begins to prepare for the next, everyone in basketball looks ahead. They all began again on October 15, 2005. The first goal for each is to get to the Dance. The next goal is Indianapolis. Then comes getting to Monday night to walk onto the court, tingling because they are there, knowing that only two teams who started on October 15 will still be playing on April 3, 2006. Only two get the Last Dance.

And only one will get to hear that sappy song.

Afterword: Next Dance

ONE YEAR LATER, the team that got to hear the song was one that *none* of the so-called experts picked before the season began: the University of Florida.

Six years after taking the Gators to the Final Four in Indianapolis as a thirty-five-year-old coach, Billy (the Kid) Donovan brought the Gators back to the same city and the same building, and this time did not come up one game short, as they had against Michigan State in 2000. Picked in no one's top ten and almost no one's top twenty-five in the preseason after losing several players to the NBA, Florida started 17–0, dropped off briefly at midseason, and then became a dominant team when it mattered most in March and early April.

The Gators never really came close to losing. Georgetown, another surprise team, made them work the entire forty minutes in the round of sixteen, but no one else came close. For the second time in three years (Connecticut over Georgia Tech in 2004) the national championship game was over by halftime. Florida completely outplayed UCLA from the very beginning and coasted to a completely unsuspenseful 73–57 victory.

None of 2005's Final Four approached a repeat performance.

North Carolina and Illinois were beaten in the second round. Both had excellent regular seasons given the number of players they lost (Carolina lost its top seven scorers but had a remarkable freshman class), but they did not have the experience to repeat their respective accomplishments of the previous season. Michigan State lost in the first round. Louisville took the biggest plunge of all, having to rally late in the season just to qualify for the Big East Tournament before ending up in the National Invitation Tournament. It was the sort of fall from grace that happens surprisingly often in college basketball.

Florida was a surprise national champion. UCLA, in Coach Ben Howland's third season, was a surprise finalist. LSU, which shocked heavily favored Duke in the round of sixteen, was a surprise Final Four entrant. But that's all they were: surprises, exactly the kind that happen every year in college basketball. For all three schools, their 2006 runs simply represented a return to past glories. Florida had been in the Final Four in 1994 and in the championship game in 2000; LSU had been to the Final Four in 1981 and in 1987; and UCLA was, well, the UCLA of college basketball, with eleven national titles, by far the most of any school, the most recent having come in 1995. All three were power schools from power conferences, Florida and LSU from the Southeastern Conference, UCLA from the Pacific-10.

Nice stories all. Florida was a very deserving champion, clearly the best team when it mattered most. Donovan came out of Indianapolis having elevated himself from coaching prodigy to coaching star. "He's not Billy the Kid anymore," his former coach and boss Rick Pitino joked. "Now he's Billy the Coach."

All that being said, there was one story and one team that completely overshadowed everything else that happened in college basketball in 2006: George Mason.

Yes, George Mason University, a state-funded commuter school in Fairfax, Virginia, about twenty miles or two hours, depending on traffic, from downtown Washington, D.C. George Mason, a school that began the season with the exact total of *zero* NCAA Tournament victories. That's not zero titles, that's zero *games*. George Mason, a school that didn't become an independent college until 1972 and didn't start playing Division 1 basketball until 1978 — three years after John Wooden won his tenth national title at UCLA.

George Mason played in the Colonial Athletic Association, a league that had produced teams in the past that had pulled some memorable tournament upsets. In 1986, one year after the league had changed its name from the ECAC South to the CAA, a David Robinson–led Navy team beat Tulsa, stunned Syracuse (at Syracuse), and beat Cleveland State to make it to the elite eight. There, the Midshipmen were crushed by top-seeded Duke. Navy had left the league in 1990 to join the Patriot League. Richmond had also been a giant-killer through the years. It had stunned Charles Barkley and Auburn in 1984, defeated Indiana (the defending national champion) and Georgia Tech to reach the Sweet Sixteen in 1988, and had become the first No. 15 seed to win a tournament game when it beat Syracuse in 1991. All those wins had come under Dick Tarrant, arguably one of the least-known great coaches in recent college basketball history.

In 1998, as a No. 14 seed, Richmond, coached by John Beilein (now at West Virginia), stunned South Carolina in the opening round of the tournament. A few years later, the Spiders also left the league, moving to the Atlantic-10 in search of bigger TV dollars and more long-term glory.

In spite of those victories, the CAA had become a one-bid

league. The last time it had received an at-large bid had been in 1986, when Richmond was invited to the tournament along with the conference champion, Navy. That had been it, in spite of the conference's reputation as an early-round giant-killer. Like many midsized leagues, the CAA had seen its share of defections: Richmond, Navy, East Carolina, and American had all departed. Longtime commissioner Tom Yeager had aggressively rebuilt, expanding the league geographically and in overall size by bringing in schools like Northeastern, Hofstra, Drexel, and Delaware. The result had been a league that was far more competitive from top to bottom than most people around the country — including, most importantly, the basketball committee — seemed to understand.

The first clue about how good the CAA had become may have come in November when Drexel reached the semifinals of the preseason NIT and, playing in Madison Square Garden, barely lost to both Duke and UCLA. The Dragons had been picked to finish seventh in the CAA's preseason poll.

"If this is the seventh-best team in the CAA, then that league must be loaded," Dick Vitale said on the air during the NIT. "No way can I see this team finishing seventh in the CAA."

He was right. Drexel finished eighth.

Even so, the lingering question in the league all season was whether the twenty-year at-large drought would be broken. Several CAA teams — Mason, Hofstra, North Carolina Wilmington, Old Dominion, Northeastern, and Virginia Commonwealth — all had impressive victories and, at times, very high RPI rankings. And yet, knowing how the committee tended to manipulate the RPI to justify taking teams from power conferences while ignoring teams from mid-major leagues, everyone worried.

Jim Larranaga was in his ninth season as Mason's coach. He

had grown up in the Bronx, had been a very good player under Dave Gavitt at Providence, and had been to the Final Four as an assistant coach while working for Terry Holland at Virginia. He had gone on to become the head coach at Bowling Green, where he had known consistent success but not great success, before coming to George Mason in 1997 because he saw potential in both the school and the league.

In some ways that potential had been realized. The Patriots were a consistent contender in the CAA and had twice reached the NCAA Tournament under Larranaga. In 2001, they had been one play away from upsetting Maryland (which went on to the Final Four) in the first round. But the upset hadn't happened. Over the next four seasons, the Patriots averaged just under nineteen wins a season and went to the NIT twice — winning two games in 2004, the school's first postseason victories ever. Larranaga turned fifty-six just prior to the start of the 2005–2006 season and, deep down, he was beginning to wonder if his destiny was to always coach solid basketball teams that would occasionally make a cameo appearance in the tournament and nothing more.

"I don't think I'm the jealous type," he said at one point. "I've seen good friends of mine like Jeff Jones and Dave Odom advance deep into the tournament [both had been to the elite eight], and while I've been very happy for them, I've wondered what it would feel like to accomplish that myself. You get to my age, you do begin to wonder."

Mason's season began like many others. There was a close call at Wake Forest — an overtime loss — and an embarrassing defeat at home to Creighton. The day after the Creighton game, Larranaga all but locked his team in the locker room to make the players look at a tape of how poorly they had played defense the previous night. The defense picked up, and the wins began to come. A February victory at Wichita State on a late three-pointer by senior point guard Tony Skinn, in the school's first regular season national TV appearance (ESPN), vaulted Mason into the top twenty-five in one poll and to nineteenth in the RPI. An at-large bid if the team failed to win the CAA Tournament seemed a virtual lock.

"Nothing is a lock," said Larranaga. "Not if you look at history."

Larranaga had become obsessed with one of sports' newer and more annoying terms, *bracketology*. He had drawn up lists and charts of who got at-large bids each year and what their RPIs were. All of his research confirmed what everyone knew: the committee was a lot more likely to pick a fifth ACC team or a sixth Big East team than a second CAA team. That made Larranaga — and everyone in the CAA — nervous.

After the victory at Wichita State — which was in first place in the Missouri Valley, another upstart league looking for multiple bids — George Mason went to Hofstra and lost. The seedings for the CAA Tournament were: UNC Wilmington, George Mason, Hofstra, and Old Dominion. No fewer than six league teams had at least nineteen victories. Vitale's team, Drexel, not only finished eighth, it lost in the opening round of the tournament to ninth-seeded Delaware.

UNC Wilmington beat Northeastern in the opening semifinal game, setting up a meeting in the final with the George Mason–Hofstra winner. That turned out to be Hofstra, which beat Mason for the second time in ten days. Unfortunately for the Patriots, the loss was not the worst thing that happened that night.

Late in the game, with Hofstra leading by 7, Tony Skinn drained a three-point shot to cut the margin to 4. Since there was less than a minute to play, Mason had to press full-court.

Larranaga was off the bench, his usual manic self, pointing in fourteen different directions at once, when he heard the whistle blow. He looked out on the court and saw Hofstra's superb point guard, Loren Stokes, crumpled on the ground, writhing in pain. He looked at Skinn, who had been guarding Stokes.

"Tony, what happened?" he asked.

Skinn didn't answer. Larranaga waved him over to the bench.

"Do you know what happened to him?" he asked.

In response, Skinn nodded, dropping his head in such a way that Larranaga knew instantly that Skinn had been responsible for what had happened to Stokes.

"I've been doing this a long time," he said. "Call it coaching instinct. I knew Tony had done something wrong, and I also knew that Tony already knew it was wrong. I felt like I had no choice but to take him out of the game."

Remember, this was the biggest game of the season for Mason — its NCAA Tournament hopes very possibly hanging on the outcome. With Skinn on the floor and just under a minute to play, a 4-point deficit was far from insurmountable. But without him handling the ball or available to hit the kind of deep three-pointer he had just hit, Mason's chances to pull off a comeback win went to almost zero. Many coaches — *most* coaches — would have left Skinn in the game. After all, Larranaga didn't *know* what had happened. When the game was over, he could say that he had to see a tape of what had occurred to be sure any punishment was merited. When the officials went to the TV tape to try to determine if a flagrant foul had occurred, they couldn't see what had happened because it was away from the ball, and the camera had been following the ball.

Without Skinn, Mason had no chance to rally. Hofstra won 58–49, a devastating defeat for the Patriots. Shortly after the game, someone from the UNC Wilmington coaches TV show approached Larranaga. "I just happened to get what happened with Stokes and Skinn on tape," he said. "You want to see it?"

In truth, Larranaga didn't. But he knew he had to. The tape was from a fairly good distance away, but there was no doubt about what had happened: Skinn had let his frustration get to him and he had sucker punched Stokes in the groin. It was, Larranaga knew, an inexcusable cheap shot.

"A good kid, a very good kid," he said later, "doing a very bad thing."

Before he went to address the media, Larranaga met with both Skinn and Tom O'Connor, his athletic director — also a basketball committee member. He told them both he believed there was no choice but to announce immediately that Skinn would not play in George Mason's next game — whether it was in the first round of the NCAA Tournament or the first round of the NIT.

"I wasn't going to wait for anyone else to take action," Larranaga said. "Tony had to know, all our kids had to know, that I found this unacceptable. There wasn't going to be any excuse-making."

By suspending Skinn, Larranaga knew he might be further jeopardizing his team's chances to make the tournament. When UNC Wilmington beat Hofstra to get the automatic bid, most people believed that (at best) either Hofstra or Mason would get an at-large bid. The teams had similar résumés except that Hofstra had beaten the Patriots twice.

The day after the Hofstra game, the Wilmington TV tape had found its way into the hands of every TV network in America. Larranaga finally stopped watching television because there was the punch, time and time again. But the news wasn't all bad. When word of Larranaga's quick and decisive action began to get around, many big-name coaches heaped praise on him.

"I'd like to say that I'd have the guts to do something like that at a time like this in the season," Duke coach Mike Krzyzewski said. "But I can't swear to you that I would. If Jim were here right now, I'd give him a hug. We need more coaches to send the message to kids that when they're wrong, they're wrong — no excuses."

Maryland's Gary Williams, hardly a close friend of Larranaga's, was succinct when the subject came up. "It's easy for any of us to say that's the right thing to do," he said. "Jim *did* it."

Krzyzewski added one other thought: "I don't know what will happen to Jim's team this week. But I believe in the basketball gods. I think they get it right — not always right away, but eventually. I hope they have something good in store for Jim. He deserves it."

Selection Sunday was as frenetic as ever. Many coaches in the TV leagues, especially those on the bubble, were in a state of panic because several of the mid-major conferences — notably the Missouri Valley and the CAA — had teams with very high RPIs that the committee would have a difficult time ignoring. Gary Williams said that the Missouri Valley had "cracked the RPI code," as if it had broken the law by doing so. For a second straight season, Maryland went to the ACC Tournament needing a big weekend and failed to get it: after beating a bad Georgia Tech team on opening night, the Terrapins were blitzed in the quarterfinals by Boston College.

"We're done," Williams said, walking out of the Greensboro Coliseum just before midnight. "I'm not sure it's fair that we're done, but we're done."

Actually it was fair. Teams from the ACC — and the Big Ten, Big 12, Southeastern Conference, Pacific-10, and Big East —

have myriad advantages over mid-major schools. They can schedule guarantee games to pad their record (Maryland and Florida State, the ACC's two bubble teams in 2006 had done a good deal of that); they get more exposure on television; they rarely play nonconference road games; and they can prop up their RPI rating by *losing* to highly rated teams during conference play. If all of that isn't enough to make them a clear-cut tournament team, that's their problem, not the committee's.

And yet, going into Selection Sunday, there were serious doubts at George Mason that they would get a bid, in spite of their RPI rating, in spite of the win at Wichita State, in spite of a difficult nonconference schedule (at Wake Forest, at Mississippi State, at Manhattan, at Creighton), and in spite of playing in a very tough conference. Larranaga gathered his team in the basement of his home to eat pizza and watch the brackets go up. He had Skinn sit right next to him because he was easily the most nervous person in the room, feeling as if he might be personally responsible for his team not getting a bid.

One bracket went up. Then a second. Commercial. After the commercial, host Greg Gumbel began working his way through the "Washington Regional." Connecticut was the number one seed and would play first- and second-round games in Philadelphia. He went through the top half of the bracket. Then the bottom half. "In Dayton, Ohio, on Friday night it will be the number six seed Michigan State — a Final Four team a year ago — taking on number eleven George Mason, an at-large team . . ."

The rest of Gumbel's sentence was drowned out as the Larranaga basement erupted in cheers. Skinn was hugging Larranaga and crying, and everyone else in the room was hugging one another. The rest of the brackets went up, and the biggest surprise in the Larranaga house was that Hofstra did not get

in. Everyone knew — especially with O'Connor on the committee — that eyebrows would be raised about that.

In fact, Hofstra should have made the field, but not at Mason's
expense. For reasons no one ever fully explained — patriotism perhaps? — Air Force was selected in spite of a terrible nonconference
schedule. Hofstra, kicking and screaming, was sent to the NIT.

As pleased as the Mason people were with the bid, they were
somewhat stunned to find themselves under attack before CBS
went off the air. In their traditional postbracket interview with
the committee chairman — in this case Virginia athletic director
Craig Littlepage — Jim Nantz and Billy Packer were extremely
critical of the committee's decision to give four bids to the Missouri Valley (the same number that the ACC received) and two
to the CAA. George Mason was singled out as a team that didn't
belong. Nantz went so far as to read from Mason's schedule before asking Littlepage, "How does that schedule justify a bid?"

Packer has always been more than willing to be outspoken
about selection and seeding. As far back as 1979, he was critical
of Indiana State, led by Larry Bird, being ranked number one
nationally because he believed they played in a weak conference.
In 2004, he blasted the committee for making Saint Joseph's a
number one seed. Now he was cast as the spokesman for the
power conferences, who were stunned that the committee had
broken from tradition and given bubble bids to mid-major
schools rather than to power schools.

Larranaga and his players knew that the best way to shut
down the controversy was to go to Dayton and beat Michigan
State — no small feat with Skinn out of the lineup. And yet they
believed they could win the game. They had played tough
against good teams all year. They led Michigan State from the
start, teetered near the end, but held on to win. It was a stunning

upset. Two days later, they took that poise a step further when —
after a terrible start that put them in a 16–2 hole — they came
back and beat North Carolina. That meant they had beaten two
Final Four teams — including the 2005 champion — within
forty-eight hours. The Tar Heels had been a number three seed,
a team that had played so well down the stretch that some people
were picking them to return to the Final Four. No one thought
that dream would die at the hands of George Mason.

The Carolina victory elevated Mason to a completely different level of fame. It had become the NCAA Tournament's Cinderella 2006. Larranaga spoke emotionally after the game about
calling his son Jay, who was playing professionally in Italy, with his
younger son Jon by his side, not long after the victory. Both sons
had played for him — Jay at Bowling Green, Jon at Mason. Skinn
kept thanking his teammates for giving him the chance to play
again. The three seniors — Skinn, center Jai Lewis, and shooting
guard Lamar Butler — were quickly becoming familiar names
nationally. During an interview in his kitchen, Larranaga was so
overcome while talking about what it meant to take a team to the
second week of the tournament that he broke down completely.
Tears in his eyes, he looked at his wife, Liz, and said, "What's the
matter with me — there's no crying in the Sweet Sixteen!"

Getting to the Sweet Sixteen is a lot harder than it looks. In
2006, Duke reached the round of sixteen for the ninth straight
season. No one else had been there more than two straight years.
None of 2005's elite eight made it past the second round.

Traditionally, Cinderella — whether she be Richmond or Gonzaga or Wisconsin-Milwaukee — bows out in the round of sixteen.
Gonzaga had broken that mold once, making it to the elite eight in

1999. One school was guaranteed to do that in 2006 because George Mason and Wichita State were matched (rematched, really) in the round of sixteen in Washington, D.C. Wichita State had routed a Big East team (Seton Hall) in the first round and beaten number two seed Tennessee (SEC) in the second round. With the number two, number three, and number four seeds gone, most people expected Connecticut to roll through the regional to the Final Four.

The Huskies were favored by many to win a third national title in seven years. They were, however, a team considered tainted by many people. The previous summer starting point guard Marcus Williams and A. J. Price, his backup, had been arrested for stealing — and trying to sell — computer laptops from dorm rooms. Both were sentenced to community service because athletes are almost never sentenced to jail time. The school then announced that Price would be suspended for the season. Williams would be allowed to return after fourteen games — thus missing none of the team's key games.

The given explanation was that Williams had confessed to his crime when confronted by authorities and Price had not. More cynical observers thought it had more to do with Williams being arguably the key to the team's chances to win a title. Everyone at UConn was careful to point out that this had been the school's decision, not Coach Jim Calhoun's, as if those on the academic side never made decisions based on money and glory.

With Williams in the lineup, Connecticut played well enough to earn a number one seed, although it never dominated teams the way many people had thought it might given that it had four potential number one draft choices in the starting lineup, great experience, and great depth, not to mention a Hall of Fame coach.

The Huskies got a surprising scare in the first round, trailing number sixteen seed Albany by 12 points in the second half before waking up and pulling away to win during the final ten minutes. They had a tough time with number eight seed Kentucky — but one could expect to have a tough time with Kentucky, even if it wasn't one of Tubby Smith's most talented teams. "All I know is this," Calhoun said. "A lot of good teams aren't in the round of sixteen. We weren't in the round of sixteen a year ago. Now we are. I'm very happy about that."

UConn should have lost to the University of Washington in the round of sixteen but rallied miraculously to win in overtime. That set up David versus Goliath in the elite eight: two-time national champion UConn, a team filled with future NBA players, against George Mason, which had just won its third NCAA Tournament *game* in the round of sixteen and was filled with future CBA players. The general consensus was that Mason had had a wonderful run. If it could just make the game respectable on Sunday, everyone could walk away with their heads held very high.

UConn led by 12 in the first half and by 9 early in the second half. But then the Patriots began making every shot they looked at from outside. Jai Lewis and sophomore Will Thomas were suddenly unstoppable inside. The lead went away. Connecticut began looking nervous. The noise in the Verizon Center kept building. Disbelieving fans wanted to think a miracle could happen but were not yet completely convinced.

Mason took the lead. It built the lead to 7. UConn rallied. Mason held on. Lamar Butler made two free throws with sixteen seconds left, and the lead was 74–70. But UConn was like Dracula. The Patriots couldn't find the wooden stake. With the lead 74–72 and five seconds left, Skinn — who hadn't missed an important shot in three games — missed the front end of a one-and-one. Larranaga had taken his team off the foul line so they would be back on defense in case of a miss.

Except they forgot to play defense. Perhaps stunned that Skinn had missed, they stood like statues while UConn's Denham Brown drove straight to the basket and put up a reverse layup at the buzzer that hit the rim once, twice, three times — and dropped through. Overtime. No one in the building thought Mason could recover. After blowing a similar lead on Friday night, Washington had lost by 10 in overtime.

"Okay, you forgot to play defense for five seconds," Larranaga told his players. "So now you have to play it for five more minutes. I have no doubt you can do it."

They played defense — and offense — for five more minutes. They made five of six shots from the field in the overtime. Again they led by 2, 86–84, with five seconds left. Jai Lewis went to the foul line. Again Larranaga pulled his players off the foul line to set up on defense. Lewis missed. Again Brown charged down the left side of the court. This time, though, Larranaga's players remembered to play defense. They cut him off 23 feet from the basket and forced him to throw up an off-balance three with under a second to play. For one split second it looked as if the shot might somehow find the net. But it hit the back rim and bounced high into the air as the buzzer sounded.

Complete bedlam broke out. Larranaga sprinted across the court, waving his arms manically at Liz. Apparently there *is* crying in the Final Four, because everyone from Mason was in tears. Tears of joy, tears of disbelief. Calhoun handled the loss with grace and dignity. And eloquence. "What George Mason did," he said, "is why basketball is such a beautiful game."

*   *   *

The ride ended in Indianapolis against a Florida team that was too talented and wasn't about to make the mistake of taking George Mason even a little bit lightly. "Look at who they've beaten," Billy Donovan said. "How can you take them lightly?"

UCLA routed LSU in the second semifinal, and then Florida easily won the championship game. After two weeks of extraordinary upsets and finishes — none of the four number one seeds (Duke, Connecticut, Memphis, Villanova) made it to Indianapolis — the Last Dance of the 2006 season fell flat. The band went home a little too early.

That statement is not meant to demean Florida in any way. The Gators were a worthy national champion, and when all of their underclassmen, led by sophomore center Joachim Noah, surprised everyone by opting to return to college for another year, they were installed as co-favorites for the 2007 title along with North Carolina. Ohio State, which landed six-foot-ten Greg Oden — considered the next Next One — was installed as the young team most likely to join the Gators and Tar Heels and UCLA? Kentucky? Texas? George Mason? — who knows? — in Atlanta for the first weekend in April.

As teams began to gather for another season in October, no one could possibly know who would cut down the nets and hear the song on April 2, 2007, in the Georgia Dome. It might be Florida or North Carolina or Ohio State. It might be a team like Florida in '06 — overlooked early, dominant when it mattered.

But one thing was certain as a new season began. There would never be a more unlikely journey to the Last Dance than the one taken by George Mason in 2006. As Calhoun said, the Little Team That Did was living proof that basketball is, in fact, a beautiful game.

Acknowledgments

I HAVE BEEN ACCUSED, on occasion, of being a name-dropper. Actually, I learned the art from perhaps the greatest name-dropper of all time: Dick Schaap, who could begin a sentence by saying something like "One night when I was having dinner with Jack Kennedy, Frank Sinatra, and Muhammad Ali, Billy Crystal stopped by the table. . . ."

I will never be in Dick's class in the name-dropping category (he wanted to call his memoir *Name-Dropping*, but some publishing genius came up with *Flashing Before My Eyes*, which is silly and meaningless), but when I started to think about the acknowledgments for this book, it occurred to me that Dick would be proud of me if he could read them.

Consider the following people I need to thank for taking the time to talk to me about their Final Four experiences: John Wooden, Dean Smith, Roy Williams, Bill Bradley, John Thompson, Jim Calhoun, Jim Boeheim, Gary Williams, Lefty Driesell, Dick Vitale, Billy Packer, and Rick Barnes. I haven't even mentioned Mike Krzyzewski, who not only talked to me at length about his Final Four experiences but agreed to write the introduction for the book. That's a pretty good group of names for starters. There's more: Jay Bilas, Greg Anthony, Jay Buckley, Bruce Buckley, Clay Buckley, Tom Brennan, Rollie Massimino, Jay Wright, Frank Sullivan, Doug Wojcik, Digger Phelps, Dave Odom, Jeff Capel III, Mike Brey, Phil Martelli, Jeff Jones, Jim Larranaga, Ralph Willard, Pat Flannery, Emmett Davis, Jim Crews, Billy Taylor, Fran O'Hanlon, Bill Lange, Jimmy Patsos, Billy Hahn, Tom Abatemarco, George Raveling, Bruce Bell, Johnny Dawkins, Tommy Amaker, Chris Collins, Steve Wojciechowski, Kenny Dennard, Rich Clarkson, Dick Weiss, Jim O'Connell, and Bill Brill. Special thanks to Wes Miller, who agreed to keep a journal for me during North Carolina's trip to St. Louis. I also owe thanks to Jack Kvancz, Gene Corrigan, Wayne Duke, Dave Gavitt, and Terry Holland, who talked to me about their experiences as members of the basketball committee, and to Tom Jernstedt, who is a walking encyclopedia of tournament history. Whether I could have finished this book at all without the help of Bill Hancock is something I seriously doubt. To say he will be missed by those of us who cover the tournament each year is a vast understatement, but if anyone can straighten out the BCS, it is Bill. Thanks also to Steve Kirschner and Rick Brewer at Carolina, to Mike Cragg at Duke, to Bill Bennett at UCLA, and to Bruce Bosley at Vermont. More thanks: to outgoing committee chairman Bob Bowlsby and incoming chairman Craig Littlepage. Also to Hank Nichols and many of his refs, most notably Larry Rose and Tim Higgins, who are Final Four refs every year as far as I'm concerned.

That's the group that played a crucial role in *this* book. Then there are the people who play a critical role in *every* book I write: Esther Newberg, my agent for life, and Michael Pietsch, who truly is a wonderful editor and exhibited great patience on this particular project, especially when my shoulder surgery put the book way behind schedule. Esther and Michael have great assistants: Chris Earle (aka FA/FW) and the precocious Kari Stuart put up with both Esther and with me — which is pretty close to miraculous. They learned, of course, from Andy Barzvi. Michael is aided immeasurably by both Stacey Brody and Zainab Zakari. Heather Fain (Murphy Brown to her friends) has promised to promote this book as she has promoted no other, since her alma mater won the 2005 national title. I'm not certain that Heather Rizzo, Katherine Molina, and Marlena Bittner will be as enthusiastic, but if they're not, Holly Wilkinson will ride in and crack her whip. Extra thanks are owed to Steve Lamont, who copyedited two of my books in a short period of time and saved me from myself on countless occasions. (That's not hyperbole, that's fact.)

Friends (still, I'm pleased to say, a long list): Barbie Drum, Bob and Anne DeStefano, David and Linda Maraniss, Jackson Diehl and Jean Halperin, Lexie Verdon and Steve Barr, Tom and Jill Mickle, Shelley Crist, Jane Brill, Terry and Patti Hanson, Bob Zurfluh, Pete Teeley, Al Hunt, Bob Novak, Vivian Thompson, Phil Hochberg, Wayne Zell, Mike and David Sanders, Bob Whitmore, Andy Dolich, Mary Carillo, Doug and Beth Doughty, David Teel, Beth (Shumway) Brown, Beth Sherry-Downes, Erin Laissen, Bob Socci, Pete Van Poppel, Frank Davinney, Scott Strasemeier, Eric Ruden, Billy Stone, Mike Werteen, Chris Knoche (still a bitter man), Andrew Thompson, Joe Speed, Jack Hecker, the perennially fabulous Dick Hall, Steve (Moose) Stirling, Jim and Tiffany Cantelupe, Derek and Christina Klein, Anthony and Kristen Noto, Roger Breslin, Jim Rome, Travis Rodgers, Jason Stewart, Tony Kornheiser (still angry after all these years), Michael Wilbon, Mark Maske, Ken Denlinger, Matt Rennie, Mike Purkey, Bob Edwards, Tom

Goldman, Jeffrey Katz, Mark Schramm, Kenny and Christina Lewis, Joanie Weiss, Bob Ryan, the soon-to-be-married L. Sandy Genelius, Jennifer Proud-Mearns, David Fay, Frank Hannigan, Mike Butz, Mike Davis, Mary Lopuszynski, Marty Caffey, Jerry Tarde, Mike O'Malley, Larry Dorman, Marsha Edwards, Jay and Natalie Edwards, Len and Gwyn Edwards-Dieterle, Brian and Laurie Edwards, Chris Edwards and John Cutcher, Joe Valerio, Rob Cowan, Andy Kaplan, Chris Svenson, Dennis Satyshur, Billy Andrade, Davis Love III, Jim Furyk, Mike Muehr, Tom Watson, Andy North, Joe Ogilvie, Joe Durant, Bob Low, Don Pooley, John Cook, Jeff Sluman, Peter Jacobsen, Lee Janzen, Brad Faxon, and, of course, Paul Goydos. Norbert Doyle has attended, I believe, every Final Four. Thanks also to my team of orthopods: Eddie McDevitt, Bob Arciero, Gus Mazzocca, and Dean Taylor.

Thanks, as always, to Howard Garfinkel, for understanding, and to Tom Konchalski, the only honest man in the gym, who checked on me constantly after my surgery.

The swimmers: Jeff Roddin, Jason (sorry I can't make it) Crist, John Craig, Mark Pugliese, Carole Kammel, Margot Pettijohn, Susan Williams, Amy Weiss, A. J. Block, Danny Pick, Warren Friedland, Marshall Greer, Tom Denes, Peter Ward, Doug Chestnut, Bob Hansen, Paul Doremus, the peripatetic Penny Bates, and the remarkably patient Mary Dowling. The FWRH group remains intact: Clay Britt, Wally Dicks, and Mike Fell.

The China Doll Gang: Red Auerbach (toughest guy going), Morgan Wootten, Hymie Perlo, Aubre Jones, Sam Jones, Rob Ades, Jack Kvancz (again), Joe McKeown, Stanley Copeland, Reid Collins, Arnie Heft, Pete Dowling, Bob Campbell, Chris (the Rookie) Wallace, Stanley Walker, Harry (the Champ)

Huang, Herman Greenberg, Joe Greenberg, Alvin Miller, Johnny Auerbach, Charles Thornton, Bob Ferry, and the ombudsman, George Solomon. Zang is still there, too.

The Rio gang: Tate Armstrong, Mark Alarie, Clay (LB) Buckley, and secretary to the group, Terry Chili.

The Feinstein Advisory Board: Keith Drum, Frank Mastrandrea, Wes Seeley, and Dave Kindred. Sadly, I didn't consult any of them during the fourth quarter of the Navy-Duke game.

Last, never least, my family: Jim and Arlene; Kacky, Stan, and Ann; Annie, Gregg, Rudy, Gus, and Harry; Jimmy and Brendan. Also Dad and Marcia; Margaret, David, Ethan, and Ben; Bobby, Jennifer, Matthew, and Brian. Danny and Brigid are a joy (most of the time), and Mary Clare Gibbons Feinstein is a remarkable mother, wife, and person. They put up with a lot dealing with a cranky cripple last summer.

My thanks and love to all of them.

John Feinstein
Potomac, Maryland
October 2005

Index

Look for these other books by John Feinstein

LET ME TELL YOU A STORY
A Lifetime in the Game
with Red Auerbach

"When stories flow out of Mr. Auerbach's mouth, and then get shaped by Mr. Feinstein's nimble hands, they leave the reader wanting more." — Talmage Boston, *Dallas Morning News*

THE PUNCH
One Night, Two Lives, and the Fight
That Changed Basketball Forever

"If you've seen the videotape, you've never forgotten the horror. . . . Now, thanks to John Feinstein, one of our finest sports journalists, NBA fans will better understand the fallout from what has simply become known as 'the punch.'" — Mark Luce, *San Francisco Chronicle*

THE LAST AMATEURS
Playing for Glory and Honor
in Division 1 College Basketball

"Mr. Feinstein's strength, as always, is his access, and there are numerous behind-the-scenes anecdotes that keep the pages turning." — Larry Platt, *Wall Street Journal*

A MARCH TO MADNESS
The View from the Floor
in the Atlantic Coast Conference

"A basketball junkie's nirvana." — Charles Hirshberg, *Sports Illustrated*

BACK BAY BOOKS
Available wherever paperbacks are sold